BI 3393039 2

LCAAN

KV-051-893

BIRMINGHAM CITY
UNIVERSITY
DISCARDED

THE NEW GLOBAL REGULATORY LANDSCAPE

The New Global Regulatory Landscape

Impacts on Finance and Investment

ROSS K. McGILL

AND

TERENCE A. SHEPPEY

UNIVERSITY OF
LIBRARY
SERVICES
CENTRAL ENGLAND

palgrave
macmillan

© Ross K. McGill and Terence A. Sheppey 2005

All rights reserved. No reproduction, copy or transmission of this publication may be made without written permission.

No paragraph of this publication may be reproduced, copied or transmitted save with written permission or in accordance with the provisions of the Copyright, Designs and Patents Act 1988, or under the terms of any licence permitting limited copying issued by the Copyright Licensing Agency, 90 Tottenham Court Road, London W1T 4LP.

Any person who does any unauthorised act in relation to this publication may be liable to criminal prosecution and civil claims for damages.

The authors have asserted their rights to be identified as the authors of this work in accordance with the Copyright, Designs and Patents Act 1988.

First published 2005 by
PALGRAVE MACMILLAN
Houndmills, Basingstoke, Hampshire RG21 6XS and
175 Fifth Avenue, New York, N.Y. 10010
Companies and representatives throughout the world

PALGRAVE MACMILLAN is the global academic imprint of the Palgrave Macmillan division of St. Martin's Press, LLC and of Palgrave Macmillan Ltd. Macmillan® is a registered trademark in the United States, United Kingdom and other countries. Palgrave is a registered trademark in the European Union and other countries.

ISBN-13: 978–1–4039–4281–4
ISBN-10: 1–4039–4281–1

This book is printed on paper suitable for recycling and made from fully managed and sustained forest sources.

A catalogue record for this book is available from the British Library.

A catalog record for this book is available from the Library of Congress.

10   9   8   7   6   5   4   3   2   1
14 13 12 11 10 09 08 07 06 05

Printed and bound in Great Britain by
Antony Rowe Ltd, Chippenham and Eastbourne

UNIVERSITY OF
CENTRAL ENGLAND

Book no.   33930392

Subject no.   332.042 Mac

LIBRARY SERVICES

Contents

Figures and Tables

FIGURES

TABLES

Preface and Acknowledgments

In the last three years more has changed in financial services regulation than in almost any other industry sector. The main reasons for this are geopolitical, and related to:

- corporate governance
- money laundering
- international terrorism
- investor activism.

The effects of such issues include both direct and indirect regulation of probity, processing, and data protection with their concomitant reporting requirements. Direct regulation affects the ways in which financial institutions behave both in their own right and also with respect to the affairs of their customers—both private and institutional investors. Indirect regulation affects the customers of financial institutions but often impacts shareholders as well.

Much has been written about each of these individual regulatory frameworks on its own account. However, to date, no work has taken the practical viewpoint to deliver an overview of the intent and operational impact of all these regulatory frameworks in a holistic "gestalt." This is important for investors and intermediaries because many elements of the different regulatory frameworks have significant areas of overlap, some of which are constructive (an institution can resolve its compliance just once and meet both requirements) while some are destructive (and the way in which compliance to each framework is achieved must be different and thus increase costs and risks).

This book is structured in four distinct parts.

Part I takes a strategic overview of several current or proposed regulatory frameworks as its starting point, outlining the macro factors, political, geographical, and sociological that form the background to much of the regulatory focus at present. Chapter 2 also provides some historical context on how the current global regulatory position was arrived at, and how the history of these regulations can and will affect future changes to them.

In **Part II**, the authors review several specific sets of regulations from the perspective of investors and their intermediaries in the financial services sector. It is important to note that the review of each regulation is a general one, not intended to be detailed or exhaustive. The intent is to give investors and intermediaries a general picture of the major issues raised by each regulatory framework in order that they can have a better general understanding of intent.

While neither of the authors is legally qualified, and their comments are observational, each is respected in the industry and has many years experience of identifying the strategic as well as practical implications of complex regulations.

The authors provide a review of each regulatory system with three elements:

1   A tabular summary of the regulations.
2   A more detailed review of content.
3   Practical tips to address the major operational and investor issues raised.

Part III provides an analysis of the key areas of overlap and conflict that create issues for both investors and intermediaries, together with practical tips to deal with them. It also deals with practical compliance issues for intermediaries.

In **Part IV** the political and other developments that will shape the future of regulatory frameworks and should form the basis of long-term planning for investors are discussed.

DISCLAIMER

The views and opinions expressed in this book are solely those of the authors. Although the authors have made every effort to ensure the complete accuracy of the text, they do not accept any legal responsibility whatsoever for consequences that may arise from errors or omissions or any opinions given. Nothing in this book is, or is intended to constitute, the provision of taxation or investment advice. Readers are strongly advised to take professional independent advice on these matters.

ACKNOWLEDGMENTS

We gratefully acknowledge advice and assistance provided by the following:

Martin S. Foont, Globe Tax Services Inc., United States.
Charles Witney, Witney and Co, England.
David Bender, lawyer with White and Case LLP, United States.

About the Authors

Ross McGill graduated with Honours in Materials Science and Education in 1978 from Bath University in England. Since graduating, he has held increasingly senior management posts with major international companies in the United States, the United Kingdom, and Continental Europe. Ross has since worked for nearly a decade in both the retail and wholesale financial services sector and was, from 1997 to 2002, CEO of a group of five companies specializing in the automation of compliance to complex international regulations and treaties. He is particularly well known in the industry for his public work with SWIFT, the US Treasury, IRS, and global custodian banks dealing with the effects of new regulatory structures. His current portfolio includes working as director of marketing for GlobeTax, leading business process outsourcing of tax reclamation in the UK and Europe, consultative services to financial services firms relating to regulatory compliance, and authorship of several key regulatory analysis texts.

Ross has had numerous publications including a review of US regulatory issues in the *Financial Times*, and trade visibility, with many articles on international withholding tax regulations. He has also been a prolific speaker at international conferences including Global Custody Forum. He was co-chair of SWIFT Market Practice Group on US Section 1441 NRA regulations for ISO standard messaging and co-chaired an Operational Impact group with the IRS, the US Treasury, and Deloitte and Touche LLP. He is also the author of two acclaimed and bestselling books, and co-author of another, including *International Withholding Tax: A practical guide to best practice and benchmarking* (September 2003) and *Relief at Source: an investor's guide to minimizing internationally withheld tax* (2004).

Terence Sheppey has had a successful career spanning 20 years in networking, communications, consultancy, and partnership management. He is now the managing director of Precision Texts Ltd, a publishing and documentation consultancy. Since the 1980s, Terence has held management roles in major American and British hardware companies such as UB Networks, Newbridge, and European software vendors. He has global experience developing operational and business support systems for service providers from China, through South-East Asia, Europe, and North America. As a consultant with Cap Gemini Ernst and Young, Terence provided knowledge management expertise and infrastructure advice to major finance companies. In the late 1990s he held the post of director of alliances for specialist workflow and billing software companies, globally managing integration partners, HP, IBM, KPMG, Logica, and Cisco, and he spoke at major conventions in Europe and Asia.

Recognized for showcase projects and cited for outstanding contributions with many companies, Terence has considerable experience of the technical environments in which modern financial institutions operate, and has a profound grasp of the practical solutions needed to manage change and compliance. He has distilled this experience into technical guides for a variety of audiences, and contributed specialist articles to many publications. He is currently working on a series of guides for finance and health sector compliance managers on the implications of the Sarbanes–Oxley regulations.

Both authors provide consultancy services to the financial services sector including custodian banks, investment managers, fund managers, brokers, and private banks, on practical impacts of multiple regulatory structures.

Abbreviations

ADR	American Depositary Receipt
AICPA	American Institute of Certified Public Accountants
AMF	Autorité des Marchés Financiers, France
ATM	automatic teller machine
BSC	Building Societies Commission
CDGF	Conseil de Discipline de la Gestion Financière, France
CEBS	EU Committee of Banking Supervisors
CEIOPS	EU Committee of European Insurance and Occupational Pensions Supervisors
CEO	chief executive officer
CESR	Committee of European Securities Regulators
CFO	chief financial officer
CGAA	UK Coordinating Group on Audit and Accounting Issues
CIC	community interest company
CMF	Conseil des Marchés Financiers, France
COB	Commission des Opérations de Bourse, France
COSO	Committee of Sponsoring Organizations of the Treadway Commission
CSP	certification service provider
CTO	chief technology officer
DPA	data protection authority
DPRA	data processing risk assessment
DTA	double tax agreement
DTI	UK Department of Trade and Industry
EBC	European Banking Committee
ECB	European Central Bank
EFTPS	US Electronic Federal Tax Payment System
EIOPC	European Insurance and Occupational Pensions Committee
FASB	Financial Accounting Standards Board
FESCO	Forum of European Securities Commissions
FISMA	Financial Services and Markets Act 2000
FRC	Committee on Corporate Governance Financial Reporting Council
FSA	(UK) Financial Services Authority
FSAP	European Financial Services Action Plan

FTC	US Federal Trade Commission
G10	Group of Ten
GAAP	generally accepted accounting principles
GLB	US Gramm–Leach–Bliley Act 2002
GRIA	Global Regulatory Impact Assessment
IAS	International Accounting Standards
IASB	International Accounting Standards Board
IASC	International Accounting Standards Committee
ICAEW	Institute of Chartered Accountants in England and Wales
IFRIC	International Financial Reporting Interpretations Committee
IFRS	International Financial Reporting Standards
ILM	information lifecycle management
IMRO	Investment Management Regulatory Organisation
IRS	US Internal Revenue Service
ISD	EU Investment Services Directive
KYC	know your customer
LIFFE	London International Financial Futures and Options Exchange
LSE	London Stock Exchange
NASD	(US) National Association of Securities Dealers
NCIS	National Criminal Intelligence Service
NQI	non-qualified intermediary
NWQI	non-withholding qualified intermediary
OFR	Operating and Financial Review
PAI	private arrangement intermediary
PCOA	portfolio compliance overlap analysis
PCOAB	Public Company Accounting Oversight Board
PIA	Personal Investment Authority
QI	qualified intermediary
RAS	relief at source
RIA	regulatory impact assessment
RIE	recognized investment exchange
SA	signature alternative
SAC	Standards Advisory Council
SEC	(US) Securities Exchange Commission
SFA	Securities and Futures Authority
SIB	Securities and Investments Board
SOX	US Sarbanes–Oxley Act 2002
STP	straight through processing
UCITS	Undertakings for Collective Investment in Transferable Securities
UKLA	UK Listing Authority
UTHC	(US) unitary thrift holding company
WQI	withholding qualified intermediary

Part I

Part I

The New Global Regulatory Landscape

The last three years has seen a sea change in the number and interaction of regulatory frameworks across the globe. Whether they are reactive to events, as with the Sarbanes–Oxley Act of 2002 in the United States, or pre-emptive, as with the European directives on data protection dating back to the late 1990s, the result is the same: an expanding system of rules by which financial firms and their clients must abide.

Compliance with any one of these regulatory frameworks would be difficult enough in itself. Many however have both explicit and implicit areas where the intent and/or letter overlap. It is with these areas of overlap that this book is concerned. We have tried to explain the broad intent and mechanisms of a number of global regulatory structures, as well as the interaction they have with each other. We have explicitly not tried to give a definitive and detailed exposition of each regulatory system. This is for others with more specialist knowledge of each individual system.

The financial services sector holds a special place in this global regulatory system. Many of the regulations that apply to citizens as well as bodies corporate do so because of some historic or potential financial irregularity or risk.

The financial sector's peculiar position exists because it must act not just on behalf of its clients in ways that meet general regulatory compliance standards, but also on behalf of itself as a body corporate. As an example, a wholesale custodian bank managing the assets of its clients must, as an expert institution empowered to do so, act in such a way as to ensure its clients are in compliance with a range of appropriate regulation. At the same time, however, the bank itself must act and report as a body corporate in terms of its compliance with domestic as well as transnational regulation. So, for example, a bank may have to maintain client-based procedures to ensure compliance with regulations such as data protection as part of its service contract (directly or indirectly). On the other hand regulations such as Basel II affect the bank's operations directly in terms of its liquidity.

It is useful at this early point to establish what we mean in this book by a "regulatory framework." In order to encompass its widest context and most use, we use the term "regulation" in this book to describe any set of rules by which the behavior of others is prescribed. This may include for example not just formalized regulations, but also acts of Parliament, EU directives, and statutory instruments. The issue here is not what form the rules take, it is the fact that, from an operational perspective, they are rules that must be implemented in order to achieve compliance to some definition of best practice or control structure. In some countries this is achieved by overt regulatory structures. For instance in the United Kingdom and many countries in Europe it includes the existence of independent regulatory bodies, such as the UK Financial Services Authority (FSA), whose role is to police the activities of its remitted sector. However, the term "regulation" also applies to countries such as the United States where, from a financial services perspective, regulation is self-imposed in many areas and thus (from an EU perspective) less effective. Also, importantly, the term "regulatory structures" in this context also applies to countries where there is no "regulatory structure" as the phrase is normally understood, including for example India with respect to data protection. We shall see examples of all of these in later chapters. The key to this discussion is that, for any given combination of countries that are capable of laying down rules, each will apply its own methods as far as it can. From a compliance perspective the fact that one country uses explicit independent regulation and another uses self-regulation or another set of rules for a given set of circumstances is irrelevant. The issue is what actually happens on the ground based on, first, the rules themselves, and second, the way in which those rules are monitored, interpreted, applied, and policed. In later chapters we will see that failure to adhere to a given rule can result in a serious consequence in one country while it has an entirely different effect in another.

Most regulatory frameworks suffer from a common problem. They are designed primarily in isolation from other regulatory structures. This is of course not entirely true of purely domestic regulation, where the framework of rules must fit in with other existing or planned law. However, virtually every recent piece of domestic regulation has had within it some element of transnational impact.

In many instances this amounts to extraterritoriality, and the degree to which any two or more independently created regulatory structures fit has as much to do with the subject matter as it does with the outlook and experience of the relevant lawmakers.

At best, such regulatory interactions cause "gray areas," where individual cases of conflict or misconception are resolved on a case by case basis. At worst, fundamental conflicts can exist, of which many in the industry are unaware, or for which they presume an answer that suits their purpose.

Such has been the case in data privacy. At one level most governments have some policy with regard to the levels of privacy their citizens can expect. In the European Union, this is encoded in Directives such as those on which the UK Data Protection Acts have been founded. The reasons for such Directives are based in a long history, longer than the history associated with freedom of information. Since 9/11 international terrorism has led at many levels to fundamental reviews of the conflict between freedom of information and data privacy. The difficulty in many cases is that the basis of "regulation" in its wider context—the structures designed to implement, monitor, and police this activity—is entirely different from one country to another. For example, the European Union uses a regulatory approach to data privacy, while the United States uses a more sectoral approach. Both have the same objectives but they use different methodologies to achieve them. So, even when disparate rule systems have similar end results, their methodologies can be fundamentally in conflict.

It is in this context that this book is written, to highlight the issue and to use some practical examples to illuminate the subject matter.

The number of regulatory structures is increasing all the time, and it would be folly to try to describe each one definitively at any given point in time. We hope in this book to identify the major issues and the major overlaps, and in future editions we hope to drill deeper into each one to provide a useful benchmark for those involved in compliance as well as operations.

WHO SHOULD READ THIS BOOK AND WHY

Compliance officers, operations directors, and senior management, as well as risk management staff and client relationship managers, at any financial institution will find this book useful. There are several areas discussed in this book that have the capacity to create competitive advantage for firms that address them effectively. This is a concept alien to many financial firms because of the way most are structured. Different departments have different reasons for being, and therefore have different priorities and drivers.

Most compliance functions are not concerned with marketing except to ensure that client relationships comply with appropriate law. They have no interest in the firm's profit other than to make sure that costs of compliance are controlled as far as practicable. Operations functions, on the other hand, seem to categorize compliance as a necessary evil detracting from their day-to-day work. One aim of this book is to provide examples of how joining up the thinking about such matters as regulatory compliance between departments can create new ways to interpret regulatory compliance.

Compliance is not a necessary evil. The degree to which any firm manages its clients and itself is one of its fundamental values. This could be thought of as the airplane seat scenario. Passengers just want to get to Barbados for their holiday, and are not interested in technical details of the aircraft's functioning. But when the arm of their seat wiggles loosely, they might well question whether the level of attention the airline pays to the condition of the armrests relates to the attention it pays to the engines. From that perspective, most passengers would pay a higher fare for the privilege of knowing their airline had gone the extra mile. This book helps uncover the extra mile.

Institutional investors, including client-side fund managers, hedge fund, pension fund, and insurance fund managers will also find this book useful. Shareholders, are increasingly aware and concerned about complex inter-related regulatory requirements, and how the custodians of their assets are meeting their responsibilities. This is one of those areas where the regulatory framework can have a dual effect:

- First, failure of attention to the major issues of regulatory frameworks can have a major effect on investment performance through the share price and the dividend delivered.
- Second, financial firms acting on behalf of such investors will increasingly be held to account either directly (in liability) or indirectly (by moving to a new firm) for any perceived loss or otherwise avoidable administrative cost of compliance.

2004 saw the first set of corporate governance guidelines published for issuing companies and for proxy voting firms, in response to increased shareholder activism. Among other issues these require enhanced attention to both the letter and spirit of international double tax agreements between countries. These guidelines encourage awareness and the facilitation of regulatory compliance by companies at the behest of investors or their proxies through the medium of the annual general meeting.

Students involved in courses related to financial services qualifications, accountancy, and legal or paralegal aspects of investor relations will find this book useful too. It is often all too easy to focus on one or a small number of regulatory structures that apply to a limited set of circumstances. Those in training should find in this book a top-level reminder that there is a world out there, and that there can be consequences for those who do not have peripheral vision.

THE INVESTOR'S PERSPECTIVE

There are some basic questions that investors face.

1   What is the balance of yield delivery in my portfolio?

2   How does regulation impede my ability to invest and obtain maximum returns?
3   How do I protect the confidentiality of my information from competitors?
4   How does my choice of intermediary affect my returns and my probity?

Yield strategy and activism

Yield is a critically important point for an investor to consider in the context of regulations. Yield in securities is formed primarily of two factors, margin on buy/sell, and dividend income. In the past dividend income has been the poor relation to margin, and so it was natural that investors were not particularly concerned with probity or regulation. They were in, then out, and the regulatory and probity issues were only relevant in the period during which the securities were held. This was an issue of pure risk management. Nowadays, however, many institutional investors are holding shares "long" as a matter of policy. In other words their mind-set, even if only subconsciously, is that of a long-term investor. In this scenario, the probity of the board and the regulatory impacts of financial services controls have a much more significant impact. This is why investor activism has grown so significantly in recent years. The difficulty is that historically, this activism has been restricted to the probity of the board because this is the most visible aspect of a company to an investor.

Institutional investors need to read this book for two reasons. First, it should give them a broader picture of what they can be active about. This broadens the scope of potential activism to how well companies as well as intermediaries behave under regulations.

Second, it should give them a reasonable understanding of the scale and scope of such regulations. Once they have understood the range of topics on which they might choose to be active, they can focus their questioning, based on the potential impact on their investments.

Put simply, beyond activism at issuer board level there is a massive area of regulatory activism which can be questioned within the investor community, within the issuer company, and also within the chain of inter-mediaries that act between issuer and investor.

Regulatory impacts on investment returns

Typically regulation impedes an investor's ability to invest and obtain returns by setting up barriers in the form of rules which either prohibit investment or curtail it either in a qualitative or quantitative way. (Double tax agreements are an example of this.) The presumption of obedience to such rules is axiomatic, but the penalties usually associated with these types of rules give an indication of the way in which regulatory authorities establish degrees of tolerance. For example, US Section 1441 NRA regulations are set up to encourage good practice in taxation of investment income. The fact that failure to abide by these regulations can result in investment income being taxed at 50 percent or more, with massive penalties for intermediaries, shows how seriously the IRS takes compliance.

From an investor's viewpoint it is not enough to have a yield model for each target market in a portfolio. It is also necessary to have a regulatory impact model to offset the yield by a factor that takes into account the costs associated with compliance (qualitative factors) and any regulatory rules that specifically impact direct income (quantitative factors). As regulatory overlap becomes more complex, the costs of compliance to intermediaries will increase. In a market where margins are already thin, it is likely that regulatory compliance will be used more frequently as a reason to pass on price rises to investors.

Protecting information

Protecting information is a more difficult task for investors. As far as an investor is concerned, it would be easier to presume that following the occurrence of an activity, the nature and impact of that activity is public knowledge. This is a result of the number of people who know of it, those that can take action based on it, and regulators that may impose sanctions based on it. Several parts of this book focus on data protection, and the tension between this principle, based on protecting the confidentiality of an investor's information, and freedom of information regulations and regulations on money laundering and anti-terrorism, which give many people access to investment information. It does not matter that the transaction concerned is innocuous; an investor's concerns are based on the fact that the data is "out there." While regulators may have created the rules to catch criminals and terrorists, it is obvious that not every breach is monitored. The answer for investors is to understand the degree to which their data is accessible and the use to which it is put, as well as where it is processed. This is a complex area, and in most cases even intermediaries are not able to demonstrate a clear risk profile.

The intermediary chain

The complexity of the chain of communications between investor and issuer is very often underestimated by investors. Most importantly, the chain is not a serial entity but serial and parallel, split by market. There may be up to 30 permutations of intermediary involved in a typical portfolio, spreading out from the original buy instruction, including various intermediaries involved in the corporate actions that flow from an increased "long" position strategy. The choice of intermediary is critical for investors.

Cheapest is not always best, and a rigorous analysis of intermediaries is vital. However, benchmarking amongst intermediaries is still relatively new, and is almost always done at a qualitative level. There are very few quantitative benchmarks available to investors which allow them to quantify risk and compliance.

The net result is that investors' best defense is to become better educated about regulatory issues in order to identify the right questions to ask, and be able to interpret the answers for their own protection.

Confidentiality and yield damage are of course just two of the potential issues. Probity can indirectly have just as damaging an effect on institutional performance. So corporate governance at fund level interacts with intermediary processing in an almost unique way. The intermediary can affect fund value directly by failing to comply, which results in lower yield or expensive remedial penalties. Lack of probity at fund level can affect confidence and reputation with similar effects. There are a growing number of corporate governance-related regulations which can add a layer of cost and risk, including Sarbanes–Oxley for example.

Intermediaries typically try to minimize costs in operations by making them carry across as much of the organization as possible. So if the effect of one given regulation is a reporting requirement, it may be that the whole client base is practically affected by the regulation even though only a small proportion should be affected. Sarbanes–Oxley, to continue the example, directly affects only about 3000 firms (those listed on US stock markets). In reality it affects many more. Interpretations of impact are not wide enough at investor level. At intermediary level it is easier to impose systems that report across all clients than to filter out only those to whom the regulations apply.

CHAPTER 1

The Strategic View

Most of the regulation that affects financial services and investors today is about information. Who has it? Who is supposed to have it? What is its content? What can be done with it? Who knows what is being done with it? Who monitors it? For the investment community, the sensitivity of such questions cannot be underestimated.

CORPORATE GOVERNANCE AND E-GOVERNANCE

Many would consider that corporate governance is not an area that affects financial services other than at the level of investors' concern relating to the conduct of a firm in which they invest. Historically, this is where the focus has been, leading to several well known and documented corporate "scandals" across the globe.

This view is too narrow because it does not take account of the investor's own compliance to corporate governance, nor that of the investor's intermediary or the interactions between them. In other words, the issue of corporate governance for investors and intermediaries is much more complex that would seem at face value. Some of the more high profile cases, such as the Martha Stewart case in 2004, highlight this by showing an intermediary, in this case the broker, as an explicit participant.

The way in which the world works has also radically changed in just the last three years, to the point where straight through processing (STP) initiatives, originally designed primarily to reduce cost through increasing automation, are now increasingly mandated to reduce compliance risk as well as cost. This has led directly to the concept of e-governance and to the US Sarbanes–Oxley Act, UK Data Protection Act, and the UK Combined Code, all of which have specific clauses dealing with the way in which electronic communications and web based commerce should be dealt with.

Yet in the financial markets, probity and corporate governance are at the root of how and why the markets work and why they continue to maintain an overall level of long-term stability.

MONEY LAUNDERING

The issues of money laundering and international terrorism are, as we now know, inextricably linked. However, not all money laundering is related to international terrorism, and not all terrorism is funded through money laundering. It is also true that not all countries are either on a level playing field or equally up to date in the implementation of regulations to control these problems.

It would be logical to assume that facing such a ubiquitous problem, there would be one set of general rules that would apply globally, with perhaps some localized variations to take into account regional issues. However, this is not the case. There are a wide range of different organizations that have some interest in making policy in this area.

As with terrorism, the net result of the activities of the relatively few is to impact the whole. For intermediaries the overall impact is an increase in the control and supervision of "know your customer" or KYC rules as the foundation of good practice. However, while intermediaries have the ability to identify account holders, they have a lesser ability to identify the use to which funds transfers or investments are put. Some of these can be identified indirectly: definitions of "suspicious transactions" by reference to their frequency or absolute amount provide a basic test, but hardly a sophisticated one, and certainly these methods, being gross, can create unwanted administration for the intermediary and potential disclosure for the account holder.

For the investor, the net result of such regulation is a breakdown in the degree of confidentiality enjoyed between intermediary and investor, as well as an increase in administration, more forms to fill in, and increased cost.

The difficulty for a global investor and indeed for global intermediaries is that the way in which this administration is proceduralized by different jurisdictions both affects the cost of doing business in that jurisdiction and creates potential conflicts, for instance, in the degree and manner in which client confidentiality is affected. What may be defined as suspicious in one jurisdiction is not in another. That which generates a secret report to a criminal intelligence service in one jurisdiction may not in another.

INTERNATIONAL TERRORISM

No one really needs any reminders about terrorism any more. Its threat is with us all on a daily basis. It affects investors through volatility in financial markets. It affects intermediaries in that they are often strategic targets, either because they represent a capitalist structure that terrorists disavow, or because they offer a soft target, damage to which could easily destroy Western civilization's ability to keep running.

The BBC aired a program in December 2004 which demonstrated, if only at a theoretical level, the impact that derivatives trading has had on the financial markets in the last ten years, making it this area one of the most vulnerable to "unfriendly attention." The program in question was a drama documentary called *The Man Who Broke Britain*. It was made by Wall to Wall Television. Terrorism was also at the root of the development of the US Patriot Act, and we are beginning to see signs within the United States that it is being very broadly interpreted in law enforcement.

FINANCIAL DISCLOSURE

Flowing from corporate governance initiatives, increasingly fund managers are being required, under regulation, to disclose more about their financial decisions. It is unsurprising that most of the regulatory structures mentioned in this book, and globally, have a common structural cycle:

1   Identify the regulator.
2   Establish the rules.
3   Define monitoring responsibilities and what constitutes a breach.
4   Require reporting (disclosure) to the regulator for enforcement.
5   Apply penalties as a deterrent.
6   Review and amend the regulations.

This is a useful model because it allows an investor or an intermediary to easily construct a model of compliance; it also highlights the importance of disclosure as the fundamental "dot" that connects the regulator's demands with industry compliance.

It is certain that this trend will continue, as it extends into areas of financial management currently undisclosed, which have an impact on performance.

INVESTOR ACTIVISM

Investors have been more active in the last five years than they have been in the previous 50. The degree of trust between investor and issuer has been damaged by high-profile probity cases and this has led to regulations such as Sarbanes–Oxley. Laws based on this are now proliferating around the world. Intermediaries have not been immune to this effect, and some, but by no means all, cases have resulted in high-profile fines from regulatory bodies.

The net result of all these factors is that the degree and extent of regulation has increased in response to concerns over probity and the use of the financial services system to promote terrorism and, supporting it, money laundering.

Most of the regulatory changes currently being made expand the access of policing and regulatory bodies to financial investment information, and increase the requirements on officers. When these changes are translated into regulatory structures, three fundamentals arise:

- identification
- data protection
- controls.

However, each jurisdiction is taking an independent approach to these matters, and while there is increasing international cooperation at the police level, there is a more fragmented approach at regulatory level.

TECHNOLOGY

A dominant trend for regulation, as for all aspects of business and social interchange, involves the possibilities unleashed by the constant changes in technology, especially communication. Simple step changes in capability have an unpredictable large step impact. E-mail, initially anticipated as having a supporting role to telephone transactions, has largely replaced telephony as the primary mechanism for transactions. Institutional investors place as many e-mail calls as telephoned transactions; intermediaries, in line with the rest of the financial sector, use e-mail as the workflow for managing business. E-mail matches the new expectation on speed. Electronic exchanges drive new product possibilities, with further opportunities for risk and malpractice in a cycle of experimentation and control. Regulation of electronic commerce is discussed later, but its role in enabling new types of interchange and new sources of regulatory evidence is striking.

For the finance sector this means that technology, generally now associated with computerization and electronic communications, defines the possibilities of business and largely constitutes the operational risks associated with providing these services. It also dictates what regulators regard as feasible when defining regulatory requirements: for example, the speed of response to an investigative question and the assumptions made about stored data on transactions and the speed of access to this data. It does not follow that all firms have the same capability. This represents a major hurdle to compliance. Not surprisingly technology has a hand in most of the trends such as the internationalization and diversification of markets, the creation of new products with increased competition, and pressures on overall profitability. There are some very specific business opportunities that technology have made possible.

The storage, transmission, and processing of data

The role of possession, especially certificates, is critical in handling transactions. Recent developments have made electronic certification acceptable. As a result business operates at a different speed, with all the advantages that electronic processing confers in terms of operating costs and speed of response to exchange updates.

Access to data, remote banking, and e-money

The enabling of regional and global economies is centered on technology. Communications systems are the hidden assumption on which the whole edifice is constructed. Linked exchanges now dominate 24-hour investing. Investors can now track and manage their investments full-time, if they so wish. In effect technology has united the world's markets for the investor, allowing instant transactions from one location. It also allows the true effect of gearing and virtual money transactions to proceed as swiftly as clearing houses and banks allow. If anything it is operational procedural bottlenecks that slow the process here, not technology itself.

The overall impact of technology is enormous and still understated. It allows:

- The globalizing of national entities. An investor can add a Japanese or South American bank's equities to its portfolio and manage these as if they were global operators and accessible as such.
- Bringing formerly distinct markets together: The extension of banking operations into mutual funds and vice versa, adding insurance and portfolio management on the way, is only possible because of the accessibility to the mechanisms of these markets. This accessibility is based on the computerization of these markets making the process feasible and profitable. It also makes complex cross-regulation possible.

Institutional investors and intermediaries are having to re-examine their management structures to reflect these impacts. As firms consolidate, blending similar lines of business, the push is to repackage products as new and constantly expand the range, introducing products, vehicles, and instruments that until recently were only available to larger, more sophisticated investors. Technology operates on the personal level too: the face-to-face, personal touch of the past is replaced by an alternative in call centers; and the necessary management of distinct lines of business is handled by distinct workflows, still focused on single product lines.

CHAPTER 2

The Historical Perspective

In order to properly understand the impact of overlaps in regulatory structures and how these might develop, it is useful to have some perspective on the reasons for regulations in the major markets. This chapter is presented to allow the reader to develop a more holistic picture. When we come to discuss the future of global regulatory change, this chapter will form the focus for extrapolation into what we can expect in the next few years.

THE UNITED KINGDOM

The United Kingdom has seen a transformation in the financial services landscape in recent years, particularly at retail level. Until recently every high street in every town bore its quota of outlets for the "big four" clearing banks: Barclays, National Westminster, Midland, and Lloyds. There was a consensus on how their customers would be managed, how they would charge, and what services they would provide. Customers typically accessed their money through clerks serving at counters during limited hours.

By 2000, all this had changed. For the retail sector, many bank customers never went near a bank but banked remotely, gaining their cash through automatic teller machines (ATMs) instead of counter clerks, or accessed money from outlets such as supermarkets, tied into an infrastructure where financial services have expanded beyond their traditional outlets. The high street picture still lingers, there are bank buildings and they are staffed, now at more accessible hours for customers. However, the days of dressing up to see the bank manager for a loan or to discuss an account or overdraft, where the customer was very much in the subservient role, have passed. Banks are more open, more anxious to gain market share, and encourage retail customers to take up new services. They have embraced the changes that have swept through financial services.

By 2003, the six biggest banks reflected the changes that had taken place, as brand names were absorbed, expanded, or simply disappeared in a period of merger and acquisition. This coincided with a market that was changing, breaking down the older rigid divisions that enforced the provision of services in vertical sectors: banking, insurance, mortgages and mutual funds, pensions. The regulatory climate had changed dramatically, moving from self-regulation and the "club" approach of the City of London to a focus on government powers, the transfer of responsibility, and a new spotlight on boardroom activity. This was the background to the changes that produced new lead companies that were hybrids: HSBC; the Royal Bank of Scotland (RBS), which now includes the acquired NatWest; Barclays; HBOS, a combination of the Halifax Building Society and the Bank of Scotland; and Abbey National, an ex-mutual funds building society now absorbed by the Spanish Banco Santander. These players reflect the change in fortune for some of the old big players:

■ Barclays—absorbed the Woolwich Building Society
■ NatWest—absorbed by RBS
■ Midland—now disappeared into HSBC (Hong Kong and Shanghai Banking Corporation)
■ Lloyds—merged with the Trustee Savings Bank to become Lloyds TSB.

Much of this change was, and is, a reflection of the change in competitive climate, but it is also a result of regulatory (and deregulatory) pressure wrought by the opening up of financial markets and the introduction of a new generation of CEOs and CFOs in the boardrooms of these venerable British institutions. These managers are marked by a different outlook:

■ They tend to be global operators with an eye on the international market as well as domestic possibilities.
■ They negotiate higher salaries and bonuses tied to performance and profits; their status is determined by money and performance.
■ They are business people foremost, no longer solely drawn from an old school network or tied to ancestral inheritances.
■ They are international in make-up, coming from the new economy of Europe, the United States, and globally.

Whether this change means a greater sensitivity to the interests of customers, or consumers (as the retail sector have been reclassified by the FSA and government), is another matter. There are a far greater range of products to consider and work with, but although these financial operations have new captains, they still may not better reflect the interests of their customers.

For the United Kingdom, the sector where a real transformation has taken place is at the level of investment banks, or what were known as "merchant banks." Global investment banks dominate domestic capital markets. Their focus, unsurprisingly, is corporations or rich, "high worth" individuals. These banks have seen dramatic change. The oldest, Barings, collapsed in a spectacular scandal which gripped the public imagination in the United Kingdom in a similar way to Enron in the United States. These banks operated in a way that was characterized as very English—based on the concept of a club where a man's word was his bond. The modern, more ruthless notion of profit alone, and a more aggressive approach to banking, were introduced in the 1980s when world competition became a reality. US investment banks became more established in London, led by a new breed of CEO focused on maximizing profits and the "productization" of the market as whole. In 1986, the "Big Bang" was another defining point for the UK. It marked the end of an era, as more US and European banks gained access to the London money markets and a number of traditional names disappeared. Critical qualities that the new arrivals possessed over the local entities were:

■ the size of the assets held
■ the ease with which they could raise capital
■ the higher "risk tolerance" of their endeavors.

The period was marked by mergers and sales to foreign arrivals. Goldman Sachs was already established, and players such as Deustche Bank, the French Société Générale, Citigroup, UBS Warburg, and Dresdner became major names. By the end of the millennium it was safe to assert that the "City" was no longer a purely British institution. The role of the Bank of England, although still important, was no longer dominant. The relationships and web of human interaction that had characterized the City's way of doing business were replaced by electronic interchange and a legalism that saw the spawning of specialist law firms linked to every deal.

One of casualties of this era, and one that some believe contributed substantially to the problems to come, was corporate ethics. A free-wheeling approach to corporate ethics now became acceptable. Pursuit of profit became an ethical yardstick in its own right. There is no doubt that the infusion of aggressive competitive players into the UK financial sector brought an energy and a new dynamism to the market. Nevertheless there was a sense of loss among the more traditional players in the City who perhaps were always aware of the corruptive nature of money separated from industry or everyday life, and now saw that corruptive power loose in the boardroom. In a sense this was a foretaste of what in the United States would lead to Enron and the scandals that have littered the decade before and leading into the 21st century.

These factors were manifest in a number of ways, and they are very relevant to any understanding of how regulation has developed as a practical response to change. Depending on the market and its drivers we might discern:

- a separation of what might be in the best interests of the organization from what might be in the interests of senior executives and or the board
- a lack of focus on what might be now thought of as ethical behavior, with weak lines of accountability
- a lack of attention to governance in general, resulting in shareholder concern.

This weakness in corporate governance can not only be traced back to a lack of willingness to be accountable at the top. There was no political will to tackle reforms during the 1980s, when the City was seen as a powerhouse of enterprise and the newcomers a badly needed tonic for a settled and somewhat atrophied system. The backlash began to be felt in the late 1990s, as the failure of financial systems to deliver on basic promises shocked the nation. Pension scandals and mis-selling of products on a large scale seriously undermined the credibility of the institutions as a whole, even as business boomed and mergers and acquisitions continued apace.

Reforms were introduced, and by the end of the century the Financial Services and Markets Act (FISMA) 2000 had created a central regulator. This Act transferred responsibility for banking supervision to the Securities and Investments Board (SIB), which has been one of the regulatory bodies in place since the 1980s, and responsible for the regulation of investment business, the supervision of other regulatory organizations, and recognized professional bodies like the Law Society. It also brought together the insurance supervisory functions of the Insurance Directorate of the Department of Trade and Industry, the functions of the Registry of Friendly Societies, the Building Societies Commission, and the Friendly Societies Commission into one regulatory body. Subsequently the SIB was renamed the Financial Services Authority (FSA). Many observers saw this as an overdue move; they noted that these bodies vied for control of their sectors and were characterized by in-fighting.

Organizations saw, for the first time, real attempts to address insider dealing, and the erection of "information boundaries" between research and practical advisory arms to reduce the dangers of speculative insider dealing. In the United States, the Securities Exchange Commission (SEC) admonished banks for the amount of spurious research they purported to undertake when backing up new products, with many brokers selling shares to small investors that would never pass muster with institutional investors, though even these were not immune from such mis-selling.

Major players such as Citigroup and Merrill Lynch found themselves under investigation for such practices. This all undermined trust to the extent that the projected proliferation of lawyers was self-fulfilling: They were employed to monitor deals on behalf of regulators and shareholders because deal makers could not be trusted to perform ethically.

An abiding concept in finance has been liquidity. Underpinning this vital condition has been the assumption that trust is vested in the parties trading and the system within which they trade. Banks, in particular rely on this; the spectacular failure of such trust in the Crash of 1929 is still a bitter memory, a specter that haunts all systems of finance. The political dimension supports (and ultimately, since all investors are constituents, controls) this process, and fosters this trust. In the end it is not the energy of unbridled capitalism that ensures the prosperous long-term growth of stable systems, but the quality of the systems themselves and how well they operate within mutually beneficial rules and controls. The realization of this has led to a greater focus on the processes that maintain such control, and the agencies that impose this control: the regulatory bodies that have come to dominate the present financial climate.

Globalization has brought about many things. Among these is the way it has spread a tendency in a major financial center such as the United States to all corners of the globe. As the energies unleashed by unfettered corporate aggression have rippled outward and were copied as models of best practice for many, so has the backlash of regulation backed by legislation become a worldwide phenomenon. At the same time as the marketplace became more global, the players in it saw their interests transcending local, national, and even regional controls. The global movement of capital owed no allegiance to nationality or region, or so it seemed. But the wheel has turned. Transnational companies are now facing blocs such as North America, the Asia–Pacific, and now the European Union, which have a new determination to ensure their constituents have a voice in these matters. The European Union has shown a deal of aggression in this matter—the tussle with Microsoft, so used to dominating its market, is a case in point. However, this is not over. Currently the trend is toward more regulation, but the regulation is tempered by local interests. The US regulators such the SEC are keen to ensure no real competitive disadvantage stems from their actions. So too are the EU and other regional and national regulators. Self-interest serves all. All regulation is proclaimed to be on behalf of the consumer. All implementation is tempered by the claims and interests of the regulated. It is a question of degree. Much as we might celebrate the grass-roots nature of investor activism, the real deals are struck between the largest financial players and their dependants—national governments.

Financial services

Talk of institutions in the world of finance has, for some time, been short-hand for a range of organizations that have become so entrenched in our imagination as the sound, stable basis of economic life that they have been "institutionalized," made part of the given fabric of life: It is assumed they have always been there and are immutable. Of course this is not historically the case, but these organizations have an image, which they happily exploit, which provides them with a sense of purpose and destiny that cannot easily be dismissed.

In this context, "institutions" is shorthand for the banks, life assurance companies, and pension funds that manage the bulk of all investments transacted on stock exchanges and in major financial centers. They are the recipients of our savings and investments, and holders of the vast majority of shares and stocks that make up the value of so much of our global economy. Often also known as "institutional investors," these organizations operate as hugely influential intermediaries between ordinary citizens, as savers or investors, and the financial markets that underpin all monetary activity. We trust them to operate efficiently in our best interest and to have the professional expertise to match the claims they make in their sales literature. The markets could operate without them, we could save and invest directly and the whole economic machine could grind on, but only with great difficulty. Without their collective clout and economic muscle, individual investors would be at the mercy of a mercenary and unscrupulous marketplace. Trust and hope—the two pillars of institutional certainty—enable us to sleep well, assured of financial security in a complex and confusing world.

There was a time, perhaps apocryphal, when it was possible to separate such organizations from the speculative players taking huge risks who moved in the markets, using considerable personal wealth to support a gambler's drive for profit and gain. The image of the institutions still has much of this aura: certainty, surety, probity; aversion to risk; an almost benevolent concern for those who entrust their money to them. But this is much more an illusion than a reality. As players in an increasingly complex system of markets and meta-markets that feed off illusion, blurring the boundaries between what is financial reality and fiction, the institutions are now prominent speculators. Ordinary citizens' assumption that their money goes in as *savings*—understood as money that will be returned (hopefully with a gain)—is translated into the reality of money that is handled as an *investment*—money that may not be returned—by the institution. This money becomes no more than a useful vehicle for creating new money—as with banks; as the source of chips on the gamblers' table, as shares, stocks, bonds; or as geared risks with the promise of great gains or losses, with derivatives; all "hedged" against disaster through more abstract arrangements where contracts lose sight of intention and value. The institutions are investors not only for their customers and clients but also for themselves.

Markets and players

The key agents in the web of relationships that characterize the process of markets absorbing and using investments are numerous, including:

- brokers
- dealers
- advisers
- fund managers
- asset managers
- portfolio managers.

Some of these agents have undergone a change in function, and the definition has slowly been catching up. A broker, prior to the 1980s, meant a member of the Stock Exchange who was entitled to transact share deals on behalf of clients. Today this function has expanded to include small firms that focus on the "retail" market, the general financial consumer. The term also refers to a firm that links a company, its shareholders, and the exchange and regulatory bodies. In the Lloyd's market, the broker had a specific sense of acting on behalf of clients in placing risks with underwriters. And now, in the general consumer market we talk of brokers used by salespeople pushing a range of packaged investment products.

These agents manage and develop a range of financial services that are generically linked to the idea of investment, but represented by concepts more popularly known as:

- debt ownership
- retirement funds—annuities
- insurance schemes—life, health and sickness, property, goods (cars and so on)
- securities—capital markets, asset-backed, derivatives, exchanges.

They work on behalf of and involve:

- investors—individual private investors and institutional investors
- mutual funds—building societies
- banks—commercial, credit unions, industrial, investment, merchant.

Other important forces shape this market:

- regulation—statutory or self-regulated, transnational, regional, and national
- technology—in its many manifestations: enterprise systems, communications including telecommunications, electronic payments systems, clearing systems, and ATMs.

These players now shape the life of ordinary citizens; and extraordinary citizens, financially speaking (those of "high value" or "high net worth") sit alongside the institutional investors who accumulate the small investor funds and use this capital to create wealth. Throughout the period just covered the change in finance has been matched by a change in attitude to these players, at the governmental and the public level:

- Generally, consumers have become more aware of the complexity of finance and the need for good advice.
- They are now the target of financial "products" and "packages" that play a more important role in accumulating funds.

Consolidation

The period of consolidation in the finance sector has lead to the emergence of more complex groups such as National Westminster and Lloyds TSB. It is these groups that will face the biggest challenges from regulatory overlap. They will experience it as:

- organizations subject to broadly based company regulation
- organizations subject to sector-specific regulators—such as those that oversee their new undertakings in other finance markets
- organizations subject to regional regulation such as EU directives.

There are other complex entities emerging that do not have their origins in the finance sector itself, but are becoming part of its body through their expansion into finance services based on the market pull of brand name. They are examples of a trend towards the creation of different channels of delivery. They are typified by the:

- entry into retail financial services of non-financial retail firms such as major retail suppliers Marks & Spencer and Tesco, or multifaceted enterprises such as Virgin
- competitive response from existing finance firms
- creation of new combined groups such as Prudential and M & G.

These groups have the potential to become financial supermarkets, offering their own financial products and services, marketed through their customer base built from retail activities. So far these offerings have been domestic, but there is the potential for cross-border financial "hypermarkets" built on brand name. However, these essentially non-financial organizations will find themselves subject to a range of regulations governing their activities in banking, investment business, insurance, and other markets, in a number of countries with different régimes. Investors and intermediaries will need some convincing that such hybrids can satisfy their sophisticated demands, and it is likely that these organizations will continue to appeal to the retail market for the near future.

The UK picture is by no means unique. It has its peculiarities, skewed by the dominance for many centuries of the City of London and an empire that gave its banking system global reach. Governments have responded to the change in climate through regulation, with one eye on the concerns of investors and one on the institutions that support their coffers.

The UK regulatory map

Although the United Kingdom has seen a major consolidation of regulatory bodies, most regulatory activity on the ground has been driven by committees producing reports and guidelines for compliance. Most of these are not statutory and therefore enforceable under law. The system still has a strong self-regulatory feel, with bodies making recommendations and offering guidance rather than mandating under law. Generally it is an approach that assumes the financial industry knows what is best for itself. This is a debatable position, and creates many contrasts with international efforts.

The responsibility for financial services legislation and policy lies with Her Majesty's Treasury, and responsibility for overseeing the conduct of regulated activity rests with the FSA. The FSA fulfills its regulatory responsibilities within a framework established by FISMA and related legislation. This Act determines what constitutes regulated activity, such as dealing with investment activities and giving investment advice.

Regulated activity can only be carried out by authorized entities or exempted entities such as recognized investment exchanges (RIEs); the London International Financial Futures and Options Exchange (LIFFE) falls into this category. The FSA manages the requirements of authorization, and HM Treasury addresses competition issues.

The RIE

The RIE is an important part of the financial landscape in the United Kingdom. Its statutory obligations require it to provide proper protection for investors and ensure trading occurs in an orderly and fair manner. All transactions must be recorded, and contractual transactions must follow timely rules, enforced either by the RIE's own offices or through a recognized clearing house. The RIE is required to monitor compliance with its rules and to enforce them to maintain high standards of integrity, and cooperate with other regulatory bodies.

LIFFE (Euronext.liffe)

LIFFE is an RIE that is also a regulated market for the purposes of the European Union's Investment Services Directive (ISD). In this instance, such a regulated market is one which meets requirements dealing with trade reporting and publication, and is recognized by the home state regulatory authority (in this case the UK FSA). LIFFE is now generally known as Euronext.liffe, the international derivatives business of Euronext, after its acquisition in 2001. This comprises the Amsterdam, Brussels, LIFFE, Lisbon, and Paris derivatives markets.

Since the acquisition, Euronext.liffe has become the world's leading exchange for euro short-term interest rate derivatives and equity options. It is a good example of how regional acquisitions can help create an effectively single market aided by technology, and how a fixture of the UK financial scene has been transformed into a regional entity. Euronext.liffe is practically a single market for derivatives. It has used technology to combine its derivatives on a single electronic trading platform: LIFFE CONNECT®. LIFFE CONNECT greatly speeds up the execution of transactions. It provides access at over at over 500 locations in 26 countries worldwide.

The ambition is to replace multiple trading venues with a electronic trading system, with the benefits of reduced costs for the exchange and its customers. It should be able to cut significantly the cost of cross-border trading. It is a good example of technology enabling change in the market and making possible new types of service and new regulated entities.

Throughout the 1990s, a number of committees were set up in the United Kingdom, sometimes by government, to examine and define the responsibilities of directors for corporate governance and to ensure transparency in the boardroom and in the expression of the company's public statement— the annual report. Of these committees, the most significant were the Cadbury Committee (1992), the Greenbury Committee (1997), and the Hampel Committee (1998). They produced reports that sought to provide best practice for listed companies in the protection of their assets and the interests of shareholders. Investment had become truly international, as technology enabled small and large investors to operate at speeds that changed the nature of investing.

The Committee on Corporate Governance Financial Reporting Council

(FRC) issued a final report which, together with material from the Cadbury and Greenbury Reports, was merged into a single body of thought. In June 1998 the Hampel Committee saw the London Stock Exchange publish new listing rules; these, together with the Principles of Good Governance and Code of Best Practice reinforced by the previous reports, become known as the "Combined Code." Internal controls had been coming to the forefront ever since the Rutteman working group on internal controls in 1994 concluded that a system had to be established in order to provide reasonable assurance of effective and efficient operations of internal financial control, and compliance with laws and regulations.

This theme has grown in importance until it has come to be central to a report such as Turnbull and at the heart of much international legislation.

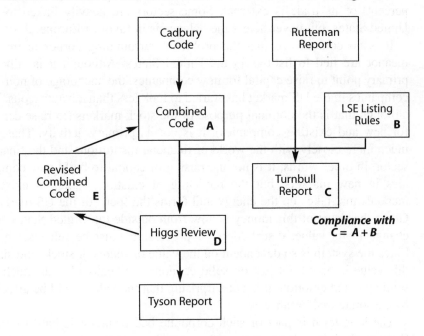

Figure 2.1 The UK regulatory web
Source: the authors.

Figure 2.1 outlines some of the lineage of the key pieces of "legislation" in terms of codes and guidance reports issued in the last decade of the 20th century and to date.

THE US SITUATION

When the US economy sneezes, the world catches a cold. This aphorism, or words like it, has reflected a truth underlying the financial relationship between the United States and the rest of the world, which until quite recently has held true. The current US deficit does not look set to go away, however, and the fact that the United States now relies heavily on external investors to provide capital for its consumer market is only obscured by the power of the US economy and the richness of its diversity. The growth of China, the stabilization of Japan, and the convergence of Europe, as independent trading blocs of growing power and significance, also indicate a gradual and significant change for the status of the world's largest economy.

The economic links between these trading blocs are diverse, but that should not lead to a dramatic knock-on from US problems. Perhaps it is the fact that is the net beneficiary of the world's investment that makes a US wobble felt everywhere else. For example, Europe as a business region trades largely internally. Only a relatively low percentage (about 16 percent) of its trade is external. Some sectors are heavily linked to the United States, but nevertheless the balance is in favor of Europe.

It is no coincidence that the problems surrounding corporate misdemeanor are tied to listings in the United States. Although it is still the primary point to raise capital for new companies, the anchorage of non-US companies in the US market has started to look less than advantageous. Yet although that is the nominal purpose of the stock markets (to raise capital for new and existing companies), it is not its primary activity. That sits much more closely with the world of financial institutions and the finance sector. In other words, it is not the raising of capital to build new companies in new markets, but the recycling of existing capital in existing markets, that takes up the energy and forms the focus of the US markets. Given that most of this money is now from outside the United States, any change in its value, distribution, or processing must be felt elsewhere. Since the system is so dependent on the value of shares or stock, and since this value is based not just on solid economic indicators but as much on sentiment and emotion, it is not surprising that the value could be affected by corporate malfeasance.

The long-term impact of such corporate bad behavior is hard to read. Whereas there have been traditional assumptions made about how to behave corporately, trends establish themselves. Such trends spread through many routes, one of which is through the community of financial service providers, including investors and brokers, and their perception of the similarity between financial regulation in the United States and Europe. Regulation is largely reactive. Governments do not focus too much on the future, their concerns tend to be short-term. When obliged to, often based on a perception of what is required, they will act, and sometimes overreact. There is a danger that regulatory rules introduced to ensure the integrity of financial systems can help prolong a downturn by weighting the system. Some rule regimes assert selling triggers when certain risk conditions occur. Selling triggers in a movement-sensitive market push further risk-based sales.

Sometimes these rules are relaxed when they are seen to be counter-productive, but they have to be reintroduced. Regulating a fluctuating market without accentuating rises and falls is not easy.

The balance between the way equities are funded in the United States and in Europe is accentuated in this way. The risk factors are different. In Europe there is a greater use of mortgage contributions and mutual funds to fuel the equities market. In reality the diversity of the US market is its strength, which tends to even out regulatory interventions. In Europe the markets are smaller, and the number of institutions involved fewer; investors also tend to be of a kind, and traditionally there have been fewer instruments and products on the market. Certain sectors are heavily weighted by certain types of company, such as telecommunications and technology-based enterprises. The hit on technology in the 1990s and the telecommunications 3G disaster left many telcos and technology companies in a downward spiral of share loss and market collapse. The scale and diversity of the US market places it in a unique position, and able to absorb the costs and demands of stringent regulation.

THE EUROPEAN UNION

The emergence of the European Union has huge significance for the way financial services will develop for Member States. The issues that have energized the United States have also found cause in Europe. Parmalat is a recent example, and this too was instructive in that it involved the US SEC, which was anxious to interview and follow through with key people involved in that scandal. Recent years have seen the evolution of the single market in financial services across the European Union, partly because of changing economic circumstances and partly as a result of political will. The European Financial Services Plan is a structure that is now largely in place, founded on a set of directives for implementation at national level. From this perspective there are number of factors of note when looking at contemporary and future European regulation on financial services:

- There is an undeniable trend towards consolidation within the EU region and within financial sectors of Member States.
- There is an opening up of cross-border access.
- Member States all have regulatory structures in need of reform, with some degree of consolidation likely.
- Member States will have to respond to the need for consumer protection and effective delivery of this protection.
- A single regulator on the UK model may not be appropriate for all states; however, international cooperation is a background activity to

the general trend of integration and consolidation and may be a viable alternative to central regulation in some instances.
- Harmonization is a term used loosely that encompasses cooperation as well as forcible measures, as EU legislation maintains momentum within a fast-changing sector.

Critical to the overall awareness of the need to manage and control the conduct of economic activity is the principle of "separation" as applied to the activities of banking and regulation in particular, and the creation of monetary policy and its implementation for states and markets.

There will be further major changes in Europe's financial markets, which will continue to involve the markets, key players, and governments, as well as international trends and factors generated by political and social change. Institutional investors cannot be expected to predict the future any more than can anyone else. Intermediaries fulfill a role whether the market moves up or down, contracts or expands. However, in a period of squeezed margins and a market dominated by price as risk, shaped by irrational developments, it is as well to be as prescient as possible. An awareness of the trends outlined is a start.

Consolidation

Regulation does not happen in a vacuum, it is governed by forces that are external to finance as much as changes in the market itself. Two key factors influence the way regulation is drawn up and implemented. The first is the speed of change, which accelerates in a period when trends take hold. The second is the complexity of the changes under way, devising regulation in national states for many sectors at a time with regional integration (in the case of the European Union) or cooperation (in the case of the Asia–Pacific region).

Other factors also heavily influence the construction of regulation:

- Consolidation among banks and insurance companies within countries. In the United Kingdom Commercial Union and General Accident have merged; Axa now owns Sun Life and (nearly) Guardian Royal Exchange.
- Cross-border consolidation across Europe, especially in Scandinavia and the Low Countries. And international takeovers such as Deutsche Bank's purchase of Bankers Trust, ABN Amro's growth to be the largest foreign bank in the United States, and HSBC's equivalent position in Canada.
- The acceleration in minority cross-share holdings, particularly involving banks in Germany, France, Italy, and Spain.
- The broadening of product ranges by banking entities by:

- the addition of investment banking by commercial banks
- the acquisition by European and North American banks of firms in London
- the creation of entities combining banking, capital markets, investment management and insurance businesses
- the increase in many countries of domestic players combining to develop a more competitive presence.

Single regulator

Globally, there have been moves to simplify the number of national regulators to manage the increase in complexity. Sweden, Denmark, Norway, and the United Kingdom already have single regulators. In some circumstances, banking and investment market supervision have been combined, as in Luxembourg, and across Europe there are debates around these issues. Banking is always a case on its own. Outside of Europe, Japan has a prime regulator. In the United States the SEC, although not a single regulator, nevertheless acts as a reference point for all financial regulation, and new Acts tend to comprise amendments to its charter.

As an example of what such a single entity might mean, consider the United Kingdom, where it was believed that a single regulator could deliver advantages, both for financial institutions and for investors and savers. The UK view of what a single regulator might bring to the market is applicable globally within a national context. It provides:

- a one-stop shop for institutions
- a simplified point of reference, introducing the consolidation of rule books on the conduct of business, including the different rules of professional bodies
- the clarification of accountability
- a reduction in costs through efficiencies in scale and reduced complexity
- a solution to the overlap in regulatory processes for similar tasks, especially on capital adequacy and systems of internal controls to be addressed
- encouragement and simplification for cooperation on international regulatory initiatives
- an authoritative view of the global risks being run by nationally based institutions.

The future of regulation in Europe

It is not necessarily the case that introducing a central, single regulator is the correct direction for all Member States in Europe. It is certainly a trend but not definitive. The United Kingdom is a complex and concentrated example. The supply of information is critical to the success of investing in general, in all its many forms and through its many instruments. This may well be best served by more diverse sources of information.

Nearly all financial institutions are rooted in a geography and allied to a Member State. Debate has covered the ground of "stateless" entities that operate beyond national markets although anchored within one of them; this compounds confusion on who supervises such entities. EU Directives generally assume that an organization is registered nationally.

Funding has and will probably always will be a source of debate. Pragmatically, government-sponsored regulators are provided for out of the public purse, funds being voted by national parliaments. Other contributors include central banks and private money provided by market participants. Generally there are provisions that in the event of bank failures and a lack of financial support from the central bank, national measures would come into force. Again the United Kingdom, as a single regulator, is a case in point on some of these issues.

The United Kingdom now has greatly reduced numbers of people directly employed in regulatory activities compared with many other EU regions. In 1999, the combined staff numbers of the regulator and central bank in the United Kingdom amounted to about 4500, while the numbers employed in the central banks and banking supervisor alone, excluding other regulators, in each of the other three largest EU countries ranged between 9000 and 16,000. Partly for historical reasons but partly as a result of economies of scale, the cost of regulation in London is significantly less than other European countries, and nearly half that of in the United States. This adds significantly to the attraction of London as a financial center for intermediaries and investors.

For the investor there are other advantages in there being a single regulator:

- As a single point of reference, expertise tends to accumulate there.
- A single organization with the consumer as its central concern has a keen focus.
- As the entity regulating a complex environment it is empowered with statutory authority.
- In the United Kingdom there is provision for an ombudsman and a compensation scheme for badly advised investors, which has been very active in the endowment mis-selling scandal.

Balancing these advantages of a single regulator, it is the case that many financial markets do not have and are unlikely to have such a centralized approach. The United States has a number of regulatory bodies, and some smaller countries have many regulators. In Appendix A the chief regulatory entities for a number of countries are listed. Some countries have many such bodies. But the creation of single entity is an opportunity for a government-imposed focus. In the United Kingdom, when the FSA was created it had statutory responsibilities:

■ to promote consumer education about the financial system and its institutions, and clarity and quality of information
■ to protect investors and facilitate effective measures to ensure this protection.

Ultimately the balance struck is a practical one, subject to the pull of a number of constituencies, often with different agendas. To satisfy them all is an impossible task. When regulation is accused of being negative, this negativity can be compounded by a centralized approach, as with:

■ the erection of entry barriers to a market
■ price controls and restrictions on competition
■ constraints on innovation
■ limitations on product development.

All these factors and more are the inevitable consequences of a trade-off between control and freedom of operation. The single regulator can act as reference point for consumer and consumers' interests. However, the self-regulatory instinct of many markets and their inherent complexity may make this centralized type of regulation insensitive, especially to the variation in size of entity and its market drivers. It is not surprising to find the SEC in the United States revising its view of draconian legislation, such as the Sarbanes–Oxley Act, to allow for a cost–benefit assessment to be introduced for smaller companies caught in the regulatory net. Investors and intermediaries should be aware of the role and power of single regulators, and the fiscal challenges of regulation that all but the largest corporates challenge; and the way that they have been acknowledged and are now under review.

Enforcement

This is still very much a national issue for the European Union. There is no provision for any form of "federal" enforcement procedures through "federal" courts such as the SEC has available in the United States. To some extent the centralized aspect of regulation finds an answer in a single national regulator rather than a single pan-European regulator. In the near future the trend will probably push towards a forum for regulators rather than a federalized board of regulators.

Although the European Central Bank (ECB) seems a good candidate for a central regulator, given that banking services are merging with other financial services within the portfolio of offerings from services organizations, it seems unlikely that something like the ECB is the best option. Besides, it would need trans-European powers of enforcement, which is politically unlikely. In the United Kingdom the separation of the central bank, the Bank of England, from direct political control is an example of a counter-trend towards liberalization. These conflicting dynamics—centralization and liberalization, central regulation and deregulation—demand constant reassessment and rebalancing in the light of market changes and consumer tolerance of systemic weaknesses and failures.

However, the Committee of European Securities Regulators (CESR), an independent committee of European securities regulators, represents the interests of Member States and national regulators in a committee comprised of one representative from each Member State. Its role is to improve coordination amongst securities regulators, act as an advisory group to the European Commission, and ensure more consistent and timely day-to-day implementation of community legislation in the Member States.

INTERNATIONAL COOPERATION

The other trend that much of this book demonstrates is the requirement for more international cooperation and effective coordination between regulatory regimes. This is not just an aspect of regional developments, but global in scope. Financial markets are located in regions and countries for practical reasons, but these reasons are not necessarily financial in nature; the global financial system, if it can be so described, is ubiquitous. Anyone can trade in securities in Asia, the United States, and South America at the same time as in Europe. It is possible to trade these securities on specific regional and national exchanges, but the activity is common and the risks too. For supervision to be variable according to geography does not sit well with the underlying logic of trading. A common, agreed, and enforced regulatory regime should mean traders have a greater level of confidence in such trades. While it is true that specific markets have specific trading conditions attached, and need specific oversight, nevertheless from the investor's perspective the underlying objectives are the same, regardless of the type of trade, investment, or "saving." Investors want the best return based on accurate, reliable, and understandable information.

There are fora for international cooperation, notably those sponsored by the G7. Europe has encouraged such developments:

- The informal "Groupe de Contact" brings together all the banking regulators of the EU Member States.
- The Banking Advisory Committee includes all the banking supervisors

and ministries of finance, and discusses matters of EU legislation and regulation.

- Most recently, the Banking Supervision Committee of the European Central Bank gathered in a single group each of the EU central banks and banking supervisors.
- There are also well-established insurance committees operating both under the auspices of the European Commission and cooperatively between the supervisors.
- The EC Insurance Committee is broadly equivalent to the Banking Advisory Committee, involving both finance ministries and supervisory authorities in discussions on insurance regulation.
- The Conference of Insurance Supervisory Authorities of the European Union provides a forum for the exchange of information and debate among supervisors.

In December 1997, the Forum of European Securities Commissions (FESCO) was created at a time when the euro had emerged and an alliance between European exchanges was evolving and driven, in turn, by technological developments. FESCO consisted of 17 securities commissions from across Europe and a secretariat made up from among these members. As examples of the work on which FESCO is engaged, we offer two issues arising out of the existing EU legal framework.

European passport

Exchanges regarded as competent authorities are issued "passports" under the ISD. This allows an exchange to provide market facilities in other Member States, for example through remote terminals.

However, this is still an area fraught with difficulties. The key idea is that of a regulated market, and the difficulty is in determining what this means in practice. There are no tightly defined international definitions that act as standards; Rather there is an understanding of what a regulated market means within a national context. The enabling nature of technology can also introduce problems of misuse of the passport, and this is a sensitive area given the lack of true internal recognition of money laundering and computer fraud.

Difficulties in gaining agreement

There are many levels of difficulty in arriving at agreements between EU jurisdictions. The pattern of regulatory responsibilities is complex, and legal frameworks are largely national and likely to remain so for the near future. Agreements tend to result from balancing the need for cooperation between regulators with the legislative and political responsibilities of the European Commission and national governments.

Underlying this effort to gain agreement is political will. The introduction of the single currency has been a dominant factor for moving towards unified capital markets. The major exchanges in Europe, notably London and Frankfurt, have started down the path of cooperation. Other European exchanges are taking initial steps. The final realization of this remains to be seen. Much is at stake. The geographical location of one or many instances of a pan-European exchange or something similar will be shaped by considerations that are political as much as financial. This poses questions about the status of national regulators, as regulators of intermediaries operating as a remote central exchange. Harmonization is need to allow an exchange to operate in a number of different countries.

One of the most obvious prerequisites for such harmonization is a common legal framework. However, that is a Herculean task mired in political processes; it is unlikely to happen in the short term. Meanwhile there is scope for coordination at the regulatory level:

- Cooperation between securities commissions. This already exists through forums such as the CESR.
- Greater harmonization between national markets. Initiatives come through from the European Commission.
- A common approach to listing, prospectus requirements, trading rules and the control of market abuse. This is a process issue, and current practice is a product of cultural and historical factors as much as pragmatic responses to market conditions. In some ways this may be more difficult than the other considerations.

The EU program has a vision of a single market. This is marginally closer but still dependent on events and trends outside of financial control. The UK FSA has been an advocate of an overhaul of the existing regulatory framework in Europe. It has suggested:

- a more consistent implementation of legislation by Member States
- an agreement on the meaning of legislation
- active and consistent enforcement of EU requirements
- placing consumer protection at the heart of cross-border business
- clarifying consumer protection and building expertise and a more widespread understanding of its advantages.

The dilemma for any jurisdiction is matching the requirement for legislation, driven by day-to-day events and pressures, with the machinery of careful decision making and accountable implementation. This is an issue for the investors and intermediaries too; they work in a changing world, under tremendous pressure to be innovative, to introduce new products in response to changing market conditions, and manage the opportunities afforded by investment technology to meet a shifting demographic customer environment. Meanwhile, supervisory and regulatory regimes have to recognize and implement bodies of guidance and legislation which more than ever seem to date rapidly, with the supervised seeking sometimes to evade the strictures of compliance in the struggle to stay competitive.

In a response to the Commission, the FSA commented on this process of maintaining as up to date a regime as possible by prioritizing and suggesting key topics for the European Union to consider:

- Develop broader enabling legislation, with clear and effective guidance, free of too much prescription.
- Creatively use fast-track legal amendments for speed of update.
- Utilize non-legislative alternatives, such as self-regulatory agreements arrived at by loose federations of market players.
- Consult more widely and thoroughly before drawing up legislation, to save considerable delay in the process of passing legislation and to anticipate issues that often severely hamstring implementation later.

The European ideal has founded itself on the concept of consensus. It is this which should be fully exploited in any regulatory framework process. The point is that the best and most appropriate method should be used to achieve the agreed objective.

European Financial Service Action Plan (FSAP)

An example of the way consensus has helped reinforce initiatives for financial services in Europe is the development of the European Financial Services Action Plan (FSAP). This is now a central plank in the efforts to harmonize EU financial regulation. It has the ambitious aim of harmonizing European financial services in order to promote a Europe-wide financial services market. This is probably the major longer-term development in European securities legislation, which strives for an efficient and competitive regional marketplace. The FSAP has a number of specific objectives:

- a single wholesale market
- a single point of entry to all markets for investors and intermediaries
- to allow investment service providers offer services across borders without encountering unnecessary barriers
- to establish a well-integrated investment framework for fund managers
- to create a positive climate of legal certainty for trading in securities safe from counterparty risk.

In essence FSAP is a collection of 42 legislative proposals to be implemented by 2005. The last of the European Commission's progress reports on the FSAP indicated that 36 of those measures had been completed. Some of these proposals have introduced important concepts that directly affect issuers, investors and intermediaries:

- The **Prospectus Directive**—introduced to promote pan-European issuance. This is to be implemented by July 2005.
- The **Market Abuse Directive.** Three proposals have now been adopted by the European Commission, establishing a formal European legal framework in relation to both insider dealing and market manipulation, based on the advice of the CESR.
- The **Directives on Markets in Financial Instruments** and **Transparency Obligations**. These form a key aspect of the FSAP. They are to replace the influential ISD and create a set of compliance procedures for pan-European investment business.
- The **Transparency Obligations Directive.** This was introduced to harmonize the disclosure of regulated issuers and support the existing EC regulation on International Accounting Standards (IAS) as well as Member States' national company law. The directive introduces new quarterly and half-yearly reporting requirements, and requires boards to publish responsibility statements.

At the same time as the FSAP was moving forward, an influential report emerged that help catalyze activity across the European Union, and found especial favor in the United Kingdom.

Lamfalussy

In July 2000, a group of senior European figures chaired by Baron Lamfalussy gathered to review wholesale markets securities regulation in the EU and to make proposals on improving them. The Lamfalussy Group produced its final report in February 2001. The report contained many conclusions including some that addressed the process for creating securities legislation, which needed to be much more flexible. The recommendations were approved by the Stockholm Council in March 2001. Lamfalussy proposed that there should be four elements to the lawmaking process:

1 Directives made by the EU Parliament. These should be high-level, concentrating on key issues of principle. (They are referred to as framework directives.)
2 Each framework directive should outline areas where more detailed

rules are required, and these should be drawn up by a committee bene-fiting from advice from an advisory committee made up of the EU Member State regulators.

3   Levels 1 and 2 concern the making of EU law. The securities regula-tors would operate at Level 3, with the EU institutions determining common standards and approaches.

4   Additionally there would be a need for continuing monitoring and enforcement by the Commission to ensure that EU law passed at levels 1 and 2 was implemented.

In December 2002, the Lamfalussy arrangements were extended from the securities sector to the banking, asset management, and insurance and pension sectors. This was agreed by the European Parliament in March 2004, and two new Level 2 (under FSAP) committees were created:

■   the European Banking Committee (EBC)
■   the European Insurance and Occupational Pensions Committee (EIOPC).

In addition, new Level 3 banking and insurance committees were established:

■   the Committee of Banking Supervisors (CEBS) based in London
■   the Committee of European Insurance and Occupational Pensions Supervisors (CEIOPS) based in Frankfurt
■   the existing Committee of European Securities Regulators (CESR) based in Paris.

The FSAP initiative supported by ongoing efforts such as the Lamfalussy process has made considerable progress in shaping the future for financial services regulation in Europe.

DEREGULATION AND LIBERALIZATION

Historically, the financial services sector in Europe has been segmented. Boundaries between types of institution and between the provision of different types of service were the result of a severity in the regulation of institutional structures (which govern the markets within which institutions operated) and institutional conduct (regulation of which manages exchange controls). In this landscape, banking and other financial offerings were separated as services, and provided by separate institutions. Banking alone saw a range of families from commercial banks through to savings banks and cooperative institutions. This landscape has undergone a radical change. This change, although evolutionary, has accelerated over the last few decades driven by two trends, deregulation and privatization.

Deregulation

This has been a feature of financial life for a while now, but its appearance was initially limited. Broadly it concerned the way the financial sectors existed as historical structures, especially during the 1980s and 1990s, at a time when misdemeanor and bad management began to undermine public confidence in the sector. This evolved into a focus on behavior, elevating governance as a concern, and with practical implications for exchange controls.

Privatization

This was a parallel trend that accompanied deregulation. State controlled and owned institutions were sold off into the market. Consolidation and the heat of competition, stoked by an influx of new packaged "products," opened the market as a whole. Some Member States moved faster than others, motivated by national, political, and economic agendas; others responded when prompted by centralized moves such as the European Union's Second Banking Directive. A significant impetus was the introduction of the single European currency, reinforcing a growing market liberalization and forcing the issue for "Euro-zone" countries on opening their often heavily regulated national markets to foreign entrants.

The impact of deregulation, although varying from Member State to Member State, has been significant.

- Structural boundaries have been dismantled. Financial institutions can now conduct business and offer services and products in all areas of financial service provision.
- The privatization of state-owned institutions means they now compete in the same markets as their privately-owned equivalents. This has seen a switch to a sector subject to market rather than government and political conditions.
- The financial services market has been internationalized. Many barriers between national markets have been removed. One aspect of this and deregulation has been an increase in the number of consolidations and mergers natural to a sudden growth in a sector, and the emergence of financial services multinationals.

Inevitably, these trends have exerted different pressures on different EU Member States, and they have responded accordingly to change. The harmonization efforts of the European Union must be seen in a context of sometimes conflicting national circumstances. For institutional investors this a key consideration, and it is worth examining the outline of these concerns for investing states.

France

The French financial services market has, like many in the European Union, undergone considerable change. It has operated on a model characterized by considerable segmentation. Smaller players, under deregulation, have faced the same challenges as elsewhere. As an ex-colonial power, its financial system always has had a global outlook, but one constrained to the interest of a French hegemony. However, the so-called Anglo-Saxon approach, typified by privatization and deregulation, has taken hold. The traditional banks are major competitors in the newer market, and indeed are market makers forcing smaller entities to innovate with new product offerings to survive. Traditional regulation and their established position make the large banks touch competition. This is also true for foreign entities trying to establish a foothold in the French market.

Many local players have looked outside France on the back of the creation of the single European financial service market. Although this is another steep hill to climb in terms of investment and time, the experience of expansion, and the efficiencies forced by working in unfamiliar territory, may ensure such players are more effective in the longer term in their home country.

France has by no means been insulated from the shocks to the financial system of the late 20th and early 21st centuries. In early 2003, the French Council of Ministers working on "Projet de loi sur la sécurité financière," passed draft legislation on financial security as a local response to the general loss of confidence in the financial sector. It introduced reforms of the financial services supervisory authorities. Among its measures were some protecting non-institutional investors and the public with insurance policies based on investments. It also, in common with so much legislation of the period, detailed ways of supervising corporate accounting and governance. As measures to encourage the more efficient and transparent operation of the financial regulatory framework, it suggested:

- A single authority consisting of the of the primary regulators: Commission des Opérations de Bourse (COB), the Conseil des Marchés Financiers (CMF), and the Conseil de Discipline de la Gestion Financière (CDGF).
- In a move similar to that in the United Kingdom with the creation of the FSA, these regulators were to be part of the Autorité des Marchés Financiers (AMF). Its powers were to be strengthened.

■ To support this process a number of advisory bodies were included for their expertise on financial legislation and regulation in the financial sector.

Denmark

Denmark finds its financial services sector linked to other Nordic countries for historical reasons. To an extent there has always been a Nordic regional economy, notably in the logic of telecomms mergers over the last decades. Given the high degree of communications technology infrastructure and the relative sophistication of the Scandinavian telecomms market, it is not surprising that the competitive agenda is set by this and the drive to cut operating costs and develop web-based services and products. Customers and markets are part of this segmentation.

Sweden

Swedish financial services providers now feel the pressure of deregulation and globalization. Historically this sector has been mixed, with a system of national and regional banks. Meanwhile, banks with a local, personalized service remain important, fulfilling a role the major banks miss. Competition has increased as other regional Nordic banks have entered the market, and deregulation has opened up the opportunities for financial institutions to market products in non-traditional areas; for instance, insurance companies, mutual funds, and other financial services providers have entered the banking market. In response, many established organizations have taken the expansion route to manage change and opportunity. Some have seen a radical shift in business from predominantly national activity to foreign markets. Electronic banking is now a necessary part of the customer services now offered in the region, and gives smaller entities an added advantage. E-business as a whole has the effect of creating a level playing field where business is won through brand marketing and flexible service offerings. The move to external markets is one that the Swedish Bank has followed. Mergers and acquisitions are natural mechanisms for achieving this.

Ireland

The Irish financial services market is under intense pressure from external organizations, notably from the United Kingdom, bent on acquisition and rationalization. A response based on protectionism runs counter to the general trend, and the Irish FSA is busy implementing regulations. The Irish economy has long made much of the benefits derived from joining the European Union. When it comes to regulation there is an instinctive appreciation of the benefits that centralized control from the heart of Europe can offer.

Italy

Italy has seen a major expansion in financial services as a result of dereg-ulation and privatization. The transition of public banks into joint stock companies is an example. The traditional Italian model was dominated by family-owned companies and state-managed entities. The transition to a market-led economy is all the more remarkable. As with all national finan-cial sectors, the pressure now comes from this increasingly competitive market, and to a lesser extent potential competition through foreign inward investment. Organizations that continue to operate in a bureaucratic manner or to rely on past strategic successes are less likely to maintain their market position than they were in the past. Competition means reduced costs and innovative products. Italy also has its own level of notoriety in the Parmalat affair, which reflects a complexity unique to the country as a result of political involvement in economic institutions.

Spain

The Spanish model is typical of a "continental" or German model, with banks as the main source of corporate financing. Until recently this model was typified by a range of savings and loans specific to the Spanish sector. Liberalization started comparatively early, with the development of "universal" banks contending for the whole market, and a deregulation and privatization process has had similar effects within the Spanish financial services.

A major effect has been the internationalization of the sector, with the removal of barriers for foreign entities. As we have seen, this process tends to have an expansionist dimension, and Spanish banks have begun a process of overseas acquisition, a recent example being the acquisition of the Abbey National in the United Kingdom by Banco Santander. Spain, like the United Kingdom and France, also has an external ex-colonial linguistic "home" market in South America.

The Spanish banks have not simply consolidated, they have also expanded nationally through increased branch networks, especially savings banks. This contrasts strongly with the tendency to cut and reduce branches in other countries, notably the United Kingdom.

United Kingdom

Change in the UK financial services sector began comparatively early. The dominance of the London markets has long centered international activities in the United Kingdom and kept it in the forefront of economic develop-ments. A liberalization process was initiated in response to market reforms earlier on.

The United Kingdom has, to a large extent, been the European pioneer in the deregulation of financial markets. This has resulted in the privatization of a large number of mutually owned insurance companies and building societies. By 2000 this process was largely complete; only a handful of mutual building societies and insurance companies remained. Pressure from shareholders still threatens these.

The mixing of functions between savings and investments and current account services is a reality, although the two distinct activities differentiate the traditional banks from the new de-mutualized entities. All this activity sees the United Kingdom as a merger-prone financial services market. Structurally the market is very open, and intensely competitive, with new products continually presented to a heavily differentiated investor audience.

However, a counter-trend of regulation and tightening of controls has emerged in response to publicly aired scandals and industry misdemeanors. By 2000, uncompetitive behavior through prospective mergers and excessive charging for services led to a movement to coordinate regulation and join up the disparate bodies responsible for overseeing financial activity. This sensitivity has seen fewer internal mergers but some acquisitions by external players, such as Banco Santander, which is seen as widening rather than narrowing competition. This has left the United Kingdom with a more complex regulatory and political environment than most, even though the creation of the FSA was a move to ease the burden of previous complexity.

Germany

While it is true that German financial services began to introduce regulation at an early stage, it remains one of the most stable and least liberalized markets in the European Union. Nevertheless liberalization has made changes. Banking is currently in a phase of transition under the pressure of competition within Germany and in international markets. The German model has *Sparkassen*, or savings banks, and cooperatives as the main providers of retail financial services, divided along regional lines. This model is under attack from investor activism and external models of transparency. There is a move towards "shareholder capitalism," where profitability is rated more highly than longevity and durability. This has generated pressure to cut costs and become more efficient, often through a wider uptake of technology, so that parts of the German financial economy are well advanced in communications infrastructure.

If you want to be a pan-European global financial services success, however, you have to succeed in Germany. Germany, for many, is seen as the largest market in Europe. Geography, history, and economic scale all make the nation and its financial markets impossible to ignore. In the broad sweep of globalization which has seen US ideas and business practices dominate markets such as the United Kingdom, Germany retains far more in common with its European neighbors than with the United States, and Germany and its business partners know the market can and must play a pivotal role in the emerging European funds market.

The recent deal between insurer Allianz and German banking giant Dresdner to create a so-called bancassurance facility was just one example of the growing appetite for change and development in the German financial services sector.

Custodians who wish to be active in this market must be adept enough to cope with a changing financial landscape. For them there are some key issues:

■ It is unclear how far historic domestic players or aggressive new market entrants will take best advantage of Germany's strategic position and strengths.
■ Success in the complex German domestic custody market will leave providers well placed to capitalize on growth in the emerging European securities markets.

The German national scene also poses several challenges which relate to:

■ complex legislation and labyrinthine regulation
■ the cost of technological development
■ margins for providers being squeezed.

To date, recent foreign forays into the German custody market have met with mixed success. Some foreign players, such as Citibank, can point to a lengthy presence in the market and a genuine understanding of its requirements. But new foreign entrants have found unexpected pitfalls such as an entrenched traditional investment and banking network suspicious of new entrants, and potential clients whose definition of commitment differs from that expected—emphasizing longevity, solidity, and staying power. To custodians comfortable with US notions of outsourcing, investment management, and custody in a liberally regulated environment, the German market can seem bureaucratic to the point of being hostile to outsiders.

History plays an important role in the tight regulation of foreign financial services companies. Foreign investment funds initially played an important role in developing the post-war German market, but the 1960s saw a dramatic implosion of the Investors Overseas Services, which had encouraged foreign investment. This had long-term regulatory implications, and there has long been a lack of enthusiasm for change.

Control and innate conservatism were typified in March 2003 when Germany's finance minister Hans Eichel responded to the need of retail investors for German hedge fund products by planning to allow the sale and marketing of German and non-German hedge funds by early 2004.

The advent of foreign entities operating in the German market has helped in a number of ways. In the German market, services were typically "bundled," making it difficult to separate and unpick custody costs, which generated transparency issues. Unbundled solutions were not widely accepted as the way of doing things, and there has been resistance. Foreign entities have helped change this.

The German market is typically strict and rich, with specific laws such as the KAG law which govern the handling of unit trust and public mutual funds. All investment and banking organizations in Germany have faced rigid control by regulators. Domestic investment managers, or KAGs, are recognized as banks, and are subject to Banking Act provisions and state supervision.

In Germany, banks have traditionally acted as both asset manager and custodian to institutional and retail investment clients. Mutual and so-called *spezialfonds* have been dominated by national rather than international entities. Until the late 1990s, the term "global custody" was almost unknown in Germany, and some funds specialists still feel unfamiliar with the term. Custodians serving the German market face extremely tight controls, not least achieving so-called *depotbanken* status, or using affiliates with this distinction. The choice of custodians has to be approved by the central regulator, the BAK, and custodian banks are required to have an equity capital of at least DM10 million and to be a member of a deposit protection scheme.

German banks have dominated the custody market. However, a shift in legislation to liberalize German financial services and encourage limited foreign involvement appears to be changing that. Others are now focusing on administering and servicing German *spezialfonds* and KAGs. This has resulted from:

■ a trend towards cross-border investing
■ the implementation of the euro
■ the need to diversify the national asset base
■ the EU process of harmonizing pensions
■ the advantages of a common reporting and accounting procedure.

As a result of liberalization, foreign companies now manage a range of pension funds, corporate investors, and banks. Chase Manhattan was one of the first banking organizations in Germany to offer an investor service focusing solely on custody. State Street and Chase Manhattan Bank are among the foreign entrants to this market. The changes in 1966 in regulation were seen by these entities as openers for the closed German market.

No domestic German bank looms as large as Deutsche Bank. It is a true global giant, and a dominant presence in the national and international market for global custody services. Unlike new entrants to the market, Deutsche Bank can point to a central historic role in supporting the German investment and banking sector. Deutsche Bank projects itself as one of the key global custody providers in the emerging funds market, predicting a shake-out in the marketplace with only a handful of providers remaining. However, on the custody front Deutsche Bank does not see a unified European investment market emerging for some time, and until then it seeks to dominate a regional market.

A distinction is made in Germany between the German and Anglo-Saxon models. The variety of regulation in securities processing, for example, contrasts with that of the United States. This puts US companies at a disadvantage, not an uncommon experience for US entities entering Europe, given the national differences they encounter. But additional complexities within each country or region adds to the burden.

This can not all be put down to German businesses being awkward. They are often openly glad of competition. They too suffer from Euro politics which sometimes puts them at a disadvantage in their own EU sphere. They might welcome tax harmonization and a truly pan-European cross-border funds industry. Europe is often more expensive to trade in than, say, the United States. The failure of the proposed merger between the London Stock Exchange and the Deutsche Börse was symbolic of differing interests at work, and a failure to realize the opportunity to consolidate financial market infrastructures, which would reduce complexity and cost.

Consolidation confers competitive advantages in the world market, and these are well understood in Germany. In the longer term, consolidation of lengthy settlement processes is critical if Europe is to be an option. Other domestic players such as Commerzbank, as well as international entities such as the Paris-based BNP Paribas, utilize their European connections. Perhaps these will draw together the logic and provide the energies needed for such consolidation. However, it seems that a solid presence in the home market is critical to success.

One significant area for potential growth in the German market is private pension provision. The US, and now the UK, markets are rich in such provision. In the case of the United Kingdom the success of private against state and company final salary provisions has yet to be shown. However, it is a growing force for change. The other major EU countries have a different legacy, one based on state provision. The funding of these pension systems is beginning to unravel, and it is likely these states will look to the private sector to take the strain, however unpalatable this may be politically. The new landscape is likely to be characterized by:

- an emergent hybrid system, private and publicly based
- the need for political face-saving pushing through stronger regulation over such schemes
- openness and accountability, the touchstones for reforms in the United States, to accompany these moves.

At some point we can anticipate a trend towards private pension schemes in Germany, and this is an real opportunity for those companies used to handling private pension schemes in a heavily regulated world. Other trends reinforce this. The adoption of Internet-based technologies is now stronger in Germany. Efficiencies in IT systems deployment are now more appreciated, and Internet banking has great potential in a country that has long had extensive deployment of broadband links to home environments through ISDN. Well-implemented technology can enable considerable cost savings and build new efficiencies into the value chain.

A German investment bill was announced, and a draft released in summer 2003, which almost immediately disappointed the target audience by its limitations. Foreign players in Germany, mainly banks, responded by presenting proposals for its amendment. The progress of this initiative has been slowed by a reluctance to make fundamental changes. But it is as well to remember that there is a culture unique to Germany, and that this is characterized by a very discerning investor public focused on reliability and service, with little tolerance of non-compliant players. The emphasis is not necessarily on the range of new packaged products, but on high-value tailored offerings.

COMPLIANCE

When it comes to managing compliance in Europe, it is essential to have local expertise to match the local requirements of EU directives implemented through national legislation. While in theory we can talk about using external consultancies that understand local variants on transnational legislation, nevertheless the reality is that financial services companies are very much thrown back on their own resources when facing the practicalities of getting themselves into shape. This, along with breaking new ground in business against a historical climate that is not supportive of external involvement, can be more than a challenge even for the largest of newcomers. There has to be a real and substantial market driver to make this all happen. Germany is an example of where such drivers exist, because of the scale of market and its potential through the regional domination of its economy in Eastern Europe.

Another school of thought sees legislation, centrally generated from the European Union, as a way of slowly but surely knitting together these markets. At the same time, the behavioral change implicit in much remedial legislation aimed at protecting the public from the darker side of business impropriety can change, and is changing, corporate attitudes. If there is a identifiable advantage to change then it will come. The influence of US practice at boardroom level is very significant. The moves aimed at tightening control of executive and non-executive directors are spreading. The United States and the United Kingdom, representing the Anglo-Saxon world, have taken this on, albeit they have enforced it in different ways. Nevertheless, the strength of intent is there.

As with all these things, the devil is in the detail, and so we move from the general to the specific, and look at instances that illustrate the variety of issues this new regulatory landscape presents to the institutional investor, the intermediary, and those whose livelihood depends on the way legislation shapes their markets.

Part II

Part II

CHAPTER 3

Regulatory Overview

In this chapter we analyze several sets of regulatory structures in some detail. The format, as indicated in the preface, is based on a summary table, followed by some contextual explanation of the particular regulations, followed by some practical tips for investors and intermediaries on how to achieve best practice or support their best interests.

It is important to note again that these descriptions are not intended to be detailed expositions of every factor of each regulatory framework. The objective of this book overall is to raise the awareness of the inter-connectedness of regulatory frameworks at structural as well as practical levels. So this chapter sets out to establish a baseline of some of the more important regulations, and explain the major issues that these regulations raise for investors and intermediaries.

Several of these regulations have a primary focus on one aspect of financial services. So, for instance, the Combined Code in the United Kingdom deals with corporate probity at issuer level. Clearly this is of primary concern to the issuers themselves, as they relate to their investors. To that extent, most intermediaries would ignore such regulation at their peril. If the reader gains any benefit from this book, its primary message has to be that what might appear not to have any effect may actually have a significant effect. These sections are also critical when we come to consider the overlaps that exist between seemingly otherwise unconnected regulations in Part III.

The implications for financial services on regulatory overlap are significant, as are the more traditionally associated risks for investors who do not encompass these types of regulation into their increasingly "long" portfolio yield strategy.

UNITED KINGDOM

The Combined Code on Corporate Governance

What is it?
The "Combined Code" combines the recommendations of the Cadbury, Greenbury, and Hampel Committee Reports.
What does it do?
Provides best practice for boards of directors and establishes responsibilities for them.
Who does it affect?
All UK listed companies.
Why does it exist?
It combines the elements of a number of codes and guidelines and the work of the Financial Reporting Council.
Will it change?
Since publication it has undergone one revision and influenced other reports.
Who are the regulators?
The London Stock Exchange (LSE), the market and self-regulation.

Following the work undertaken by the Hampel Committee, in June 1998 the London Stock Exchange (LSE) published new listing rules together with related Principles of Good Governance and Code of Best Practice that have become known as the "Combined Code." This Code carries a charge of responsibilities for the directors of limited companies across all industries. It is a central piece in the edifice of corporate governance in the United Kingdom, and its sentiments reflect an international outlook. However, it has been the subject of considerable criticism. We look later at how the debate reflects developments in the industry, and consider how well the code maps to international developments.

Since its first publication, efforts have been made to change the Combined Code. The most effective changes have resulted from the Higgs Review, which led to a revised version of the Code.

In summary, the key provisions of the Combined Code state that:

- The board should meet sufficiently regularly, and there should be a formal schedule specifically covering its responsibilities.
- Management should provide receive timely and accurate information, which directors should question as necessary for clarification.
- There is an onus on the chairman:

- to ensure that board members maintain suitable skills and are suitably acquainted with the operation of the company
- to ensure that the views of shareholders are communicated to the board
- to communicate, and discuss matters such as governance and strategy, with major shareholders
- to hold meetings with the non-executive directors.

■ Performance is a critical consideration in a period where public confidence had been shaken by the perception of poor performance being inappropriately rewarded. The board must undertake a searching annual evaluation of its own performance and that of its committees and individual directors.

Further critical requirements of the original Combined Code address the following issues:

■ In the code, all internal controls are to be the subject of the responsibility of the board of directors, not just financial controls.

■ Annual reports must include a narrative statement that describes how the defined principles of good corporate governance have been applied.

■ The board of directors will report to shareholders directly on remuneration.

■ Remuneration for senior executives should reflect performance. To make this a reality, incentive schemes must be tied to performance, and these schemes should be demanding.

■ Non-executive directors must be identified and named in annual reports. They are to play a more significant role: The remuneration and audit committees are to be primarily staffed by independent non-executive directors.

The code is structured to cover "principles" of good governance and a code of best practice focused on companies, listed, and institutional shareholders:

1 Principles of Good Governance
   1.1 Section 1 Companies: directors, their remuneration, relations with shareholders, accountability and audit
   1.2 Section 2 Institutional shareholders: institutional investors
2 Code of Best Practice
   2.1 Section 1 Companies: directors, their remuneration, relations with shareholders, accountability and audit
   2.2 Section 2 Institutional shareholders: institutional investors

The importance of the Code was acknowledged by the UK Listing Authority, which requires listed companies to disclose how they have applied its principles and whether they have complied with its provisions. A new Listing Rule (12.43A) requires a UK incorporated listed company to make a disclosure statement on:

■ how the company has applied the principles of Section 1 of the Combined Code
■ whether or not a company has complied throughout the accounting period with the provisions established in Section 1 of the Combined Code.

Another piece of regulatory guidance is closely connected with the Combined Code: the Turnbull Report. The significance here is that a company complying with Turnbull also complies with the Combined Code and the Listing Rules, such is the interplay and overlap between the two. Both these reports are sets of guidelines for voluntary compliance; they do not have legislative force.

The Code talks of a system of internal control. The importance of this is raised for the board to consider, in order to safeguard shareholder investment and the company's assets, as enshrined in Principle D.2. The Code goes further than other guidelines in requiring directors to review the effectiveness of all their internal controls, not merely financial controls. However, the Code does not explicitly look for an opinion on the effectiveness of this system of internal control, and provides no guidance on the matter. This is something the Turnbull Report addresses as a set of supporting guidelines on the Code in practice.

Although it is nominally aimed at companies listed on the LSE, the principles of the Code apply to all limited companies in so far as they represent a body of best practice guidelines. There is some awareness of international developments, and they are claimed to be broadly in line with the requirements of other international stock markets, although this is an aspect that may be revisited. The Code was seen as a mechanism for establishing a benchmark by which the international as well as domestic investor could make a judgment.

Following the Higgs Review, the Combined Code was amended, and the New Combined Code on Corporate Governance was published on July 23, 2003 by the FRC. It came into effect for listed companies for reporting years beginning on or after November 1, 2003, and largely follows the recommendations made in the Higgs Review of the Role and Effectiveness of Non-Executive Directors, and in the Smith Report on Audit Committees. Some of the Higgs proposals were watered down in response to criticism, notably where Higgs required that companies would have to confirm their compliance and explain any non-compliances. They can now state more generally how they have applied the requirements. Higgs was generally thought to be too idealistic and unworkable.

Although this is a voluntary code, in effect regulation is explicit in that non-compliance brings the threat of de-listing on the Stock Exchange, and implicit in potential market threats such as shareholder activism and lapse in confidence, a lower share price, and loss of reputation.

Practical tips for investors

Essentially, as with many of these reports, the Combined Code is a collection of best practice guidelines. Investors should take its guidance seriously, and when measuring the performance of the company, use the principles and specifications as an effective checklist. Over time, more and more of the principles are being represented in company annual reports.

Interim information is available through company press releases. Website updates also provide a rich source of company information—on internal reorganization, staff changes, business growth and contraction, and market penetration.

If a company fails to meet a majority of the critical points within the Code, it is clearly failing itself and its investors. Investors should combine this view of the company with the best practice associated with the other linked reports to build a bigger picture of the true state of corporate governance.

Practical tips for issuers and intermediaries

To consider the impact of the Combined Code on financial institutions, we can visit the annual report of HBOS, one of the giants that emerged from the era of acquisition and merger. In particular, an extract from the Annual Report and Accounts of 2003, covering corporate governance, talks of welcoming "the reviews of Corporate Governance conducted by Sir Derek Higgs and Sir Robert Smith, together with their proposals for a revised Combined Code." HBOS makes the specific point of embracing "both the letter and spirit of the new Code." The report talks of reporting on compliance with the principles and provisions of the original Code. The extract notes that:

> the Company has a comprehensive programme of meetings and dialogue with institutional investors and ensures that the views of investors expressed through this dialogue, and through the Annual Audit of Investor Opinion ... are communicated to the Board as a whole, so that all directors can develop a balanced understanding of the issues and concerns of major shareholders.

We can see here the Code settling into the thinking of the board, and married with a process of dialog with investors. A pragmatic view is taken of the Code's suggestion of routine meetings between the shareholders and the senior independent director: It is claimed they are not necessary, based on shareholder feedback and existing adequate channels of communication. This is a good example of a company measuring up to the requirements of the Code, recognizing its spirit, and specifically detailing its response in a public statement.

When it comes to the practicalities of compliance, the Code stresses that external auditors are required to review the statements of compliance before publication of their report and of the company's annual report and accounts.

Higgs Review

What is it?
A report, based on an independent review led by Derek Higgs, on the role and effectiveness of non-executive directors in the United Kingdom.
What does it do?
Sets out an agenda for change, and provides recommendations and guidance on the role of non-executive directors and their recruitment.
Who does it affect?
The boards of financial institutions.
Why does it exist?
The review was commissioned in April 2002, by the UK Secretary of State and the Chancellor of the Exchequer, and published on January 20, 2003.
Will it change?
The report is a one-off, but its implications, for example for the Combined Code, are ongoing.
Who are the regulators?
Higgs takes a non-legislative approach; it relies on companies to institute best practice. Further aspects are covered in the Combined Code.

The Higgs Review, or *Review of the Role and Effectiveness of Non-Executive Directors*, was published in January 2003. In his opening letter to the sponsors of the review, the Chancellor and the Secretary of State, Derek Higgs notes that:

When corporate strategies fail or governance lapses ... attention rightly focuses on the contribution of the non-executive director. Against a background of corporate turbulence, it is very much the purpose of this Review to let in some daylight on the role of the non-executive director in the boardroom and to make recommendations to enhance their effectiveness.

This fundamentally sums up the mood and content of the report. Essentially the review seeks to explore an area not dealt with thoroughly by previous recommendations: the non-executive director and his or her critical role in good governance at board level. The review is also an attempt to rework this message into a revised Combined Code. The changes envisioned for the Combined Code are significant for intermediary investors, since they encourage:

- independence of thought and action in non-executive board members
- a better informed senior executive, leading to greater transparency and accountability
- improved formal performance appraisals
- closer relationships between non-executive directors and shareholders
- a far more rigorous process for appointing non-executive board members.

Higgs goes on to say: "The Combined Code and its philosophy of 'comply or explain' is being increasingly emulated outside the UK. It offers flexibility and intelligent discretion and allows for the valid exception to the sound rule." This also strongly indicates the way the report expects boards to respond to its recommendations—through self-interested self-regulated compliance, not statutory edict and regulatory penalties. Higgs clarifies his own thoughts on this by adding:

> The brittleness and rigidity of legislation cannot dictate the behavior, or foster the trust, I believe is fundamental to the effective unitary board and to superior corporate performance.

The report is based on a view of corporate governance which is enlightened, in that it recognizes the need for persuasion through other than legal channels, and follows a tradition of self-regulation which is not in tune with the global change to statutory methods of enforcing good governance. The aspiration that "the Code can and should regularly evolve to lead best practice in the boardroom and raise the bar for performance," is an aspiration that has yet to be fully realized.

The review has a prime focus on the effectiveness of non-executive directors, especially in the promotion of company performance and the relationship with accountability. Recommendations look for a culture change at the very top of the organization to develop transparency in the appointment process, encouraging appointment on merit and suitability to broaden the integrity and experience of UK boardrooms. These recommendations include:

- The promotion of appointment on the basis of merit and experience of relevant disciplines in the boardroom.
- Using an open and transparently fair appointments process to broaden access to prospective candidates.
- Clearer scope and definition of the role of the non-executive director.
- The separation of the roles of chairman and chief executive.
- The chief executive should not become chairman of the same company.
- A revised definition of director to include the concept of independence in those areas affecting a director's objectivity. This would apply to most of the board and the audit remuneration and nomination committees.
- Developing the non-executive director's relationship with major shareholders.
- An annual review of the performance of the board.
- Improved and more comprehensive induction and professional development for directors.
- A clarification of the liabilities of non-executive directors.

The report is sensitive to the scale of organizations that qualify for its recommendations, and suggests that some of the new Code provisions may be less relevant or more challenging for the smaller organization.

The report also includes specific guidance for non-executive directors on the need to provide leadership, especially for risk and internal controls. This guidance encourages the non-executive director to:

- be involved in strategy development
- help establish the values and standards of the company in line with its obligators to shareholders
- focus on the board-level concerns of "strategy, performance, risk and people."

A further annex provides guidance for chairmen. Given the central role of the chairman, the report lists his or her primary responsibilities for running and setting meeting agendas, ensuring the prevision of accurate and timely information, communications with shareholders, inducting new members, and reviewing annually the performance of the board.

A major annex, "Suggested Revised Code (incorporating review recommendation)," outlines in detail the Principles of Good Governance and the Code of Best Practice for companies and institutional investors, with an additional "Guidance on liability of non-executive directors: skill and dili-gence." This fulfills the aim of the review—to act as a base for revising the Combined Code.

The recommendations of the review are applicable to a wide range of companies, in effect all those affected by the Combined Code. Specifically it applies to listed companies with financial years ending on or after November 1, 2003.

The terms of reference for the review required it to build and publish an accurate picture of the current status of boardroom governance in order to generate debate and conclusions on how best to improve the effectiveness of non-executive directors. In part the agenda also implied they were a valuable resource in managing the transition from a more traditional board to one that had specific expertise and experience to take on the changes implied in new regulatory requirements. The importance of directors is central to this regulatory climate, and Higgs centers its initiative on devel-oping them to avoid the issues of transparency and deemed breach of trust that span out of Enron and so damaged the image of the industry.

To explore the background to the review and build up a body of mate-rial for review, a consultation paper was issued in June 2002. It received in excess of 250 responses across the industry. In addition, three pieces of research were commissioned. These generated a comprehensive picture on the size, composition, and membership of the boards of the United Kingdom's 2200 listed companies, and their population of non-executive directors. MORI was engaged to carry out a survey of 650 executive and non-executive directors and chairmen of listed companies, addressing patterns of behavior on recruitment, induction, and perform-ance appraisal. Senior academics were employed to interview directors on FTSE-350 boards, furthering the understanding of the practical real-ity, in terms of relationships and behavior, of being a non-executive director.

This review is a one-off. However, it is likely there will be further reviews in the future in relation to the Combined Code if other questions are raised about the state of governance in boardrooms. Much depends on the reaction of directors to the Code and the Turnbull Report. A further report, the Tyson Report, is an instance of this.

Responding to a recommendation in Chapter 10 of the Higgs Review, pointing to the need for companies to draw on a wider range of talent with skills, experiences, and perspectives that could enhance board effective-ness, Professor Laura D'Andrea Tyson, Dean of the London Business School, was asked by the Department of Trade and Industry (DTI) to lead a group to look at how companies might realize these aims. The report, focusing on the recruitment and development of non-executive directors, was published in June 2003. Its main points are:

- The promotion of diversity in the boardroom.
- Like the Higgs Review, it calls for the setting of transparent criteria for the appointment of non-executive directors, and more and better evaluation and training for board members.
- It also recommends recruiting directors from outside the usual layers of top management to strengthen experience and introduce new ideas. In particular this would help to promote more women and minorities.

The principle here is to enhance the overall capability of boards, by skilling them to monitor their business in an increasingly complex regulatory climate, eliminating many of the concerns over directors' remuneration, and making good some of the damage done to corporate trustworthiness.

The recommendations of the Higgs Review aimed at amending the Code, where necessary, are for the FRC to implement. The FRC is responsible for keeping the Code under review, and it has publicly welcomed the recommendations of the Higgs Review. It has set up a working group to produce a revised draft of the Combined Code which incorporates the recommendations of the Review.

The non-regulatory nature of the Review's outlook has been expressed by Derek Higgs himself, and he adds, "I do not presume that a one-size fits all approach to governance is appropriate." Indeed, the approach has been to encourage self-development among directors, as well as formal structured development from induction onwards, and a move to ensure that boards adjust their own behavior by strengthening their cross-functional experience, and bring fresh insight and experience to bear on their growing regulatory responsibilities.

> "The Review is not a blue-print for box-tickers, but a counsel of best practice that can be intelligently applied."

Practical tips for investors

Higgs emphasizes the best practice aspect of the Review. From the perspective of an intermediary or investor assessing a potential investment, it is important to look at the board of a company with a Higgs perspective. In particular:

- look for expressions of intent to broaden the range of the board in terms of skills and experience
- look for plans to introduce effective induction processes for new board members

■ scrutinize details about the non-executive directors to see what they bring to the board and the company

■ examine how well all the business functions are represented at top level—notably IT

■ look for clarification of roles and responsibilities of directors, the chairman, and non-executive directors

■ look for intent to follow the Higgs recommendations in general, especially the requirement to publicly document any or all of the above.

Although there are overlaps, which we will examine later, with other regulatory entities such as the Combined Code and Turnbull, the whole review in itself is a collection of recommended best practice rather than formal regulation. Investors and intermediaries should look for evidence of this spirit.

Practical tips for issuers and intermediaries

The messages of the Higgs Review are clearly stated. For issuers not yet implementing a recruitment and induction regime for non-executive directors there is plenty of scope for following the recommendations of the review. The subsequent work of Tyson is also worth following up as an example of best practice in selecting a balanced boardroom. Key recommendations are:

■ Ensure newly selected non-executive directors bring the right mix of skills and experience to the board. It has long been practice among less enlightened companies for senior management teams to follow a "like recruits like" approach to staffing the board, where the board recruits further facsimiles of its members rather than people with different sets of skills and experience. It is a form of "comfort" recruitment.

■ Ensure that the independence of non-executive directors is demonstrable. This also ensures this independence stays at the forefront of induction programs and general everyday decision making.

The FRC announced that it would take forward the recommendations of the Higgs Review for changes to the Combined Code by summer 2003. Alongside this, the Coordinating Group on Audit and Accounting Issues (CGAA) is reviewing the UK audit and accounting regime to enable a proactive regime for enforcing accounting standards.

The Higgs Review was commissioned by the Chancellor of the Exchequer and the Secretary of State, in the context of further concerns about the exposure of corporate boardrooms following the Enron scandal. The

Secretary of State added, referring the raft of reports and sub-reports issued in that period: "Together these reports make an important contribution to boosting market and investor confidence." However, how true is this? How far have the evolving groups of reports and recommendations really generated a new climate in which boards examine themselves critically and truly review the criteria by which they judge non-executive directors, and how are claims to have promoted the performance of the financial sector through such studies substantiated?

There has been considerable criticism of the review through anecdotal articles and surveys of directors. To some extent this might be expected: After all, the review is aimed at improving something thought to need improvement. Those affected may well think this is unnecessary. However, the voluntary nature of the code does mean it needs substantial buy-in from its target audience, and it is not clear that this is forthcoming. Some surveys have indicated that up to three-quarters of Britain's leading executives see the recommendations as being ineffective and another increment to the larger burden of legislation. Chief among their concerns are that directors will have to spend more time on company business, and be paid more. Estimates of the financial cost of regulation for businesses in the United Kingdom are already in the region of £100 billion. Estimates have also talked of 2.5 percent of Britain's gross domestic product being diverted to enforcement. It is also widely believed that while the review may make some impression on fraudulent and criminal behavior, this behavior is impossible to eradicate, and shareholders should not be misled on this issue.

Other concerns have been voiced: that the report is "flawed" and that it *does* have a "one size fits all" approach. This contrasts with Derek Higgs's own sentiments. The true test relates to the response the revised Combined Code meets with in the industry, and how well it reflects investors' interests.

Higgs, Turnbull, and other reviews of the industry tend to be vertically oriented and focused on single issues. The recommendations made are focused within the structure of how a CEO or board should act with respect to its shareholders. One of their biggest drawbacks is that they all fail to address the question of how these two ends of the investment chain interact through the complex web that is the financial services industry. Typically, the approach has been to presume that the "meat" in this sandwich is regulated by the FSA. This also creates the false presumption that the elements at beginning and end of the governance chain can somehow interact, subject to the report guidelines, without affecting or being affected by the conduit between the two. This is of course untrue, and later chapters will show how this area of overlap can create significant risk and liability for intermediaries.

Turnbull Report

What is it?

Guidance provided by the Institute of Chartered Accountants in England and Wales (ICAEW) to enable UK companies to implement the internal controls required by the Combined Code on Corporate Governance.

What does it do?

Provides guidance on implementing the elements of the Combined Code dealing with internal controls, internal audit, and risk management.

Who does it affect?

UK companies especially those under the remit of the LSE.

Why does it exist?

The section of Combined Code dealing with internal control needed additional guidance for directors. This task was given to the Turnbull Committee.

Will it change?

In all probability. The significance of internal control is such that it is an ongoing issue.

Who are the regulators?

The LSE endorses compliance with the report, but there is no official enforcement.

The Turnbull Report, published in September 1999, is the abbreviated name given to guidance provided by the ICAEW to enable UK companies to implement the internal controls required by the Combined Code on Corporate Governance. Prepared by the ICAEW's Internal Control Working Party, its full title is *Internal Control: Guidance for directors on the Combined Code*.

The report focuses on the responsibilities of company directors, especially for managing risk. Listed organizations must now demonstrate to shareholders that they have assessed the risk attached to all assets and activities, and that they have taken action to limit or remove their exposure to risk in each area. Of course, as with any regulation or sector-specific guidelines, companies that do not comply with the Turnbull Report face the threat of a backlash in stakeholder confidence—from customers to investors—and in theory could even be de-listed.

This emphasis on senior director responsibility for business continuity establishes how widely it is dealt with at board level, with the key drivers being regulation, the threat of terrorism, and companies' increased reliance on IT systems.

The key themes of the report are:

- Risk management—managing risk responsibly as a organization.
- Internal controls—effective controls for risk management and transparent reporting. According to the ICAEW, the guidance "indicates the company's internal control system should ... be embedded within its operations and not be treated as a separate exercise." Further:
  - the system should be able to respond to changing risks within and outside the company
  - the guidance should enable the company to apply the system effectively to its key risks.

Compliance with this report is seen by the LSE as being consistent with the Combined Code. In fact, adoption and implementation with the Turnbull Report guidance ensures a company is in compliance with:

- Combined Code provisions D.2.1 and D.2.2 and the narrative for principle D.2.
- the related listing rule disclosure requirements of the LSE.

All LSE listed companies were expected to put in place procedures to implement the Turnbull guidelines by the time they reported for the end of year on or after December 23, 1999. Full compliance was expected for the years after December 23, 2000. As part of its lineage, the Turnbull guidance replaces the Rutteman "Internal control and financial reporting" guidance of 1994.

The Combined Code, among other things, widened the scope of interest for companies on internal controls from financial system internal controls to all internal controls. However, there was acknowledgment that the part of the Code dealing with the broader concept of internal control needed re-examining, and guidance needed to be provided for directors. This task was given to the Turnbull Committee, which published draft rules in April 1999, and final guidelines at the end of September 1999. It is also consistent with the Combined Code and the Listing Rule of the LSE on disclosure requirements.

The Turnbull Report is linked to a number of bodies and other reports (see Figure 3.1). The originating body, the ICAEW, the supporting body of the LSE, and the UK Listing Authority (UKLA), maintain its links with the Combined Code on Corporate Governance.

The Turnbull Report is a response to a weakness in another report, and in turn is part of a web of reports and guidance that reflect the constant shift in emphasis taking place in corporate governance. It seems inevitable that it will be revisited, in a similar manner to the Combined Code itself. At the time of its launch in 1999, Nigel Turnbull said it should be reviewed in five years (2004) to deal with any new issues or problems that arise in practice. The reviews and consultation may occur more frequently, with the intention of implementing any revisions. One is scheduled at the beginning of 2006. However, when we come to assess its overlap with other regulation, the report is now seen to be "dating," especially with regard to the Sarbanes–Oxley Act in the United States and changes to the Combined Code on internal controls.

There is no statutory regulation per se. The Turnbull provisions are "enforceable" (by the UKLA) after a fashion, under the Financial Services and Markets Act 2000. A company can be de-listed ("suspended" or "canceled"), but voluntary compliance is sought, supported, and endorsed by the LSE. However, as with any formal guidance, codes of practice, and sector-specific guidelines, companies that do not comply with the Turnbull Report face the threat of a loss of stakeholder confidence. The key risk is a "market" risk rather than financial or personal risk: that is, a risk to brand name, reputation, and probity. Given the endorsement of the LSE and the association with listing disclosure rules, companies could be de-listed. Time and again we see the threat of exposure (that a company does not

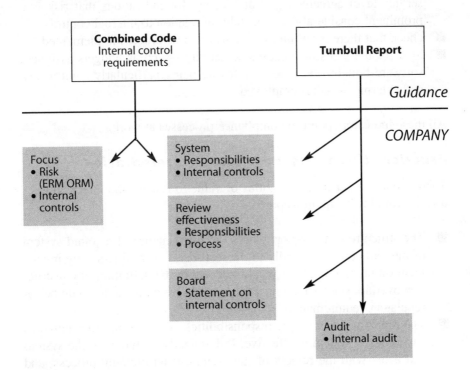

Figure 3.1 Turnbull guidance and the Combined Code
Source: the authors.

declare through its reports that it complies with voluntary codes) as a means of enforcing non-legislative regulation.

Listed organizations must now demonstrate to shareholders that they have assessed the risk attached to all assets and activities, and that they have taken action to limit or remove their exposure to risk. From the investor's perspective this should be evident from company reports and press releases. The declarations should be clear and unmistakable.

Since it affects all UK companies under the remit of the London Stock Exchange, the Turnbull Report affects financial institutions. This is especially so at board level, and Turnbull is similar to Sarbanes–Oxley in focus on board-level transparency and financial reporting. Later, in Part III when we examine examples of regulatory overlap and their impact, we visit this relationship in more detail.

Practical tips for investors

The recommendations on guidance to the Combined Code are clearly outlined in the report. Investors should:

- inspect an issuer's statements on compliance or an intermediary's service level agreements, if applicable, for indications that risk is a prominent consideration, especially in relation to internal controls
- check that there is an internal control review process implemented
- look for the signs of compliance activity—such as budgets assigned, software bought (the type of software being particularly significant), and external agencies employed.

All these indicators point to compliance processes at work.

Practical tips for issuers and intermediaries

There are a number of observations of value to issuers and intermediaries arising from the Turnbull Report:

- The structure of the report places the maintenance of a sound system of internal control centrally to the well-being of business. Any investment on internal controls would fall within the definition of constructive overlap, since sound internal controls are germane to a number of regulatory requirements.
- The report focuses on the responsibilities of executives in relation to ensuring the system is effective. It defines the elements of the system and deals with the review of the system as an ongoing process, and touches on internal audit and the board's statement on internal control. A clear demonstration of attention to internal controls is to appoint a

"champion" for these issues either from within the audit committee, or better still from the board. If there is a chief technology officer (CTO) on the board he or she will be a strong candidate, since internal controls are normally an area of focus for the IT function as much as the business function.

■ The report allies internal control with risk and risk strategies, and fundamentally tackles areas that gained prominence in the United States under Sarbanes–Oxley and SEC legislation. The issuer or intermediary that has not revised its risk strategy, in terms of its internal processes and its controls for the benefit of demonstrating compliance to regulation, needs to address this as a matter of urgency. Where such a strategy has taken account of this area, it should build in ongoing reviews, since this is not an issue that will be dealt with as a one-off. Compliance is for life.

Currently the FRC has drafted rules and has published them for UK and Irish companies listed on US stock exchanges, to help them comply with Section 404 of the Act. This is referred to again on the section on US legislation.

However, according to many commentators, Turnbull has succumbed to the tendency to respond to regulatory requirements by issuing boilerplate replies and tick lists rather than pursuing analysis and action. Many of the companies claiming to comply with Turnbull have, it turns out, failed to embrace its guidance in practice by embedding risk management and internal control within their organization. Even by 2002 there was a sense of Turnbull being a lost opportunity. Some boards were promoting themselves by publishing their attempts at analysis, drawing the attention of investors to the risks they faced, and indicating how they were going to face them. By the principle that describing a problem is half-way to solving it, such companies have used judicious psychology. However, companies are going to have to do more than describe processes to really gain credibility.

MLR 2003

What is it?
UK regulations dealing with reporting of suspicious financial transactions.
What does it do?
It establishes obligations for those involved in "relevant" businesses (training, monitoring, and reporting), and sets up the new role of Money Laundering Officer. It replaces (i) MLR 1993, (ii) Financial Services and Markets Act 2000 (Regulations Relating to Money Laundering) and (iii) MLR 2001.

Who does it affect?
A range of financial institutions are affected as well as institutional and private investors.
Why does it exist?
There is a continuing need to update the control of systems for identification of money laundering.
Will it change?
It is part of an developing body of review and reports responding to industry events. It is likely to evolve further.
Who are the regulators?
The Treasury initiated the regulations, and there are various regulatory bodies, including the FSA, Office of Fair Trading, Gaming Board, and Occupational Pensions Regulatory Authority.

The Money Laundering Regulations 2003 (MLR 2003) are a set of legislative regulations (Statutory Instrument no. 3075) which were laid before the UK Parliament in November 2003 and came into force in 2004. Their provisions, from the perspective of the intermediary or investor, can be summarized as requiring financial institutions to:

- report or prevent suspicious financial transactions
- properly identify their customers
- maintain procedures, training, and reporting controls to identify or prevent suspicious transactions.

The most high-profile general tenet of MLR is the requirement on anyone within a relevant business to report "suspicious financial activity." As we shall see in Chapter 3, this has some serious consequences when taken with other regulations, which can create problems for the relationship between investors and their intermediaries in the financial services sector.

Suspicious financial activity is categorized in three ways:

- two or more entities agreeing to form a business relationship where one of the entities is in a relevant business under the act
- one-off transactions
- two or more one-off linked transactions.

One-off transactions are any transactions other than those carried out in the course of an existing business.

Primarily, from a financial services perspective, this legislation affects the relationship between investors and their intermediaries. In order to ensure that the reporting is effective, the regulations define what a "relevant business" is, as well as the terms under which the regulations on reporting have effect.

It might be thought that, to identify money laundering, everyone would need to be subject to the regulations. However, only a specific set of entities are subject to this particular regime. They include those involved in the following activities:

- Regulated activities including
  - taking deposits
  - effecting or carrying out long-term insurance contracts
  - dealing in investments as principal or agent
  - arranging deals in investments
  - managing investments
  - safeguarding and administering investments
  - sending dematerialized instructions
  - establishing collective investment schemes
  - issuing electronic money.
- Activities of the National Savings Bank.
- Any activity for the purpose of raising money under the National Loans Act 1968.
- Several of the activities defined in the Banking Consolidation Directive.
- Estate agency work.
- Operating a casino.
- Insolvency practitioners.
- Provision of tax advice for others.
- Provision of accountancy services.
- Provision of audit services.
- Provision of legal services.
- Provision of business formation operation and management services.
- Dealing in goods by way of business where the total cash transaction value exceeds €15,000.

There are, as might be expected, a number of caveats and exceptions to the list above, so this should not be taken as an exhaustive or detailed list. It is clear that the first item alone covers any firm that is acting as an intermediary for the management of investments—custodians, brokers, investment managers, hedge fund managers, and so on. In addition, those business services that all investors use—accountants, lawyers, auditors—are all naturally included. The last item has all the look of a catch-all, and covers those who are not in the financial services or related industry. In addition, while this specific set of regulations has a narrow application, there is a requirement for the everyday citizen to report suspicious financial activity under the Proceeds of Crime Act 2002.

Once it has been defined who the regulations apply to, their text goes on to specify internal controls and systems that are necessary to prevent money laundering. The most important of these is the requirement to "know your customer" or "KYC." Basically, the need is for relevant businesses to identify their customers. It is clear that this requirement is where most effort is associated. This is so that those who are genuinely engaged in suspect activities can be located and dealt with appropriately. The section of the regulations that deals with this area is split into six separate areas:

- Systems and training—effectively requiring everyone subject to the regulations to be aware of, comply with, and be continuously trained in their provisions, under penalty of up to two years in prison, a fine, or both.
- Identification procedures—effectively requiring those subject to the regulations to ensure that in the conduct of their business there are procedures in place which will ensure that either satisfactory evidence of identity is produced or in its absence, a transaction that would otherwise have been allowable is not made. The procedures also require chains to be identified (where one or more persons is acting on behalf of others).
- Exceptions. These exist if the customer is exempt under other legislation, or is subject to another regulatory regime with similar provisions, or someone else has adequately established the identity of the customer.
- Record-keeping procedures—to ensure that copies of identity documents are kept, that their location is known, and that records are kept for five years after the end of the business relationship.
- Internal reporting procedures—these establish the concept of a nominated officer, usually called an MLR Officer, and procedures to ensure that he or she is contacted about suspicious transactions. Investigations can then be undertaken, which may lead to a report to the National Criminal Intelligence Service (NCIS).
- Casinos—this category is not strictly relevant to this book, but for completeness, this section of the regulations deals with confirming the identity of anyone about to take part in gaming activities.

There are already important consequential issues for different kinds of intermediaries. On the one hand, accountants, custodians, and brokers have no option if they come into contact with a suspicious transaction other than to report it for investigation. However, one kind of intermediary—a legal adviser—is able to use an exemption. Clause 7(3) allows the legally qualified to claim that the information they have acquired is subject to lawyer–client privilege.

It will be apparent that there are difficult relationship issues here for investors and their intermediaries. Any intermediary relationship will have already been established or updated to operate under banking regulations, but MLR 2003 brings different issues to the fore. The intermediary must decide whether a deal constitutes a one-off transaction, or is part of a series of linked one-off transactions. Since most investors ask their intermediaries to make transactions that vary in time and scale, many intermediaries take the approach that each one needs to be treated as a one-off transaction, and as such is subject to the MLR 2003 requirements.

Practical tips for investors

■ Check the terms of contracts with intermediaries, and any updates to them, to ensure you understand how the intermediary has dealt and will deal in future with your business.

■ Look particularly for clauses that indicate that you have given explicit permission for reports to be made to NCIS without your knowledge or permission.

■ Regularly review your own internal systems and policies, and ensure they are integrated with those of your intermediary, so that no gaps exist.

■ Ask your intermediary whether he or she has ever filed a report on you to NCIS. The intermediary might not give you an answer, but you do have the freedom to ask.

Practical tips for intermediaries

■ Through relationship management, make sure clients are clearly aware of the implications of MLR 2003 for their privacy and their "confidential" information.

■ Do not hide any change away in contract sub-clauses or updates. The client may not have any choice in the matter, but relationships are based on the degree of probity and openness, and clients can change their intermediary if one is clear and another is not.

■ Do not support blanket reporting policies. They will swamp NCIS with irrelevant data and stop them finding the real bad guys under the mountain of administration.

Freedom of Information Act

What is it?
A UK Act of Parliament which has independent status but also amends the Data Protection Act 1998.
What does it do?

Establishes rules for access by third parties to information held by public bodies or those providing services for them.
Who does it affect?
Everyone.
Why does it exist?
To provide access for UK subjects to information (not related to themselves).
Will it change?
Yes.
Who are the regulators?
The UK government.

The main effect of the Freedom of Information Act is its establishment of a "right to know," subject to a number of exclusions. The Act is closely linked to the Data Protection Act 1998, and indeed includes some amendments to it. However, the Act does not appear at present to have any major implications for investors or intermediaries that are not already dealt with within the Data Protection Act 1998.

The Act defines public authorities that hold information subject to it, which includes "any government department." By definition this includes the Inland Revenue, DTI, and HM Customs and Excise. These departments hold information relating to UK (corporate and natural) residents' investments abroad, as well as non-residents' (again both corporate and natural) investments in the United Kingdom.

This Act does not apply to requests from applicants with respect to data of which they are the subject: any request for such data is automatically dealt with as if it had been filed under the Data Protection Act 1998.

Clearly it would be of major concern for investors if it were possible for third parties to use the Freedom of Information Act to investigate their private financial affairs (for example, to obtain their tax return information), but this is not the intention of the legislation. This information would normally be deemed sensitive and confidential, and thus remain private, under the terms of both this Act and the Data Protection Act 1998.

Practical tips for investors

■ Establish whether anyone in the chain of investment is subject to FOI, and whether the making public of any decision such a body makes or has made could affect the value of, or return on, investments.

■ Request information on how the decisions were arrived at in order to assess a general policy for future investment decisions.

■ Take advice on potential class actions, if any historic decision reveals a potential breach of other control structures that would detrimentally affect share value.

Practical tips for intermediaries

■ Ensure that the investment chain, by investor, is mapped for potential risk of FOI information claims, since several "public authorities" in the act are financial in nature.

ISO 17799

What is it?
ISO 17799 is an internally recognized information standard consisting of a range of information security controls and best practice.
What does it do?
As a standard it sets out the requirements for an information security management system. It helps identify, manage, and minimize the range of threats to which information is regularly subject.
Who does it affect?
Any organization that needs to implement security.
Will it change?
As a standard it is subject to revisions.
Who are the regulators?
These are not enforceable regulations. The standard is a set of best practice provisions.

ISO 17799 is an internationally recognized information standard consisting of a range of information security controls and best practice. British Standard ISO/IEC 17799:2000, originally BS7799, is the British version of this standard. It is a standards code that has at its core the assumption that information is an asset, has a value for the organization, and needs to be protected.

Originally a code of practice devised by the Department of Trade and Industry (DTI) and published in 1995 by the British Standards Institute, ISO 17799 is essentially a standard that sets out the requirements for an information security management system. It helps identify, manage, and minimize the range of threats to which information is regularly subject. The standard establishes how organizations can build a system whereby they continually protect their information from threats arising from many sources—internal, external, accidental, or malicious. It provides a framework that ensures that staff are made fully aware of how they should treat the organization's information, enforce policies, and address information security threats from staff behavior, from accidental misuse to malicious abuse. It is derived from an analysis of collected best practice.

The structure and content of the original BS7799 is subdivided into a number of sections. The controls cover ten areas which are detailed in Annex A of the standard. Four of these are outlined below, and have specific relevance to the context of regulation:

- **Security policy**—providing management direction and support for information security.
- **Personnel security**—reducing the risks of human error, theft, fraud, or misuse of facilities. This reduces the risk of unintentional error by ensuring staff receive policy training and by testing user understanding. Such activity reduces the risk of malicious misuse by making staff aware of the consequences of misuse. This area also considers what security filters and monitoring are in use, obtaining agreement to abide by company policies, and establishes how to monitor these policies by keeping an audit trail of all transactions.
- **Compliance**—avoiding breaches of any criminal and civil law, statutory, regulatory, or contractual obligations, and any security requirement. These are laws, codes of practice, and regulations presented to staff in a compelling manner.
- **Business continuity management**—to counteract interruptions to business activities and to protect critical business processes from the effects of major failures or disasters, reducing the risk to the business by ensuring all staff understand and agree to adhere to key procedures.

Because of its range, the standard affects all organizations in all sectors. This includes financial information provided by a consumer to a financial institution, and the results of a transaction or service by or for a consumer, such as date of birth, social security number, credit history, and account balances.

As a body of best practice reference material, the standard is not enforceable by legislation. However, compliance is driven by the real benefits of risk mitigation. In particular, the cost of indemnity insurance is promoting acceptance of certification within many industry sectors. Insurers look to it as a sign of risk mitigation, since certification is evidence of a proactive approach to risk. The standard is not exhaustive, nor does it define all controls for every instance, but there are a mandatory sub-set. The whole standard acts as a set of best practice guides.

Practical tips for investors

The investor should include an assessment of how far a company has implemented standards such as this.

- Consider whether the standard is being used within an organization. This indicates a clear commitment to ensuring a system of control over security.
- Since it is an investment in time and budget in staff training, and an ongoing operational cost that the business believes is of value, it indicates that attention is also likely to be paid to other internal processes.
- Security is a critical aspect of a risk strategy; the two go hand-in-hand. The standard represents best practice, internationally, and if the organization is international in nature, it indicates a possible consistency across all operations.
- This normally signals a business that understands itself and how it operates; this approach makes compliance with regulation easier, since the business and operational processes are generally documented, and functional areas are working together.

Practical tips for issuers and intermediaries

The standard represents an established methodology with an international following, monitored and maintained by a reputable regulator in the form of the BSI/ISO. If at all possible the intermediary should:

- Review its operational systems to see if such a standard would be of benefit.
- Be aware of the advantages it brings for the compliance process, especially in addressing generic compliance issues such as:
  - documentation
  - operational process analysis
  - risk assessment and analysis
  - a clear view of the separation of responsibilities within the organization
  - cross-functional responsibilities and operations.

Companies (Audit, Investigations and Community Enterprise) Act 2004

What is it?
The Act implements safeguards intended to prevent the occurrence of Enron-type events in the United Kingdom.
What does it do?
It is an initiative to provide investor confidence in financial markets, strengthen the independence of the system of supervising auditors, and establish "community interest companies."
Who does it affect?

Auditors and audited companies.

Why does it exist?

To help redress the decline in confidence in financial markets post-Enron.

Who are the regulators?

As an Act of Parliament it is enforceable by law. The main regulator is the Department of Trade and Industry.

The Companies (Audit, Investigations and Community Enterprise) Act 2004 received Royal Assent on October 29, 2004, and was scheduled to come into force in January 2005. It seeks to restore investor confidence in corporate governance and accounting, and also introduces the concept of community interest companies. The DTI summarized the Act as "a package of measures aimed at restoring investor confidence in corporate governance, company accounting and auditing in Britain." In summary:

- The Act tightens the regulation of the auditing profession, and increases auditors' powers to investigate companies, and obtain information from directors, employees, and others.
- Directors are required to state that they have not withheld any relevant information from their auditors, and companies are required to publish full details about other services their auditors provide for them.
- The Act underlines the importance of the Financial Reporting Review Panel in enforcing accounting requirements.
- As part of government recognition that the needs of communities are increasingly met by social enterprises, it creates a form of incorporation for non-charitable social enterprises, the community interest company (CIC).

The government had announced plans for reforming company law in 2003, to implement changes recommended by various reviews that had been set up in response to public concern over major corporate failures. These changes were to complement non-legislative measures already in place or underway. The legislation drew on work by the Coordinating Group on Audit and Accounting Issues, and the Review of the Regulatory Regime of the Accountancy Profession.

In parallel with this legislation, the Government planned to use existing powers to introduce a statutory Operating and Financial Review (OFR) for large companies. Currently draft regulations on the OFR have been published. (We outline these measures below.)

This is part of a continuing program of reform of company law, designed to provide "a modern, cost-effective, fair and transparent framework for

business, shareholders, creditors and others." It also provides a more effective sanction for non-compliance with "section 447" requirements, with the
power for regulators to require entry into premises.

The main regulator is the DTI. A newly appointed regulator of CICs will
approve applications for CIC status, receive copies of annual community
interest reports, and police the requirements of CIC status, including
compliance with an asset lock.

It is too early yet to assess the impact of the Act on the financial services
sector. As a reinforcement of the trend towards transparency and accountability of companies, this is another move to ensure companies provide
quality information to investors.

Practical tips for investors

The institutional investor will probably be focused primarily on how auditors work within this new regime, which provides substantial new powers
to assist in investigation. However, this tends to be an after-the-event
response; the investor needs to be forewarned, and not just benefit from
more in depth-knowledge about difficulties that have already occurred.

Practical tips for issuers and intermediaries

There is a trend to strengthen the role of auditors across the regulatory
spectrum. Partly this is because auditors make excellent front-line regulators! This is not necessarily how an issuer or intermediary will see its auditor, and this type of regulation needs attention if both organizations are to
get the best from the auditor relationship.

■ As the Act increases the powers of auditors to investigate companies
   and obtain information from all levels within the organization, it is in
   the interest of the company to anticipate the type of information
   needed. This is generally the same information required under
   many other regulations, and acts as a good example of constructive
   overlap.
■ Directors are required to state that they have not withheld any relevant information from their auditors. The Sarbanes–Oxley-like
   management assessment will provide this kind of assurance; and the
   maintenance of demonstrably effective internal controls is of great
   value here.
■ It is likely that as a compliant organization, the issuer or intermediary
   will already have published the right kind of information. If this is not
   the case it is worth researching exactly how the information has to be
   presented and how it links to internal controls. Again overlap is evident
   in the pursuit of transparency.

■ A financial reporting review panel is referenced in enforcing accounting requirements. This can be addressed either as a function of the
audit committee or as a subcommittee reporting to the board.

Operating and Financial Review (OFR)

What is it?
The Operating and Financial Review is a proposed new statutory mech-
anism outlining a yearly report to be published by company directors.
What does it do?
This is likely to be a partial UK equivalent to the US Sarbanes–Oxley
Act in determining transparency for yearly financial reviews; it goes
further in that it nominally includes operational issues.
Who does it affect?
All UK listed companies must provide an OFR.
Why does it exist?
As a statutory response to concerns on financial reporting within UK
listed companies
Who are the regulators?
As it is an Act of Parliament compliance is likely to be handled by the DTI.

In summer 2004 the government published a consultative document outlining a proposed new statutory Operating and Financial Review (OFR). The
DTI also published a document, *Practical Guidance for Directors*, in the
same period—a guidance paper for directors on what processes to follow
in assembling and selecting information for an OFR. As part of this initiative the government sought help in developing supporting standards for the
OFR from the Accounting Standards Board (ASB), stipulating that these
should reflect best practice. The underlying principles are:

■ All UK listed companies must provide an OFR for reporting periods
commencing on or after April 1, 2005.
■ Directors have a responsibility to prepare a yearly OFR which must be
approved by the board.
■ The OFR must be signed by a director, on behalf of the board, or the
company secretary.
■ In preparing the OFR, directors will be expected to apply "due care,
skill and diligence." The OFR must be "a balanced and comprehensive
analysis" including:
  ● performance details of the company and its subsidiary undertakings
  during the financial year

- the main trends and indicators underlying this performance and likely to affect future performance
- a statement of the business, objectives and strategies of the company, its resources, risks and uncertainties and details of its financial set up and liquidity.

■ The OFR also should include an analysis of environmental matters and employee matters using key performance indicators (KPIs) and financial indicators where possible.

■ Auditors will be required to produce a report and state whether the OFR is consistent with the audited accounts, and point out any other relevant matter that might conflict with or cause concern regarding the OFR.

This review and its requirements are very reminiscent of the moves and stipulations that came into force in the United States through the SEC as a result of the Sarbanes–Oxley Act (SOX) of 2002. (SOX is assessed later in conjunction with the Combined Code and the Turnbull report.) The OFR is another part of the greater jigsaw of regulation being put together in response to the events of the late 1990s.

Practical tips for investors

For an institutional investor this is another piece of quality information on the state of play within a company.

■ On behalf of shareholders, the government is not looking to impose a requirement that shareholders get a full OFR as a matter of course. However it should be made available on the company website.

■ The investor should access this as yet another piece of clear evidence of how well the company is run internally.

Practical tips for issuers and intermediaries

■ As in the United States, the emphasis here is placed on the auditor to state whether the review is sound. A similar approach to that taken with the Companies (Audit, Investigations and Community Enterprise) Act 2004 is relevant.

■ In the United States the auditor's attestation is on internal controls of processes, producing a financial report or review. Building a good relationship with the auditor is critical to steer the company through the assessment process. Establishing and scoping clearly the areas of engagement is vital.

Financial Services and Markets Act (FISMA) 2000

What is it?
The Financial Services and Markets Act created the powers of the FSA.
What does it do?
Modernize financial services regulation in the United Kingdom under a single regulator, the FSA.
Who does it affect?
All financial services institutions and organizations, and allied professional institutions as well as the LSE listing authority.
Why does it exist?
To rationalize and modernize the previously diverse regulatory regime.
Will it change?
As an Act of Parliament it is subject to review and change.
Who are the regulators?
The UK government backing the Financial Services Authority.

The Financial Services and Markets Act (FISMA) received Royal Assent on June 14, 2000. It provided the statutory framework for completing the modernization of financial services regulation announced in 1997, creating a single regulator for the financial services industry, the Financial Services Authority (FSA). It equipped the FSA with a number of statutory powers, and created the Financial Services and Markets Tribunal ("the Tribunal"). The Act also established the framework for single ombudsman and compensation schemes to provide further protection for consumers, and introduced a framework for a UK market abuse regime, which became effective on December 1, 2001.

The Act comprises 30 parts. More detailed information is contained in Explanatory Notes to the Act, available from The Stationery Office. The Act provides, amongst other things, for:

- the constitution and accountability of the FSA
- the definition of the scope of regulated activities
- the control of financial promotion
- powers of the FSA to authorize, regulate, investigate, and discipline authorized persons
- the recognition of investment exchanges and clearing houses
- arrangements for the approval of controllers and the performance of regulated activities
- the oversight of financial services provided by members of the professions
- regulation and marketing of collective investment schemes

- certain criminal offences
- powers to impose penalties for market abuse
- the transfer to the FSA of registration functions in respect of building societies, friendly societies, industrial and provident societies, and certain other mutual societies.

Businesses to be authorized and regulated under the Act include:

- banks, building societies, Insurance companies, friendly societies, and credit unions
- Lloyd's, investment and pensions advisers, and stockbrokers
- professional firms offering certain types of investment services
- fund managers, derivatives traders, and mortgage lenders.

In May 1997, the UK government announced proposals to reform the regulation of financial services. Responsibility for regulation was then transferred to the newly established FSA as the logical successor to the Securities and Investment Board. The staff of the regulators were gathered together under one nominal roof, theoretically ending a period of intense rivalry among the regulatory bodies.

Regulation of financial services in the United Kingdom had been the responsibility of a number of different bodies:

- the Securities and Investment Board (SIB)
- the self-regulating organizations (SROs): most recently the Personal Investment Authority (PIA), the Investment Management Regulatory Organisation (IMRO), and the Securities and Futures Authority (SFA)
- the former Supervision and Surveillance Branch of the Bank of England
- the Building Societies Commission (BSC)
- the Insurance Directorate of the Treasury
- the Friendly Societies Commission (FSC)
- the Registry of Friendly Societies.

These functions were pulled together under the single regulator. The Act coordinated and modernized financial regulatory arrangements currently established under other legislation such as that covering credit unions, insurance companies, building societies, and banking, which has been repealed or replaced. The Act also provides for the transfer to the FSA and the Treasury of the remaining functions, including functions relating to the registration of mutual societies, of the Building Societies Commission, the Friendly Societies Commission, and the Registry of Friendly Societies.

The Act is probably one of the most significant in recent decades for financial institutions. Some functionality was transferred to the Bank of England, or contracts agreed for existing bodies to undertake regulatory functions, such as the Treasury for insurance companies. Most significantly the FSA took over responsibility as the authority for listing quoted companies from the Stock Exchange. Among other capabilities, the FSA was given powers to regulate the Lloyd's insurance market, and direction over the Council of Lloyd's. The FSA will also authorize and regulate professions such as solicitors and accountants. The Act itself does not affect the powers of professional bodies to regulate the activities of their members.

The FSMA market abuse regime provides new powers to the Financial Services Authority (FSA) to sanction anyone who engages in "market abuse," that is misuse of information, misleading practices, and market manipulation, relating to investments traded on prescribed UK markets. It also applies to those who require or encourage others to engage in conduct that would amount to market abuse. FISMA's stated objective is to fill the "regulatory gap" by giving the FSA substantial powers to punish unregulated market participants whose market conduct falls below acceptable standards, but does not rise to the level of a criminal offence.

Practical tips for investors

For investors the Act is good news. It states that a core interest is the protection of investors, and their education about the market and the way it operates. When looking at investments, the rules introduced are largely those under the regimes it absorbed:

- The rules have not changed substantially as a result of this centralization process.
- The Act stresses the importance of information, and it is this which is refined by other reports, reviews, and acts. Information is the key resource for the investor.

Practical tips for issuers and intermediaries

For issuers and intermediaries the results of the Act are manifest in subsidiary legislation and regulation and the implications of European directives translated through UK government acts and the FSA.

UNITED STATES OF AMERICA

Sarbanes–Oxley

What is it?
A US legislative Act that amends SEC rules to introduce stricter controls on US listed companies' financial reports, to restore investor confidence in the probity of corporate business activity.

What does it do?
It amends the SEC Acts (1934), introduces further regulation, defines the responsibilities of senior executives, external auditors, and introduces penalties for non-compliance.

Who does it affect?
All US and non-US companies listed in the United States.

Why does it exist?
It is a product of the climate of concern engendered by the scandals of Enron and others in the early 21st century.

Will it change?
Its measures are being phased in, and since it primarily amends existing SEC legislation, it is likely to be a vehicle for continuing to do so.

Who are the regulators?
The US SEC and its enforcement officers.

The Sarbanes–Oxley Act (SOX) was passed in the summer of 2002 in response to public debate over the state of financial probity in the wake of the Enron fiasco in the United States. It represents a sea change in the way the regulation of business at the highest level is conducted in the United States. It is a central piece of legislation in the new regulatory climate, and its implications are being felt globally.

SOX is really a series of amendments to the SEC laws governing reporting standards and requirements in the United States for US-listed companies. These amendments are detailed in the body of the Act, which is divided into "Titles" and sections. Key sections have driven major compliance programs in most large US-listed bodies. Of these, Sections 302, 404, and 409 warrant specific attention.

Section 302 establishes the responsibility of board-level management, notably the signing officers of financial reports, that is, CEOs and CFOs, for the accuracy and fairness of the reports as representations of their companies in the eyes of interested parties such as investors and regulators. It specifically indicates that the signing officers will be held accountable for any misleading facts or descriptions in these financial reports. The Act mandates that such misleading of the public can be punishable by heavy fines and imprisonment. The financial reports must now carry an additional report made by the corporation and signed off by its senior executives, which is an assessment of how effective its internal controls are in meeting the demands of fair and accurate financial reporting.

Section 404 section rounds out the Act's interest in auditors as the means by which a corporation, its board, its senior executives, and its audit committee are investigated or judged. Auditors have traditionally adopted a less than neutral stance when it came to working with clients, generally supporting their clients in efforts to be flexible with regulatory rules deemed to be disadvantageous. SOX has pushed auditors into a much stricter neutrality. They have now to "attest" to the accuracy of the management's "assessment" of the effectiveness of its internal controls in financial reporting.

Section 409 has received relatively little attention, although its demands are perhaps among the most difficult to address. In the effort to ensure as much relevant information is made available to investors as possible, and within as short a time frame as possible, this section requires ad hoc statements and reports to be issued of anything that materially affects the well-being, success, or failure of the business, and for this information to be made available in a very short time frame, generally days. The nature of this information varies but it can include almost anything that is materially relevant, from macro-events such as mergers, acquisitions, and system failures, to acts of God, political changes, wars, or micro-events such as internal system failures, changes in partnerships, product recalls, board-level changes, and so on. By and large these events must be reported in real time, that is, with some immediacy.

Nominally SOX affects listed companies in the United States, whatever sector they operate in. Financial services are particularly subject to its regulations because of their sensitivity to shareholder concerns and the central place they occupy in the economy. It is also true that many of these institutions are global. They have subsidiaries in many regions, such as Europe, Asia, South America, and Africa. It is not clear from the legalization how these subsidiaries are affected; however, as elements in the supply chain for a consolidated financial report, their systems of internal control over financial reporting will be particularly important to the US entity. The Act is specific on this, in that its requirements cannot be avoided by placing the HQ overseas. Being listed is enough. However, this does introduce a real issue for non-US companies that have listed in the United States to gain the benefits of capital generation that such a listing can deliver. This is compounded when we come to look at regulatory overlap, and decisions have to be made over potentially contradictory requirements. While it is true that we live in a global economy, and companies act as if the international market were totally homogeneous, nevertheless legislation is predominantly local, and international agreements are not so easily achieved.

As well as listed companies, there are many others, often quite large concerns, that are affected:

- auditors in the United States are affected directly by the legislation
- non-US auditors working with listed subsidiaries in the United States or elsewhere
- supply-chain partners that may have to ensure their internal controls are synchronized well through systems based on electronic data interchange (EDI) or extranets and e-commerce.

SOX is a direct product of the events that shook the US economy in the very late 1990s. In particular, the collapse of a player such as the energy company Enron, and the subsequent effect it had on the auditing firm of Arthur Andersen, very publicly uncovered just how badly things could go wrong if the "creative," aggressive approach to bookkeeping at the highest levels was allowed to go unchallenged. The real impact was the effect the fall of Enron had on the many small investors in the United States who relied on such investments for their pensions. This hit a striking political chord, and energized the US President, George W. Bush, into immediate action. The Act was born of political will in a climate of retribution somewhat tempered by realism.

The Act set up an oversight body, funded by the industry, answerable to the SEC. It is the regulatory agents of the SEC who carry out investigations, using the Act as the source of authority. As a federal measure it has a mandate across the United States, and nearly all affected organizations have responded by introducing revised internal policies to match its requirements, as well as allocating often substantial budgets to compliance programs. The cost of compliance to SOX is potentially enormous, as year on year these organizations have to find extra funding, skills, and systems to support the thoroughness of the regimes. The cost of regulation has already been recognized by the SEC, which has instituted programs and studies into how it can ameliorate some of this overhead for smaller organizations less able to absorb the costs.

Practical tips for investors

The Act appears to be a beacon of light and reason, holding companies to account for the excesses of the period, and forcing them to come up to a higher standard in corporate governance. The introduction of the management assessment of internal controls, and the attestation mandate on auditors, is the Act's way of establishing some form of cross-checking at an early stage. However, there is a price to pay for this. Under the Act, "significant deficiencies" and "material weaknesses" reported as part of this process can have a real impact on the company, especially its perception in the market and its share value. This, more than anything, hits the investor. For an investor it is as well to check that:

- The management assessment is a real reflection of the work undertaken within the company to address issues relating to internal controls. Indicators of this are:
  - spend on new IT systems, especially workflow systems and their support platforms
  - the employment of full-time or additional agency specialist skills in internal auditing and IT systems
  - the engagement of additional auditing skills with their domain knowledge
  - work being carried out in subsidiaries to support this
  - the introduction of a flurry of new internal policies
  - the acquisition of applications to support the monitoring and management of internal policies, especially for unstructured communicants such as e-mail, instant messaging, web-messaging, and texting
  - stronger corporate governance statements from the board or CEO.
- The relationship with auditors is very indicative of how things are measuring up. Many auditors are dropping "smaller" clients because now, under the Act, they are perceived as an unacceptable risk. This means that relationships which were more like partnerships, are coming to an end. Where the relationship is maintained, it is likely to be more distant, as the auditor adopts the neutral stand expected under the Act. Look out for instances where the company has dropped and changed auditors without any obvious reason. This may well indicate that "material deficiencies" have occurred.

Practical tips for issuers and intermediaries

- Map investors into the firm based on the level of impact to them of SOX, and assess whether you are subject to the Act indirectly.
- If so, assess the ways in which your firm and investors interact; assess what systems and procedures are being put into place, and how to interface with them to assure compliance at the intermediary level and failsafe at the investor level.
- If the company is directly affected as a US-listed company, consider the SEC allowance of Turnbull guidance as a recognized reference framework.

USA Section 1441 NRA

> **What is it?**
> United States regulations dealing with tax on cross-border investment income.
> **What does it do?**
> Establishes rules for obtaining relief at source from taxation. In the absence of compliance, investor income could be overtaxed by up to 30 percent.
> **Who does it affect?**
> All US financial institutions acting as withholding agents, all non-US financial institutions receiving US-sourced income directly or indirectly, on their own proprietary accounts or those of their clients, all auditors providing audit services required under the regulations, and all investors in receipt of US-sourced income.
> **Why does it exist?**
> It consolidates previous regulation and attempts to counter abusive tax activity, including "treaty shopping."
> **Will it change?**
> Yes.
> **Who are the regulators?**
> Primary regulator: US Internal Revenue Service (IRS).
> Others involved: US Treasury.

The full name of the regulation, which is a part of the IRS code, is Section 1441 of the Internal Revenue Code relating to Non Resident Aliens. Its more usual title outside the United States is the "QI regulations," where QI stands for qualified intermediary. While this section relates primarily to the US regulations, it should be noted that by 2004 both Ireland and Japan had implemented simpler, albeit nonetheless extensive, regulation to effect the same result. Some references will be made at appropriate points to these clone regulations, but in essence, readers should assume that wherever a requirement under the US regulations appears to have an impact, there is likely to be a similar type of impact for Ireland and Japan, and there may be an impact in other countries.

The US regulations deal with the taxation of cross-border income where the income was derived originally from the United States. One example of such income is income derived from shares in US firms owned by non-US persons. "Persons" in this context can mean both individuals and aggregates of investors such as mutual funds, hedge funds, pension funds, and unit trusts. There are over 400,000 dividend announcements a year in the United States. When a US firm has an annual general meeting it may reward its investors with the declaration of a dividend. The dividend, together with movements in share price, comprises investors' yield on their investments. The firm's registrar and withholding agent bank are tasked with distributing the dividend, and local law requires that unless the withholding agent has reason to know otherwise, in the United States it will deduct 30 percent and remit this to the IRS, and send the net to the intermediary representing the payee (investor). There are at least 19 other types of income where this withholding can occur, and on each, the IRS requires the money to be paid, within set time frames, to the US Treasury and reports to be sent to the IRS at the end of each fiscal year.

Overall there are two broad approaches to tax on cross-border income (known in this context as withholding tax) dealt with by the financial services industry. The first is relief at source (RAS) and the second is remedial reclaim. The principle is that beneficial owners, or more typically intermediaries acting on their behalf such as custodian banks, brokers, and investment managers, can if eligible, and if the country allows it, be taxed at a lower rate of tax if they can prove their entitlement before receiving the income. If they cannot, tax will be withheld at a higher withholding rate and the beneficial owners or their intermediaries must file remedial tax reclaims to obtain their money. The former RAS system has three subdivisions based on the relative complexity of the processes and procedures involved. They are Simple, Intermediate, and Advanced. The US Section 1441 NRA regulations are an example of an Advanced relief at source taxation system. They are, in fact, the most extensive and complex set of withholding tax rules currently in existence.

The QI regulations describe the rules pertaining to taxation of various (over 20) kinds of income received by persons resident outside the United States. The standard rate of withholding tax to be applied to such income is 30 percent unless the payer is aware of and has documentary evidence to prove that the payee or beneficial owner is entitled to a different, usually lower rate of taxation. The lower rate is most often available to a beneficial owner by reason of, first, their residency in a country with which the United States has a double tax agreement or treaty, and second, their status under that agreement or treaty as eligible for a treaty rate of taxation.

Underlying the concept of the regulations is the idea that the IRS cannot directly affect non-US persons or financial intermediaries because such rules would constitute extraterritoriality—the application of a rule beyond the area over which the United States has jurisdiction. So the IRS has established the idea of a commercial contract with non-US financial firms to control the way and degree to which they document their customers to the point where the IRS can apply tax rules and procedures beyond their direct jurisdiction and enforce quality controls and penalties that, one, effectively make unpaid tax collectors out of the financial services industry, and two, ensure that the IRS achieves its primary aims (described later).

This is probably one of the most contentious and profound pieces of regulation ever to be promulgated by the United States. It affects any financial firm outside the United States that receives income deemed to be sourced from the United States, directly for its own account or on behalf of its customers. This, however, is only the start. The regulations' requirements for documentary evidence to demonstrate an eligibility for a lower rate of taxation have major implications for beneficial owners themselves. The regulations also establish a transparency principle which applies to some, but not all, types of aggregated beneficial owner. This principle requires that documentary evidence of eligibility for lower tax rates must be applied to each beneficial owner as opposed to the aggregate vehicle through which the beneficial owners have invested in the United States.

Also affected are US entities which act as withholding agents. They may be required to withhold varying amounts of money from distributions dependent on the degree of information provided by foreign intermediaries and their status. They may also be required to submit reports to the IRS, in addition to those required under other domestic US legislation, on behalf of foreign intermediary QIs. Finally, US firms are impacted most of all by those foreign intermediaries that choose not to contract with the IRS and become QIs. These intermediaries, termed non-qualified intermediaries (NQIs), are required to send detailed information about their customers and their US source income to a withholding agent, where their calculation of withholding tax must be verified against the complex rules of the regulatory structure. This is because, in the absence of a contract with the IRS that would remove this onerous requirement in favor of summary reporting, the IRS needs comfort that a person or organization with which it has a contract, or over which it has some control and thus confidence, is analyzing the judgments and actions of those (NQIs) over whom it effectively has no contractual control.

The net result is that these regulations are extremely pervasive. They affect all persons and entities that derive US-sourced income, and all persons and entities in the United States who deal with this group.

The original reason that the legislation was brought into force was to catch US residents engaging in treaty shopping. US domestic tax rates are higher than those that apply to investors from treaty countries such as the United Kingdom and France, so some US investors chose to invest in US companies through non-US intermediaries. The typical example given is of US investors opening an account in France with a French bank. They needed only to show some evidence of residence such as renting an apartment, and their account was opened on the basis that they were French residents. Their income from dividends in the US company was then taxed at just 15 percent instead of 30 percent. This was not the only reason for the regulations, and the regulations themselves took over 20 years to come to fruition in their current form.

These regulations were changing even before they were put in place. The regulations themselves were deferred three times by the IRS at the request of the financial services community, which claimed to need more time to comply. For a major financial firm to comply with the regulations, which run to over 800 pages, really meant automation. There is no real way that any firm can deal with the complexities without some level of automation, and the major firms succeeded in deferring the regulations until 2001, when the IRS finally implemented them. Even after promulgation, pressure from the financial services industry continued to find areas where the original regulations were either unclear or did not suit the structure of the investment community.

The regulations continue to change. For those who have signed up as qualified intermediaries, the most useful publication produced by the IRS is Publication 515, which gives a summary of the rules as well as worked examples.

Originally the only firms likely to enter into a QI agreement with the IRS were custodian banks or in-country agent banks, brokers, and major financial firms. The invasive degree of information needed by these QIs, however, created pressure from what would otherwise have been the customers of those very custodians and brokers. Even though the object of the information gathering is to protect the customer from having this information sent directly to the IRS, some types of business wanted to be able to become QIs themselves so that they could manage this part of their business directly without recourse to a third party. As examples, since inception of the regulations the concept has been extended to private arrangement intermediaries (PAIs), withholding foreign partnerships, and withholding foreign trusts.

To make a lateral comment, the principle of the regulations (an advanced RAS system) has already been adopted by both the Irish and Japanese governments. Both these countries have applied the concept to a different degree and in different ways. Any financial firm with a broad portfolio of clients and investment strategies may well derive client income from the United States, Japan, and Ireland. As a result it needs to consider becoming a QI under each of the different sets of regulation from these countries.

Change to the US regulations themselves continues apace. While the regulations principally set the rules for those firms that enter into a QI agreement with the IRS, they also specify procedures and notably penalties for those who do not so engage—the NQIs. In 2001, in order to have clients taxed at the right rate, an NQI needed to document each income event for each client to a US withholding agent bank. This was originally intended to be done using a US Form W-8BEN. Calculations indicate that at the time this would have meant 900 million forms a year. Not surprisingly, pressure from withholding agents, which had neither the appetite nor the resources to check 900 million forms against the relevant income events, led to this requirement being relaxed to once per year. More recently, this has been relaxed still further, with a certification by an NQI to a withholding agent being sufficient to warrant that the proper documentation exists.

In summary, the regulations continue to change as the investment community successively identifies efficiencies it would like to leverage, and negotiates changes or amendments with the IRS. These changes are typically announced in IRS "Notices." The first real Notice in this regulatory framework was Notice 2000-12, which gave the world the text of the QI Agreement and established the ground rules that have since applied.

The issue of extraterritoriality makes the position on these regulations very important. The "regulator" of all non-US financial institutions is the US Internal Revenue Service.

The clever element of the regulations is that there are rules governing those that agree to be QIs, and these are enshrined in the QI Agreement. Any non-US firm that chooses not to sign up with the IRS is not exempt. It is subject to a more penal set of rules, and failure to behave in the appropriate way results in higher penalties than those that apply to QIs.

However, the IRS does not usually engage directly with QIs and NQIs in its capacity as a regulator. The regulations are set up to ensure compliance retrospectively through independent audit. It was rumored that one of the top audit companies made US$30 million from advice to QIs in the first six months of the regulations. The QI Agreement requires that independent audits are made on QIs in the third and fifth year of the agreement to assess their compliance. The first such audits were being performed in 2004, and subsequently the IRS announced that it had decided to audit some of the US withholding agents too, from which we may infer that the results of QI audits were not entirely to its satisfaction.

The audits take place in three phases, and success at any phase means that typically the subsequent phases are avoided. So, in a Phase I audit, a spot check of a QI's accounts is performed to set statistical criteria. If no problem is found, the QI's audit is complete. If there are concerns, a QI may be asked to undertake a Phase II audit, in which specific transactions are analyzed, in particular those areas that failed in Phase I. If any problems are found in a Phase I audit that resulted in the QI under-withholding (that is, it applied a treaty tax rate erroneously and should have taxed at a higher rate), the penalty is only that the erroneous transactions are corrected. In a Phase II audit, however, any under-withholdings found in a sample of the QI's transactions are extrapolated to the QI's entire client base. It is clear that extensive efforts must be made by QIs to avoid Phase II audits by becoming as fully compliant as possible.

If the QI fails a Phase II audit, the euphemism for a Phase III audit is "a discussion directly with the IRS on matters of concern," and it is at this point that the "regulator" becomes directly involved.

The audit rules for auditors are almost as complex as the regulations themselves, and are also subject to continuing change.

There are a number of different entities involved with these regulations both vertically and horizontally. How and with whom an institutional investor is related in the investment management chain can make the difference between being taxed at 15 percent and 50 percent on US-sourced investment income.

The IRS

Most of the people in the investment community think of the IRS as a singular entity. However, it is important to understand in the context of these regulations that there are actually several subordinate agencies involved, most of which have little or no contact with any of the others.

The principle of the regulations is that tax is levied on one of the many income types that are distributed outside the United States. This requires two issues to be resolved, both of which have two associated sub-issues. First, the money has to move, and second, the government needs to reconcile payments made with tax dollars received. This is not as simple as it seems. From the monetary viewpoint, the tax dollars are remitted to a subdivision of the IRS, the US Treasury. There is a complex date and amount-based formula to determine how frequently a withholding QI or withholding agent must send tax dollars to the US Treasury. Basically, the larger the amounts of tax due in any given time frame, the more frequently the money must be moved to the Treasury's financial agent, BankOne. In addition, if the amounts of tax being deposited exceed a certain level, the money must be moved electronically using the Electronic Federal Tax Payment System (EFTPS).

From a reporting perspective, the IRS requires annual reports from any person or organization that receives US-sourced income. A QI can report in summary based on its underlying customers, thus keeping the identity of its clients confidential. An NQI does not have such protection.

However, the IRS designates two categories of "income," reportable amounts and reportable payments. The difficulty for investment firms and institutional investors is in segregating the two but aggregating their reporting. Reportable *payments* are income types where income is distributed and withholding tax is applied and paid. Reportable *amounts* are amounts of income received where no withholding tax is applied, but the IRS still

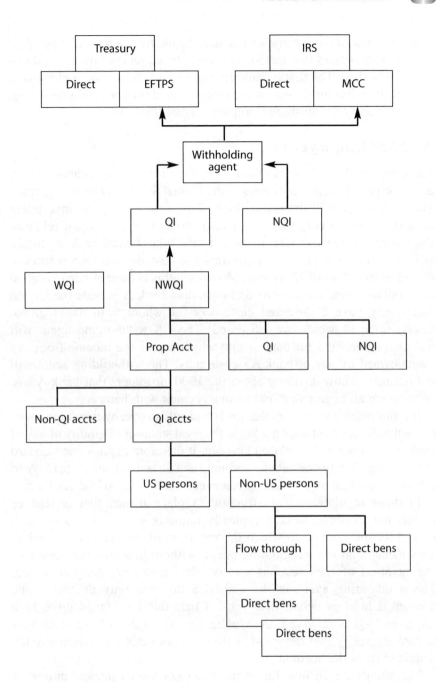

Figure 3.2 Overview of financial services model as it relates to US 1441 NRA Regulations
Source: McGill, R. (2003) *International Withholding Tax: A practical guide to best practice and benchmarking*, Euromoney.

wants to know of the income's existence. Again, from a reporting perspective, the IRS defines two methods to report based on the volume of documents to be filed. The first is naturally manual, but the second is electronic. The specification for the electronic filing method is over 1200 pages long, and is issued by Martinsburg Computer Center (MCC).

Withholding agents

These are usually US banks which have a dual role. In one capacity they act on behalf of corporate issuers in the United States and their registrars. Their job is to fulfill the instructions of the firm issuing the investment income, usually a corporate. They also often have contractual relationships with non-US financial services firms, other banks, brokers, funds, and so on, under which they perform some custody role with respect to the US assets of non-US persons. Most often this is done at what is called an omnibus level. This means that custodian bank A outside the United States may have a thousand customers for whom it manages global assets, some of which are US-based. The US withholding agent will maintain an account for bank A into which it puts the income from any assets owned by any of bank A's customers. The withholding agent will not normally know anything about the 1000 customers that bank A has, as these are all aggregated into its one account with bank A.

It is this omnibus structure that leads typically to over-withholding, since the withholding agent does not know the legal status or eligibility of any of bank A's customers for reduced taxation. It therefore applies one standard withholding rate to the whole account, and it is then up to bank A to calculate which, if any, of its customers can claim some of the tax back.

In these regulations, the structure in place means that instead of having one account, bank A typically requests several accounts, each named for the tax rate to which the members of the account are liable. This means that the withholding agent, without knowing the details of the members of each account, can tax the income correctly at source. The withholding agent in the United States can only do this if the account is held on behalf of a non-US firm that has signed up to be a QI. If an NQI is involved, the withholding agent must have some way to directly verify that the non-US firm has correctly calculated any tax deducted from the account.

The impact for an investor of receiving US source income through a non-qualified intermediary can be major.

QIs

As was mentioned, QIs are those non-US financial services firms that choose to enter into a contractual agreement with the IRS. They do this primarily to be able to protect the identity of their customers. A QI that knows its customer base because it has documented its customers according to its local "know your customer" (KYC) rules when they open accounts, can aggregate all customers with similar eligibility to a low treaty rate (or exemption). This enables the withholding agent to remit the correct amount of tax to the US Treasury and report it to the IRS, while the QI is able to distribute the net income across its client base without having to tell anyone who or what its customers are and how they invested. This is the model that is followed by most QIs: in other words, while they maintain the confidentiality of their clients they do not actually send money to the US Treasury, something that is done by the US withholding agent further up the investment chain. There are however two options for a QI. A QI can elect to follow this standard model and be a non-withholding QI (NWQI), or it can elect in its QI agreement, to "adopt primary withholding responsibility" and be a withholding QI (WQI). In the latter model, the WQI takes complete responsibility for both payments and reporting to the IRS.

NQIs

These are the firms that have not entered into an agreement with the IRS. This however does not protect them from scrutiny. Far from it: an NQI must demonstrate that it has documented its clients correctly and that it has also calculated their tax rates correctly. Failure to do so can result in severe penalties from the IRS, applied via a US withholding agent.

Auditors

Auditors have always been part of the regulatory process. Indeed, most of the top auditing firms have senior staff who were at one time with the IRS developing the regulations. Technically, any firm can be a QI auditor, although from an investor's viewpoint it clearly makes sense to engage an auditor with sufficient gravitas to negotiate with the IRS, knowledge to advise QIs effectively, and experience to be able to identify compliance issues within the three-phase audit process.

Every person or organization outside the United States that derives US-sourced income either directly or indirectly is affected, including those inside or outside the United States who audit such firms or provide withholding agent services.

Intermediaries, whether or not they are qualified, are affected in that their systems and procedures must be compliant with the regulations. One European bank estimated that it had spent US$1 million getting compliant, and expected to spend at least US$1 million a year staying compliant.

Compliance means:

1   Analyzing segregation of accounts.
2   Documentation (and renewal of documentation) of clients.
3   Management of income processing to calculate eligibility and validity to arrive at a correct tax rate.
4   Communications (electronic and manual) with other parties in the investment chain both upwards and downwards.
5   Depositing of taxes with the IRS.
6   Reporting of income to the IRS.
7   Managing traceability. For QIs, this means submitting to up to three phases of audit every third and fifth year. For NQIs this means evidencing eligibility to a withholding agent for every income event/client pairing.

Investors, including institutional investors, are affected in that they must suffer increased and regular re-documentation of their legal status and residency in order to benefit from relief at source. In itself this would be a difficult process. However, the financial services industry operates in a serial/parallel way with its investors. It was not unknown, prior to 2001, for any one investor to have investments split in terms of custody, between up to ten intermediaries. Each one of these will require original evidence of eligibility, usually through the provision of a Form W-8BEN. Since 2001, most investors have drastically reduced the number of their intermediary custodians precisely to avoid the plethora of replicated documentation.

Originally, the response of the financial services community was delay, delay, and delay, followed by muted threats of legal action against the IRS. Eventually, after three years, the regulations came into force. The suggested legal action never materialized.

Responses today vary depending on who is involved. Many brokers, for example, which historically have little interest in custody issues, have tended to apply a blanket 30 percent withholding tax rate for US-sourced income irrespective of whether the beneficiary has been documented or not, leaving the beneficiary the time-consuming task of reclaiming over-withheld tax from a country where the focus of resource is on relief at source.

As at 2004, there were estimated to be around 7500 foreign firms signed up with the IRS as QIs, leaving the vast majority of intermediaries around the world as NQIs.

As has been noted, investors have drastically reduced the number of intermediaries that act on their behalf in order to minimize paperwork. For aggregate investors such as institutional investors, pension funds, and hedge funds, there is a whiplash effect in terms of compliance, whether this is self-imposed by internal risk management or externally imposed through increasing corporate governance pressure, such as has hit the US mutual fund industry in recent times. The fact is that, in the knowledge of the complexity of the regulations and the impact on custodians, investors are becoming more alert to the potential effect on returns if their intermediaries are not fully complying with the regulations. For those investors working solely through QIs, the risk is somewhat mitigated by their being taxed at the right level, but it is increased by the workload in making sure that the QI has done the job correctly. For those using NQIs at any point in the process, these risks are compounded by potential penalties that could see tax on investments penalized up to 50 percent.

As was mentioned in the introduction to this chapter, the US regulations were the first of a number of "advanced" taxation systems to be implemented in recent years. Relief at source is generally in the expansion phase of its cycle, with several countries deciding to opt for pre-income documentation as opposed to post-event reclamation. This might seem anachronistic, since each country has a statute of limitations, and research indicates that most tax that is over-withheld by foreign governments is never reclaimed. Industry estimates vary, but range from US$60 billion a year in non-reclaimed tax to over US$200 billion. With average statutes across European countries setting the limitation period at 5.2 years, this indicates that at any one time, there could be over US$1 trillion of money that has been taken in tax and not returned to investors, and to which they have an entitlement.

The advanced relief at source system initiated by the United States has since 2001 been copied, albeit in simpler form, by both the Irish and Japanese governments, although the latter scheme applies to Japanese government bond income only.

For readers of this book dealing with multiple regulatory structures across different countries, this represents a classic example of the need for expert advice. An intermediary that manages a reasonable number of clients and their assets is almost certain to receive income for a selection of clients from all three of these jurisdictions. The regulatory requirements of each jurisdiction are different, even though they all fall into the category of an advanced relief at source system, and the Japanese and Irish systems can even be described as clones of the US system. The implication of this is that any one firm may have to segregate its accounts in a matrix format to identify which set of regulations applies. The intermediaries themselves will have to contract separately with each tax authority, report separately, and effectively wear several "hats" as different types of qualified intermediary under the various regulations.

The issue is made even more complex when it is borne in mind that the "source" of income is not always clear, and that research must be done at intermediary level and a judgment made. The potential for several intermediaries to come to different judgments, based on their own internal pressures, creates the likelihood of significant regulatory non-compliance and fines.

As these advanced systems extend geographically, they create an increasing degree of extraterritoriality that has historically been problematic for many governments. Since September 11, 2001, increased cooperation between governments has mitigated these concerns to a great degree.

Changes to withholding tax rates and procedures are often a way to create a macroeconomic effect. In 2004 President Bush, in an effort to stimulate the US domestic economy, changed the way withholding tax was applied to dividends, by establishing the concept of a qualifying period, so that the applicable tax rate was to some extent dependent on the length of time the investor had held shares prior to the dividend being distributed. While this had a debatable effect in the United States, it stimulated a major protest by the international investment community, and created a widely accepted notion that investment into the United States was becoming too expensive and labor-intensive to bother with. While this was hardly a justifiable position to take with regard to the world's largest economy, the subsequent clarification that the rules only applied in very limited circumstances to non-US investors or non-US distributions did calm the market somewhat.

Practical tips for investors

- If you derive investment income from the United States, make sure your intermediary is a qualified intermediary (either a WQI or NWQI); otherwise you risk disclosure of your investments and confidential details to third parties in the United States.
- Respond quickly to requests for W8 documentation, their existence is all that stops your investment income being taxed at 30 percent rather than the lower rate to which you may be entitled.

The USA Patriot Act

What is it?
An US Act of Congress passed on October 24, 2001.
What does it do?
Sets rules designed to deter and punish terrorist acts in the United States and around the world and enhance law enforcement investigatory tools.
Who does it affect?
Everyone.
Why does it exist?
Primarily to provide a structure of law enforcement to identify terrorists and deter any harm to the United States or its interests.
Will it change?
Yes.
Who are the regulators?
US law enforcement agencies.

The phrase "USA Patriot" is actually an acronym: **u**niting and **s**trengthening **A**merica by **p**roviding **a**ppropriate **t**ools **r**equired to **i**ntercept and **o**bstruct **t**errorism. Clearly its aim is to deter and obstruct terrorism. For the financial community this is very important, since most terrorism needs to be funded, and terrorists use international financial systems to move money around the world. There is therefore a clear focus on money laundering. However, there has been criticism that the Patriot Act is being used by law enforcement agencies to widen their ability to deal with other types of crime.

While most of the Patriot Act can be considered to be Amerocentric (that is, focused on US domestic interests), the terms of the Act encompass any form of American interest, widely defined. To that extent, harm to the United States's interests, and terrorism, can be very widely interpreted, and with that wide interpretation comes a degree of extraterritoriality. This gives the Patriot Act teeth well beyond the boundary of North America.

In similar vein, since 9/11 we have seen a dawning realization around the world that terrorism per se can be very widely defined, and cannot be restricted to the purely physical phenomena of things being blown up or the threat of biological or nuclear agents. It is equally a terrorist act to place the financial services industry under threat, since it is this industry that underpins much of modern civilization, and its failure would have catastrophic consequences. So the impact on financial services and investment is twofold. The industry is the prima facie route by which terrorists fund their activities, and it is also a clear target for terrorism. The Patriot Act therefore needs to deal with a number of issues which have overlap with other regulation both within and outside the United States.

The Act has ten titles or subject areas, each of which is "joint and several," or stands independent of the others. There are nine key areas and one "miscellaneous". The key areas are:

1   Enhancing domestic security against terrorism.
2   Enhanced surveillance procedures.
3   International Money Laundering Abatement and Anti-Terrorist Financing Act 2001.
4   Protecting the border.
5   Removing obstacles to investigation of terrorism.
6   Providing for victims of terrorism, public safety officers and their families.
7   Increased information sharing for critical infrastructure protection.
8   Strengthening the criminal laws against terrorism.
9   Improved intelligence.

One of the biggest difficulties with the Patriot Act in particular (but one that applies to a more limited extent to other regulatory frameworks) is that of clear definitions. The Patriot Act has come under particular focus since some of its terms remain internally undefined—a fact which, its critics say, gives the United States almost unlimited ability to interpret it in a way that suits its purpose. In particular for example, Title 1 includes an amendment to the International Emergency Powers Act (50 USC 1702) which includes a power to confiscate property that extends to foreign nationals or entities that have "attacked" the United States. This is at the core of many concerns about the degree of control that may be leveraged by the United States in the financial markets. We have already seen that the Act has been interpreted so widely inside the United States that some critics claim it is being abused. There is concern, for instance, that the term "attack" could be interpreted to include financial attack.

This is one of the bases on which we have chosen to discuss the Act in this context. To take an extreme example, would the US government consider that a concerted disinvestment in US securities constituted an "attack" on the financial fabric of the United States? While the markets are ostensibly free, it is questionable what would happen in them if there were to be a drastic downturn that could be attributed to a single person or small group acting through a non-US financial intermediary.

In December 2004 the BBC aired a drama documentary called *The Man Who Broke Britain* in the United Kingdom, showing how the international financial system could easily be derailed through the abuse of derivatives trading, and the reliance that the industry now has on such exotic instruments. This was considered in the program to constitute financial terrorism, and it could be argued that any such act aimed at the US market could indeed be deemed to be an attack on the United States.

The last "round" of financial scandals (including the Nick Leeson/Barings affair, WorldCom, and Enron) was treated by the industry as serious but not outside its own financial services perspective. It remains to be seen whether the next scandals, whenever and wherever they occur, have ramifications outside the financial services sector, and are dealt with by internal regulation and by the Patriot Act as an attack on the United States.

The concern here is twofold. In order to discover whether an act of an intermediary or investor constitutes an "attack" on the United States, investigation must take place. Of course in most cases such investigations will reveal no issue. However, given the concerns of the United States over this issue, it is likely that investigations will be based on "suspicions" that are very widely defined. Sections of many US government agencies were criticized in the aftermath of 9/11, for having but not acting on information that could have been of use, and for not investigating what were in hindsight suspicious activities. The result in the post-9/11 era is that "suspicion" is very widely interpreted, and the attitude rules that it is better to investigate than not. It is arguable that the USA Patriot Act gives almost carte blanche to the US authorities to collect information and investigate any transaction anywhere in the world, and this has serious implications for investors, and even more importantly for intermediaries that handle millions of financial transactions daily.

After this scene-setting on the potential applicability of the Act to the global financial system, let us go on to look at some of its provisions in more detail. Title II includes provisions covering:

- interception and disclosure of wire, oral, and electronic communications
- surveillance
- seizure of voicemail messages
- disclosure of customer communications or records.

There are however other Titles within the Act that also bear on the financial services markets, operations departments, and investment. In particular Title III takes the concerns of Title I and makes them much more explicit with respect to financial services:

> Money laundering and the defects in financial transparency on which money launderers rely, are critical to the financing of global terrorism and the provision of funds for terrorist attacks ... money launderers subvert legitimate financial mechanisms and banking relationships by using them as protective covering for the movement of criminal proceeds ... and threaten the safety of the United States.

This wording in the preamble to Title III demonstrates the concerns that the US government has about the stability and probity of global financial markets. The Act goes on to target specific types of organization that foster potential problems: offshore banking, correspondent banking, and private banking are three of them.

The Act's intention within this Title is to strengthen measures to deter and counter money laundering by providing a clear mandate to subject foreign jurisdictions, financial institutions, and classes of transactions or types of account to special scrutiny. The main way this is done is to confer powers on the Secretary of State to assess jurisdictions, institutions, classes of transactions, and types of account, and to take countermeasures if any of these are found to be potentially or actually capable of supporting money laundering. Investors and intermediaries must remember that while the language is similar to many money laundering regulations, these are found within a Title of a piece of regulation that is primarily concerned with harm to the United States from terrorism, with all that our previous discussion on interpretation implies.

Most intermediaries operate "omnibus" accounts in most countries including the United States. The omnibus account may be single or multiple, based on an aggregation factor. However, the key is that the omnibus account, interpreted within the Patriot Act, is a "payable through" account. From that perspective it can be argued that, even if an investor does not open an account in the United States but uses a non-US intermediary in another country, since that intermediary is likely to manage its business within the United States through one or more US domestic institutions through an omnibus account structure, the investor (and the intermediary) are directly subject to the Patriot Act and its consequences.

The Patriot Act also has defined links with other current legislation including Safe Harbor and Gramm–Leach–Bliley (see below). Each has different detailed objectives, but they address similar issues. Most of these countermeasures, once assessed, relate to the need to control information, its quality, its transmission, and importantly control the banking system through which this information is acquired and managed.

Overall, the Patriot Act is an unsurprising development considering the terrorist issues the United States faces, and no one really can blame the US government for its attitude. It is likely that many governments are considering, or have considered, equivalent measures, or strengthened existing legislation to take account of the changing world structure, and in particular the speed of changes to information networks and financial services structures.

Investors have increasingly come under extreme pressure with respect their US-sourced income and investment strategies, to the point where any further increase in documentation requirements, disclosure rules, and the like may have a detrimental and measurable impact on external investment in the United States. As terrorism is seen by many as almost viral in its capacity to change and adapt to new circumstances in order to subvert the system at which it is targeted, changes to the Patriot Act should be expected as new types of threat develop.

Practical tips for intermediaries

- Perform a risk impact assessment of Titles I and III of the Act.
- Review your US investment policy.
- Ensure proper and accurate account opening procedures are met.

Practical tips for investors

- Ensure that at account opening, intermediaries explicitly state in writing that they have obtained from you all documentation required under multiple regulations in order to manage the account correctly.
- For accounts already opened, require certification that all regulatory documentation has been properly supplied and is properly managed.

■ Ask for a copy of, and review, the intermediary's compliance policy with regard to account documentation.

Gramm–Leach–Bliley

What is it?
US regulations dealing with the modernization of financial services.
What does it do?
It tightens up and aggregates previous regulation, with new rules for banks and insurance companies.
Who does it affect?
All US financial institutions directly. Indirectly, all non-US financial institutions receiving US-sourced income directly or indirectly, on their own proprietary accounts or those of their clients, and all investors in receipt of US-sourced income.
Why does it exist?
It consolidates previous regulation and attempts to provide a more modern base for banking and insurance activities.
Will it change?
Yes.
Who are the regulators?
The primary regulator is the US government.

The Gramm–Leach–Bliley Act of 2002 (GLB), so named for its three sponsors in Congress, is also entitled the Financial Services Modernization Act. As a result it is clearly critical for US financial services institutions to be aware of its existence and its fundamental principles. The biggest issue for non-US financial services institutions following from GLB is related to privacy (see Title V), and this is where this particular Act has an impact, both internally within the United States in relation to the Safe Harbor Act, and thence to the EU directives on data protection.

As with most US acts, GLB consists of several sections or "Titles" which create the overall pattern of elements within the Act. These are:

1 Title I: Facilitating affiliation among banks, securities firms, and insurance companies.
2 Title II: Functional regulation.
3 Title III: Insurance.
4 Title IV: Unitary savings and loan holding companies.
5 Title V: Privacy.
6 Title VI: Federal Home Loan Bank System modernization.

Title I deals mainly with amending previous regulation or legislation that was felt to be restrictive on banks, predominantly prohibiting some elements of affiliation. This indicates the realization that modern financial services is not a simple set of straight-line relationships. To meet customer needs, both extended competition and the ability for affiliations between "best of breed" are needed. It also establishes new structural concepts that financial services firms can adopt, together with the regulatory standards for such concepts to be acceptable. While our account is not exhaustive, the main provisions are outlined below, with some commentary.

Affiliations and regulation

This Title repeals the restrictions on bank's abilities to affiliate with securities firms (under Sections 20 and 32 of the Glass–Steagall Act). It also provides that bank holding companies which are organized as mutual holding companies should be regulated on comparable terms to other bank holding companies. The Title also streamlines bank holding company supervision.

Financial holding companies

The Act creates the idea of a "financial holding company" (Section 4 of the Bank Holding Company Act), which is a construct that may be commercially advantageous.

Capitalization

The Act ensures that any such holding company's subsidiaries must be well capitalized. This has similar implications for US companies to those that Basel II (see page 113) has in Europe. Although the provisions of Basel II are much more extensive in terms of defining levels of liquidity and stability, this Title element is similar in essence, requiring that the subsidiary entities of a financial holding company should be properly managed and capitalized. The penalty of non-compliance is expressed in the Act as the ability of the Federal Banking Agency to withdraw approval for any new activities or acquisitions if the subsidiary fails to obtain at least a satisfactory rating in its CRA exams.

Insurance regulation

The Act provides for state regulation of insurance.

Title II of the Act deals with functional regulation. This relates to the activities of banks and broker-dealers with respect to functional elements of each of their respective business models. It does this by placing more restrictive provisions on the broad exemptions that banks previously had on regulated broker-dealer activity. The object was to provide banks with the ability to continue their existing activities but also develop new products. Broker-dealers on the other hand are subject to limited exemptions from registration for some types of transaction. These include:

- trust
- safekeeping
- custody
- shareholder and employee benefit plans
- sweep accounts
- private placements
- third party networking offering brokerage to bank customers.

In this way, since 2002 we have seen the continuing "graying" of the boundaries between banking and broker-dealing. It is at these boundaries that new products are most evident where competition is fierce. Underpinning the gray overlap area are the continuing efforts of the banks and broker-dealers to drive down core operating costs and drive up efficiencies in order to protect their base business models.

Title III updates some of the functional regulations that apply to banks and their subsidiaries, particularly with respect to insurance products. This covers such issues as consumer protection. In addition this GLB title preempts any state law that interferes with bank affiliations, requires consultation between the Federal Reserve Board and State insurance regulators, and allows the licensing of multi-state insurance companies.

Title IV is a brief set of rules that apply to a specific type of US entity— the unitary thrift holding company (UTHC). Prior to GLB, the UTHC was the method by which insurance underwriters could engage in banking activities: in other words, an affiliation. The effect of GLB has been to make the use of UTHCs unneccesary, since GLB permits these affiliations. So the net effect of this title is to remove any approval process for new UTHCs to be formed, and to restrict the sale of existing UTHCs to other financial institutions.

Title V is the most important section of this Act from an investor's perspective, because it deals with privacy. Of all the issues that have overlap between different regulatory frameworks, privacy is almost ubiquitous, and GLB is no different. GLB privacy provisions overlap with Safe Harbor and also with EU data protection provisions.

Clearly US banking and insurance institutions are directly affected. The implications of Title V may result in increased costs of compliance.

Practical tips for investors

■ Make sure that, if data on your affairs is being sent to the United States, irrespective of what other regulation may or may not apply, your FI's privacy policy is disclosed in conformance with GLB.

■ Find out whether your FI has joint marketing arrangements with other institutions (financial services or otherwise) and assess your degree of comfort with what is being disclosed.

■ GLB presumes that investors must "opt out" sharing of private information. Make sure you have assessed and "checked the box" where appropriate, otherwise you are presumed to have agreed.

Practical tips for intermediaries

■ GLB is a US Act that may have application if non-US financial firms send "personal data" to the United States. Perform a RIA (regulatory impact assessment) if you are part of a US group or if you send data to the United States.

Safe Harbor

What is it?
US regulations dealing with data protection.
What does it do?
Allows US firms to receive personal data from the EU legally.
Who does it affect?
All US firms which, in the course of business, have reason to receive personal data from a European union firm. Indirectly of course it also affects the EU companies sending such data.
Why does it exist?
The EU Data Protection Directive Eighth Principle prohibits transfer of personal data to "inadequate jurisdictions," which previously included the United States.
Who are the regulators?
Primary regulator: US Department of Commerce.

Safe Harbor is a US Act that was created by mutual agreement between the European Commission and the US government. Principally, the issue is that there are fundamental differences between the United States and the European Union in terms of the protection of private information. To date, the retail financial services industry has provided the main focus, in terms of the use of information provided through credit card companies, as well as increasingly through the Internet and World Wide Web. However, the wholesale financial services and investment banking communities are equally subject to the impact of this Act both in the United States and outside it, because its principal reason for existence is to harmonize the differences between two very different regulatory structures designed to address the same issue.

When it comes to data protection, the United States uses a sectoral approach that relies on a mix of legislation, regulation, and self-regulation. The European Union, however, relies on comprehensive legislation that requires, for example, the creation of government data protection agencies, registration of data bases with those agencies by firms that wish to process personal data, and in some instances prior approval before processing of personal data can take place.

The EU Data Protection Directive of 1998 established the principle of "adequacy" to assure EU citizens that their personal data cannot be transferred to a jurisdiction which does not provide an equal level of protection to that to which the citizen is entitled within the European Union. The Eighth Principle of the Directive prohibits the transfer of personal data to any jurisdiction not deemed to be adequate.

The problem is that the United States is not deemed an "adequate" jurisdiction by the European Union. As a result, under the terms of the Eighth Principle, except under limited and defined conditions, transfers of private data to the United States are prohibited. Clearly there are many occasions where such transfers might be necessary, and the United States was keen to facilitate a method by which US firms could legitimately receive such information. The Safe Harbor Act essentially provides a public listing mechanism for US firms to self-certify that they will apply and afford the same levels of data protection to EU residents as those residents would have enjoyed had such information been transferred between EU Member States.

At the time of print some 470 US firms are signed up to the Safe Harbor system, including some of the biggest and most well-known retail firms and one or two financial firms. The fact that there are no US banks or financial services firms listed as participants in Safe Harbor is a major concern. It is a classic example of the new global regulatory landscape, which can easily produce conflicts even when regulations have been implemented specifically to avoid conflict.

Safe Harbor provides a number of important benefits to US firms including:

- Participating US firms are deemed "adequate" for data protection purposes, and data flows to those companies can take place.
- EU Member State requirements for prior approval of data transfers (where these exist) are either waived, or approval is automatically granted.

■ Data protection claims brought by European citizens against US companies will be heard in the United States subject to limited exceptions.

An EU firm sending information to a US firm can ensure that it is participating in the Safe Harbor scheme by viewing the public list of Safe Harbor self-certified firms on the US Department of Commerce's website at www.export.gov/safeharbor. This list is regularly updated, so that it is clear which organizations assure their contacts of Safe Harbor benefits. (The DoC also makes the firms' self-certification letters publicly available.)

Registration by US firms is entirely voluntary. Firms that participate must comply with the Safe Harbor requirements and publicly declare that they do so. For this purpose a firm needs to certify annually to the DoC in writing that it agrees to adhere to the Safe Harbor requirements. It must also state in its published privacy policy statement that it adheres to the Safe Harbor. Firms can either join a self-regulatory privacy program that adheres to the Safe Harbor requirements, or develop their own conforming privacy policy.

The seven Safe Harbor principles cover:

Notice

Firms must notify individuals about the purposes for which they collect and use information about them, how they can contact the firm with any inquiries or complaints, the types of third parties to which they disclose the information, and the choices and means they offer for limiting use and disclosure.

Choice

Firms must give individuals the opportunity to choose (opt in or out) whether their personal information will be disclosed to a third party, or used for a purpose incompatible with the purpose for which it was originally collected or subsequently authorized.

Onward transfer (transfers to third parties)

To disclose information to a third party, firms must apply the notice and choice principles. Where a firm wants to transfer information to a third party that is acting as an agent, it can do so if it makes sure that the third party subscribes to the Safe Harbor principles, or is subject to the EU Directive or another adequacy finding. As an alternative, the firm can enter into a written agreement with the third party requiring that the third party provide at least the same level of privacy protection as is required by the relevant principles.

Access

Individuals must have access to personal information about themselves that a firm holds, and be able to correct, amend, or delete that information where it is inaccurate, except where the burden or expense of providing access would be disproportionate to the risks to the individual's privacy in the case in question, or where the rights of persons other than the individual would be violated.

Security

Firms must take reasonable precautions to protect personal information from loss, misuse and unauthorized access, disclosure, alteration, and destruction.

Data integrity

Personal information must be relevant for the purposes for which it is to be used. A firm should take reasonable steps to ensure that data is reliable for its intended use, accurate, complete, and current.

Enforcement

In order to ensure compliance with the Safe Harbor principles, there must be:

- Readily available and affordable independent recourse mechanisms so that each individual's complaints and disputes can be investigated and resolved, and damages awarded where the applicable law or private sector initiatives provide.
- Procedures for verifying that the commitments companies make to adhere to the Safe Harbor principles have been implemented.
- Obligations to remedy problems arising out of a failure to comply with the principles. Sanctions must be sufficiently rigorous to ensure compliance by the organization. Organizations that fail to provide annual self-certification letters will no longer appear in the list of participants, and Safe Harbor benefits will no longer be assured.

In general, enforcement of the Safe Harbor takes place in the United States in accordance with US law, and is carried out primarily by the private sector. Private sector self-regulation and enforcement are backed up as needed by government enforcement of the federal and state unfair and deceptive statutes. The effect of these statutes is to give an organization's Safe Harbor commitments the force of law.

As part of their Safe Harbor obligations, firms are required to have in place a dispute resolution system that will investigate and resolve individual complaints and disputes, and procedures for verifying compliance. They are also required to remedy problems arising out of a failure to comply with the principles. Sanctions that dispute resolution bodies can apply must be severe enough to ensure compliance by the firm; they must include publicity for findings of non-compliance and deletion of data in certain circumstances. They may also include suspension from the Safe Harbor and injunctive orders.

The dispute resolution, verification, and remedy requirements can be satisfied in different ways. For example, a firm could comply with a private-sector-developed privacy seal program that incorporates and satisfies the Safe Harbor principles. If the seal program only provides for dispute resolution and remedies but not verification, then the firm would have to satisfy the verification requirement in an alternative way.

Firms can also satisfy the dispute resolution and remedy requirements through compliance with government supervisory authorities or by committing themselves to cooperate with data protection authorities located in Europe.

Under the US Federal Trade Commission Act, a firm's failure to abide by commitments to implement the Safe Harbor principles might be considered deceptive and actionable by the Federal Trade Commission (FTC). This is the case even where a firm adhering to the Safe Harbor principles relies entirely on self-regulation to provide the enforcement required by the Safe Harbor enforcement principle. The FTC has the power to rectify such misrepresentations by seeking administrative orders and civil penalties of up to US$12,000 per day for violations.

If a firm persistently fails to comply with the Safe Harbor requirements, it would not be entitled to benefit from the Safe Harbor. Persistent failure to comply would arise where a firm refused to comply with a final determination by any self-regulatory or government body or where its claim to compliance claim was no longer credible. In these cases, the firm would need to notify the US Department of Commerce. If it failed to do so, that might be actionable under the False Statements Act.

So this US Act has a defined purpose—harmonization of data protections procedures between two different styles of regime, as well as defined penalties and mechanisms for complaints. Of course, this presumes on the one hand, that the data subject is aware of any transfer, and on the other, that the EU firm making the transfer is aware of, and has followed, the procedures to assure EU citizens of the safety of their personal information. For this to occur, the firm making the transfer must understand not just the Eighth Principle of the EU Directive, but also the US Safe Harbor Act and whether or not the receiving firm is a signatory and thus protected, or whether or not it has taken one of the available routes to mitigate the legal risk.

Practical tips for investors

- If you invest in the United States, ask your intermediary whether your data is being or has been forwarded to a third party in the United States that is not a signatory to Safe Harbor.
- If so, require your intermediary to demonstrate the decision path and judgment it used to establish that your data would be held and managed to the same degree that it would have to be managed within the European Union.
- Review contracts with intermediaries for simple single-paragraph clauses that give them the apparent right to send your data outside the European Union. The sample EU Commissioner's approval text for this purpose is several pages long. You may be giving your intermediary carte blanche to do what it likes with your data without you having any idea of its control processes or policies.

Practical tips for intermediaries

- Use EU-approved text to give clear disclosure, and obtain clear approval for the extent to which data will be transferred.
- Require, as a matter of policy, that any third party to which you transfer personal data of your clients is a signatory to Safe Harbor.

Securities and Exchange Commission Act 1934

What is it?

The Securities and Exchange Commission (SEC) is a US body created to monitor and oversee business activities.

What does it do?

The SEC establishes rules on the keeping and maintenance of records for affected companies and the process of auditing securities transactions.

Who does it affect?

The rules affect those who act as broker-dealers, and other individuals who trade securities or act as brokers for traders, and listed US companies.

Why does it exist?

The SEC Act was introduced to protect investors from fraud and misleading claims in the securities industry.

Will it change?

It is regularly amended by other Acts of Congress.

Who are the regulators?

The US government through the enforcement staff of the SEC.

The SEC is perhaps the globally best known of all national regulatory bodies. It is known internationally and used as a model for many other countries. The official designation of the enabling legislation is the Securities and Exchange Commission Act (SEC) 1934 17a-3/4, and the NASD 3010/3110. The Act has two central practical dimensions:

- Records to be made and kept for review:
  - SEC 17a-3 contains the requirements to make records
  - SEC 17a-4 contains the requirement to keep records.
- The auditing of security transactions.

All entities listed in the United States are affected. The rules affect the actions of those who act as broker-dealers, and other individuals who trade securities or act as brokers for traders. This includes financial institutions such as banks, stock brokerage firms, and securities firms and traders. The scope is the United States, and the SEC regulates US trading, but it is a benchmark for other jurisdictions such as the FSA in the United Kingdom and the EU Directive on Auditing.

The SEC Act was introduced to protect investors from fraud and misleading claims in the securities industry. It originated in the period after the Great Crash of 1929, when investors were left stranded by the collapse of the financial system. As its name implies, it focuses on securities and the exchange systems that dominate capital movement, borrowing, and growth in the US economy. There was a significant recent amendment to the Primary Rule, 17a-3/4, in 1997 to allow broker-dealers to store records electronically, including electronic communication and messaging, such as e-mail and instant messages.

The SEC has its own enforcement arm backed by government legislation in the forms of Acts passed by the US Congress. Amendments to the SEC rules are made through this mechanism and other Acts, such the Sarbanes–Oxley Act of 2002.

The National Association of Securities Dealers (NASD) 3010 and 3110 applies the SEC 17a-3/4 and requires relevant organizations to have a policy on the retention of reviewable customer records and transaction data.

The effect on financial services has been enormous. It is hard to measure the influence the SEC has had not only on US financial players but internationally, in the way it has helped shape legislation; because of the dominance of the US economy it has been the prime reference model for emerging markets. Yet historically it was only formed as a response to the aftermath of the crash of 1929, and much of the legislation entrusted to it is reactive; this helps define the way companies and others respond to it. Generally the United States has had an approach that is self-regulatory in spirit. The Enron debacle and the problems of that period have seen a sea-change in the zeal with which the SEC has taken up the cause of the shareholder. The

Sarbanes–Oxley Act, discussed above, is an example of how the SEC has started to use its teeth and take a more proactive approach to regulation.

Practical tips for investors

Investors have seen the SEC as a great reference point for the best practice in company assessment for the industry.

Practical tips for issuers and intermediaries

The SEC laws are a series of detailed mandates on how to manage company information for the benefit of shareholders. The relationship with other US regulatory bodies also falls into this theme of information control, management, and presentation. For issuers and intermediaries there are a number of mandated activities to undertake:

- Ensure all transaction documentation is properly captured, archived, stored and deleted.
- Ensure this documentation is available and easily accessible to regulatory investigation.
- Ensure it is tamper-proof and not subject to change.
- Since electronic data is valid as transactional information, ensure that e-mails, instant messaging sessions, and webmail interactions are all stored, archived, and subject to effective information life cycle management.

EUROPE

Basel II

What is it?
The Basel Capital Accords are a response to the changes in financial industry over the 15 years since 1988.
What does it do?
The proposed new Basel Capital Accord (Basel II) introduces a more comprehensive, risk-sensitive approach for banks for calculating regulatory capital.
Who does it affect?
Basel II applies to credit institutions and securities firms in Member States of the European Union, but application varies by country.
Why does it exist?
Its purpose is to update the 1988 Accord.
Will it change?
As it refers to an EU set of directives it is likely to change.

Who are the regulators?
In itself (although the Accord is not legally binding) it is implemented in the EU through the Capital Adequacy Directive. EU states are required to implement this Directive in national legislation by December 31, 2006.

The Basel Committee on Banking Supervision was established by the central bank governors of the G10 (Group of Ten) countries at the end of 1974. In 1988, the Basel Committee decided to introduce a capital measurement system, normally referred to as the Basel Capital Accord. The aim was to protect investors and markets by establishing a minimum capital adequacy framework and a credit risk measurement framework for banks. It sought to internationalize this, and over 100 countries (including the G10) opted to comply with the 1988 Accord.

"Basel I" represents a set of rules for measuring accurately the financial risks undertaken by financial institutions. In essence, banks have to balance the risks they take with the capital they hold. This is another piece of regulation that focuses on risk in the finance sector. We might be forgiven for believing that risk is something comprehensively covered by a sector so sensitive to its capital base. However, the history of the sector does not bear this out.

The Committee is not a supranational supervisory body; its role is advisory. It works with the central bank governors of the G10 to implement the Accord through national institutions. EU directives and the Member State legislation that implements these enshrine aspects of the Accord in law.

In June 1999, the Basel Committee decided that the 1988 Accord needed replacing with an updated version. It delivered the Basel II Accord (also called the Second Basel Accord) in 2004. The timeline sees implementation for member companies by the end of 2006. Under the Accord, banks can align regulatory requirements more closely with their own projected measurements of risk, providing a unique opportunity for banks to modernize by upgrading their risk management, internal policies, and introduce technology to manage credit, market, and operational risk. It introduces a more comprehensive approach to risk evaluation, focusing on the banks' own assessment of risk.

Basel I only took into account the financial risks carried by banks and relevant financial institutions, such as credit risk. In 1996, market risk was added. The emphasis of Basel II ensures that banks evaluate and measure other forms of risk, including operational risk, reflecting the increased importance of this area. It also includes capital charges for operational risk. Banks will have to make capital provision to effectively act as a contingency fund, to cover the direct and indirect losses that emergent operational risks could cause. This allowance of self-assessment is in tune with a self-regulatory approach. The Accord also provides capital incentives to improve risk management and measurement. It is concerned with ensuring that banks hold sufficient capital to cover their risk. It requires qualifying institutions to meet capital adequacy requirements, and demonstrate:

- an understanding of operational, market, or credit risk management procedures
- good data management, reporting, and storage procedures.

The Accord focuses on mechanisms that deliver minimum capital adequacy requirements, regulatory supervision, and market discipline.

Basel II has three key features, known as "pillars":

- Pillar 1—Minimum capital requirements, which will update and refine the rules set out in the 1988 Accord. It uses the minimum requirement of 8 percent of capital-to-risk-weighted assets from the first Basel Capital Accord.
- Pillar 2—Supervisory review of an institution's internal assessment process, risk management framework and capital adequacy.
- Pillar 3—Enhanced disclosure to strengthen the market discipline for an institution as a complement to supervisory efforts.

Basel II applies to credit institutions and securities firms in Member States of the European Union, but application varies by country. It is enforced by supervisors, empowered to intervene in bank activities and order remedial action. Markets are seen as natural enforcers, penalizing non-compliance through enhanced transparency requirements. International consultation has resulted in a flexible framework and the use of qualitative as well as quantitative factors. There is a need to develop a granular mechanism for aligning risk measurement and regulatory and economic capital.

Basel II is implemented in EU Member States through the Capital Adequacy Directive, which States are required to enshrine in national legislation by December 31, 2006.

Practical tips for investors

For institutional and private investors there are a number of observations that can be made of institutions affected by the Accord:

- Check whether they have published a clear understanding of the major features of Basel II.
- Look for evidence of a practical implementation of the new Accord, typically with risk strategies and re-definitions of risk tolerance.

Practical tips for issuers and intermediaries

Many banks are taking advantage of the Accord. These moves are directly relevant to issuers and intermediaries, which can introduce a practical and positive response to legislation by:

- developing strategies to integrate their risk management and financial reporting solutions
- moving beyond regulatory compliance and benefitting fully from best practice to achieve distinct competitive advantage.

For affected companies best practice centers on:

- assessing the practicalities of rating systems and data accumulation and architectures needed to evolve in banking
- assessing enterprise-wide risk management, based on risk-tolerance strategies and frameworks
- learning from those who are testing the quantitative impact of Basel II on their levels of regulatory capital and who are experimenting with new models to measure operational risk
- discovering how the banking industry is responding to the far-reaching implications of the new Accord's overall requirements, developing risk management, internal processes audit, and IT infrastructure
- embracing the latest thinking on Basel II employed by risk consultants and IT experts.

Industry feedback will reveal the likely impact of the Accord and, in particular, focus on the best strategies towards data capture, warehousing architecture and integration, the use of CRM data, internal rating systems, methodologies for operational risk measurement, mitigation, and overall bank strategy towards an added value way to implement Basel II.

UCITS III

What is it?
Undertakings for Collective Investment in Transferable Securities Directive (UCITS).
What does it do?
It and its predecessors lay down rules on the minimum conditions to be satisfied by unit trusts whose units can be sold across frontiers.
Who does it affect?
Any company within the European Union that trades unit trusts.
Why does it exist?

> The 1985 UCITS Directive established a set of EU-wide rules governing collective investments schemes, known as unit trusts and OEICs in the UK. These funds could then be sold across the European Union depending on local tax and marketing laws.
> **Will it change?**
> It is being amended currently and has been amended since inception.
> **Who are the regulators?**
> National entities and governments implementing the EU Directives.

Historically, unit trusts are investment funds that are available to the general public. As such they are a standardized form of asset management governed by law. They are managed by experts who attempt to spread the associated risks of investment funds for the benefit of all involved. They are, in effect, entry-level packages that give consumers access to the capital markets, but also saddle them with capital market risks. However, since the 1960s in the United Kingdom and the collapse of certain funds, the public and the political establishment has been sensitive to these risks, and a unit trust has a strong association with consumer protection. The principle has evolved whereby the consumer is assumed to know little of the way the markets operate and a deal of advice, not typical of an investment fund sale, is provided in the process. However, what works well for one market bound by national constraints and culture may not work well for another. Within the European Union, there are national differences in approach to public investment. Now, national efforts to regulate this market have been reinforced by transnational efforts.

EU Directive 85/611/EEC addresses laws, regulations, and administrative provisions on investment funds known as undertakings for collective investments in transferable securities (UCITS) (which in the United Kingdom are known as unit trusts). It was adopted on December 20, 1985. This UCITS I Directive includes minimum conditions to be satisfied by unit trusts. Under Article 4(1) the home country principle applies, whereby a UCITS-affected entity needs authorization only from the competent authorities of the EU Member State in which it is situated.

This Directive was a response to the needs of consumer protection within the investing populations of the European Union. A number of measures were put in place:

- Authorized unit trusts are limited to a range of low-risk products.
- Investments were largely restricted to shares and quoted bonds by limiting the use of high-risk securities to 10 percent of total fixed assets.
- A further limit of 5 percent was imposed on other securities to ensure that the risk was widely spread.

■ Interest-rate and hedging tools, such as options, were to be only used internally and where absolutely necessary.

■ Unit trusts were forbidden to invest in other unit trusts, such as "funds of funds."

By January 2002 two directives amending the 1985 directive entered into EU law. These directives broadened the range of assets for investment and harmonized rules for supervising firms that manage UCITS.

Product Directive

Directive 2001/108/EC, COM(1998) 449, clarifies the use of "products" and derivatives by UCITS, giving unit trusts access to more investment options in the capital markets.

Service-Provide Directive

COM(1998) 451 outlines rules for service-providing institutions. These rules clarify the minimum requirements to be met, while other provisions expand the potential range of investment activities, especially for managing individual portfolios through asset and pension fund management.

The new Directive (UCITS III) proposes to amend or change principles in line with those previously applied and found to be active in national legislation. This is especially the case for higher-risk instruments, such as derivatives. These are permitted if they are explicitly intended for use by "experienced investors," and where risk cover is sufficient. There is a revised list of investment products that unit trusts will be able to invest in the future:

■ shares that are not fully paid
■ all money market instruments, as defined at national level
■ all bank deposits, up to 10 percent per credit institution
■ investments in financial futures, options and OTC derivatives if risk cover ensured
■ units of other unit trusts.

Companies are also permitted to engage in the management of the assets of individuals and pension funds as well as unit trust business.

Delegation and simplified prospectus

The Directive amendments further permit investment companies to delegate certain functions, and manage any conflicts of interest between partners that arises from this delegation. They introduce a "simplified prospectus." With the focus still on the ordinary investor, it provides key information about the fund, its objectives, structure, and associated risks. This simplified prospectus is compulsory, and although it is supplementary to the full prospectus, it is likely, for many, to replace it.

Any company or institution offering appropriate collective investment schemes that wants to sell them across the EU market is affected. A typical example is in the United Kingdom, where the UK Inland Revenue ICTA88/S468 (6) notes that an "authorized unit trust means, as respects an accounting period, a unit trust scheme in the case of which an order under FSA86/S78 is in force during the whole or part of that accounting period." This clause notes that:

> The UK vehicles directly affected are those authorized unit trusts that are UCITS. They are known as certified unit trusts; that is, they have received a certificate from the Securities and Investments Board (under FSA86/S78 (8)) that they comply with the conditions for UCITS. Some authorized unit trusts which satisfy the conditions for certification have not applied for a UCITS certificate.
>
> (www.inlandrevenue.gov.uk)

Regulation has a specific role for UCITs. Under the Directive, investment in a range of high-risk financial products, as well as those commonly used, is permitted throughout Europe. Unit trusts are authorized under national law in a number of countries. However, for these higher-risk products, national restrictions imposed by member countries no longer apply. Like all EU directives, the UCITS Directives are implemented on a country by country basis.

The regulatory bodies vary: in the United Kingdom it is the FSA in combination with the Treasury. The FSA Handbook dealing with "Collective Investment Schemes Investment and borrowing powers," section 5.2, "General investment powers and limits for UCITS schemes" outlines: "general investment rules, with which authorized funds must comply, in order to ensure that they qualify as UCITS schemes" (source: http://www.fsa.gov.uk/vhb/html/CIS/CIS5.2.html).

Practical tips for investors

While UCITS funds generally open up the investment opportunities within the European Union, they can be problematic:

■ They can cause problems with double tax agreements as we shall see later. Investors should consider this area carefully.
■ The EU drive to open up the financial services sector is at odds with the

US approach, which has developed limitation on benefits designed to deter and identify treaty shopping. In principle, a UCITS fund could be viewed from the American perspective as a vehicle intended either deliberately or accidentally to foster treaty shopping. Investors should examine the nature of treaty shopping and see how it might apply to them.

■ Under such conditions, if the deal is not properly structured, those who invest in such funds may find that the fund's performance is understated since the fund will be excluded from treaty rate benefits under double tax regulation. The difference could be as much as 15 percent of the fund value. This difference must be identified early on so that appropriate steps can be taken to reduce the burden of risk.

Practical tips for issuers and intermediaries

■ Care must be taken by issuers and intermediaries to not only comply with the UCITS regulations implemented nationally but also take special note of the Product Directive which now gives unit trusts access to more investment options in the capital markets. These investment options may carry additional costs that need to be identified.

■ The development of products is the life blood of these unit trusts. Anything that impedes their creation and marketing has to be factored into the risk profile.

■ Service-Provide Directive rules clarify the minimum requirements to be met for service-providing institutions. These rules are specific to unit trusts and need careful attention.

■ The management of individual portfolios is covered through asset and pension fund management under the directive; this growth area has to be understood in depth to avoid additional costs.

Data protection

What is it?
EU regulations dealing with data protection.
What does it do?
Establishes eight principles of data protection.
Who does it affect?
All firms in possession of personal data.
Why does it exist?
To protect data subjects from uncontrolled dissemination of their private information, and to provide means of access to and correction of such data.
Who are the regulators?
EU national governments and national data protection commissioners.

The European Union has issued directives on data protection which have, for the most part, been adopted into national legislation. The regulations fall broadly into three areas: definitions needed, the rights of data subjects, and the obligations of those in possession of their data.

The data protection directives that apply to EU countries give individuals who are the subject of personal data ("data subjects") a general right of access to the personal data that relates to them. These rights are called "subject access rights." Requests for access to records and for other information about those records are known as "subject access requests," and can be made to the person or organization (the "data controller") who is processing the information. Personal data takes the form of computerized, or in some cases paper, records.

Clearly from the financial services perspective, intermediaries, custodians, banks, brokers, IFAs, and many others acquire much information about their clients, and prospects, that comes under the terms of the directives.

From the retail banking perspective, this may typically include name, address, copies of identification taken under "know your customer" regulations, together with information about data subjects' banking transactions. It will also very often include indirectly acquired data, including "lifestyle" information which helps the intermediary identify product sales opportunities.

In the wholesale banking environment and particularly in custody, this basic information set is enhanced with information about investments, risk profiles, and secondary information needed to process corporate actions, such as tax identification details. So the range of data can be extremely large, and one of the key issues for investors is, as with data protection in general, that data subjects generally only ask for information that they know is held. It is often very difficult for a data subject to identify precisely what data is held, and therefore there can be some uncertainty about the accuracy and maintenance of all information. To an extent, the data subject's interests are protected by the obligations of the directives imposed on data controllers.

There are eight principles put in place by the data protection directives to make sure that information is handled properly. Information must be:

1   Fairly and lawfully processed.
2   Processed for limited purposes.
3   Adequate, relevant, and not excessive.
4   Accurate.
5   Not kept for longer than is necessary.
6   Processed in line with the data subject's rights.
7   Secure.
8   Not transferred to countries without adequate protection.

Most EU Member States have had data protection legislation in place for some years, so Principles 1 to 7 are for the most part well understood by intermediaries. Those new entrants to the European Union that have not yet had time to comply will need to move towards compliance as rapidly as is feasible. However to that extent, even EU data protection directives can only be said to be consistent across the European Union to a limited extent.

For both investors and intermediaries it is the issue of cross-border transfer (the Eighth Principle) that creates the greatest risk. The issue is not well understood, and the principle is not deployed consistently by intermediaries.

The principle prohibits the transfer of personal information to countries or territories outside the European Economic Area, which consists of the 25 EU Member States as well as Iceland, Liechtenstein, and Norway. A transfer can only be made where there is adequate protection for the rights and freedoms of individuals in relation to the processing of information about them. This is intended to ensure that data protection rules cannot be circumvented by transferring personal information to a place where it will enjoy no legal protection, and where individuals will have no rights in respect of it.

The EU Commissioner has issued "good practice guidelines," which include advice on how to assess the adequacy of a destination jurisdiction as well as guideline contractual terms.

The issue of whether or not an investor's personal data can legally be transferred outside the European Union can be shown as a decision tree. The lower in the decision tree that the decision to transfer is made, the higher the risk. At the top of the tree is the principle establishing that, unless the destination country is deemed adequate, such transfers are prohibited. The Commission has so far recognized Switzerland, Canada, Argentina, Guernsey, the Isle of Man, the US Department of Commerce's Safe Harbor Privacy Principles, and the transfer of an air passenger name record to the United States' Bureau of Customs and Border Protection as providing adequate protection. This latter is why passenger manifests can be sent to the United States prior to aircraft departure so that names can be cross-checked for terrorist suspects under the USA Patriot Act.

As anyone can see, this adequacy list is not large. One notable country absent from the list, given the rise in popularity of outsourcing contacts, is India, an issue that is addressed later. The United States, as the hub of much of the world's financial transactions, is also generically not deemed adequate unless the destination firm in the United States has signed up to the principles of Safe Harbor. Of the slightly more than 240 US firms in Safe Harbor, none are banks.

The rest of the decision tree is constructed of a series of decisions which can allow such transfers, even though the destination is not "adequate" based on exemptions or other rules.

The two major exemptions are:

- if data subjects have given their unambiguous and informed consent
- or if the transfer is made to fulfill a contract involving the data subject.

In addition, the directives allow data to be transferred to destinations where adequate protection is not generally guaranteed but the "exporter" can show that adequate safeguards are in place, for example in the form of a contract with the "importer." The contract between the exporter and importer of data can either be tailored to the specific transfer, in which case it will have to be approved beforehand by national data protection authorities, or it can rely on standard contractual clauses adopted by the Commission. Generally speaking these clauses do not need prior approval from national data protection commissioners.

What should be of concern to most investors is that in many instances these contractual guidelines are not being followed, and inter alia, full and informed consent is not given by the data subject. The standard contractual clauses recommended by the EU Commissioner run to six pages. More generically, most banks adopt a "catch all" type of clause, usually in small print, which seems to give blanket approval by the data subject based on the performance of an act such as account opening. This is often found on websites. In account opening documents themselves, more detailed text is found, but often this falls short of the necessary information, as the bank or intermediary wishes to keep future options open.

The Commission has also developed some binding codes of corporate conduct designed to enable multinational organizations make better adequacy decisions. This is a category into which many banks fall.

Corporate actions and trading activity for investors create a large amount of data that is either highly personal to an individual or private to a body corporate. Ultimately, even the body corporate in many financial transactions is fiscally transparent, so that such a body must release underlying investor information for certain corporate actions to proceed. Quite often investors will be unaware of such legitimate transfers, let alone of the impact they may have. Investors should not automatically assume that their information is being managed in compliance with data protection. As with all things, investors' best interests are served by intermediaries being explicit and detailed in their regulatory compliance so as to avoid risk and liability. Investors themselves however also have an obligation to their own interests, to make sure they ask the right questions.

The nature and complexity of the financial services business model is often overlooked in such compliance issues. Typically, certainly in corporate actions, data may be transferred across borders within an organization, across borders outside an organization, and across borders via third party transactions. Most custodians operate a network of subcustodians through which transactions can be effected within a local market environment. However,

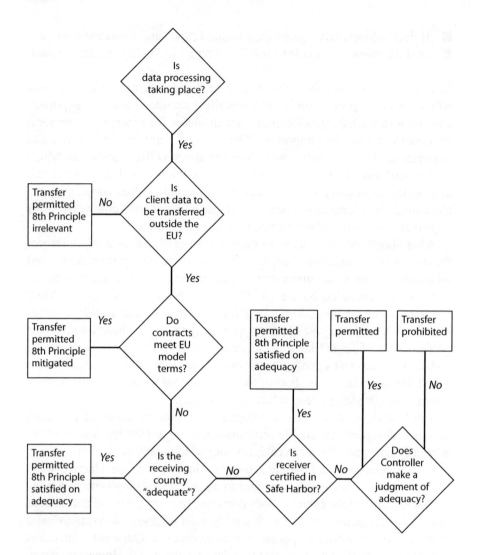

Figure 3.3 Data protection decision tree
Source: the authors.

data transfer is necessary for the subcustodian to perform these local market procedures. In some instances the third party receiver may even be a foreign tax authority.

Practical tips for investors

■ Require your custodian to provide a hard copy of its statement on data privacy, and review it for the adequacy of their procedures with respect to your data.

■ Review your portfolio for data process risk (see Chapter 4). If you reside in the European Union and invest in countries outside it, find out whether your intermediary is transferring personal data to these countries, why, and what specific protections are provided.

Practical tips for intermediaries

■ Perform a regular audit of DP compliance. In particular review the adequacy of statements made on websites and in account opening procedures.
■ If corporate actions processing is outsourced in full or in part, perform an audit of DP compliance on the supplier.

E-Commerce Directive 2000/37/EC

What is it?
The E-Commerce Directive 2000/37/EC is an EU directive widely implemented by Member States.
What does it do?
It clarifies the rights and obligations of those involved in e-commerce to promote its use and protect consumers.
Who does it affect?
Every commercial website providing "information society services."
Why does it exist?
The Directive is designed to tighten control on e-commerce across the European Union.
Will it change?
As e-commerce evolves it will be a part of a body of legislation subject to change and revision.
Who are the regulators?
National jurisdictions.

The Directive clarifies and harmonizes the rules of conduct for online businesses throughout Europe, to boost consumer confidence in this emergent market. The new legislation is intended to clarify the rights and obligations of those involved in e-commerce, and by doing so to promote greater use of it.

Key elements of the legislation

■ The legislation applies to services that are remotely provided.
■ The services must be provided in response to an individual request.

■ Faxes, gambling and lotteries, data protection laws, and cartels are excluded.
■ Information should be provided through the website to all customers, and should be "easily, directly and permanently accessible."
■ Additional information is required for those selling online.
■ Terms and conditions should explain how contracts are formed, and cover procedures for taking or refunding money (via credit cards).

Implementation

Within the Directive there is a clear objective to maintain a practical approach based on the controlling country of origin. The main aims of the Directive mandate that information society providers are subject to the law of their home Member State, and that these states cannot restrict the freedom to provide services across borders within the European Union. The objectives of the regulation will be hard to achieve without this emphasis on country of origin. The likelihood of the country of origin status being enshrined in the Directive was not an assumption. As with much EU regulation involving so many Member States with established or incipient institutions of control, there was disagreement. Nevertheless, this element is in the Directive and is now being observed.

Those states that fail to fully embrace the Directive may yet find they are at a significant competitive disadvantage when it comes to the development of electronic commerce. We can look at a selection of EU countries to capture the broader picture and the effect it may have had on their financial institutions.

■ **Austria.** The Directive was implemented through the Austrian E-Commerce Act (*E-Commerce-Gesetz*). This has chiefly affected insurance companies, and the Austrian Act notes that the controlling original country principle shall not be applicable in certain circumstances.

   Largely it has not affected investment firms; but for UCITS, certificates can be advertised under the Austrian Investment Fund Act in conjunction with the published prospectus, with standard disclaimers on fund performance past and future.
■ **Belgium.** Has not implemented these regulations. A bill has been submitted for the approval of the Belgian Parliament.
■ **Czech Republic.** The Directive has not been implemented yet. However, Czech legislation regarding E-commerce has been partially harmonized with the Directive, especially for "consumers' contracts" provided by the Czech Civil Code.
■ **France.** The Directive has not yet been formally implemented in French law.

■ **Germany.** The Directive has been implemented. Among other restrictions, the home state regulation principle is limited by German law. The explanatory statement to the implementation does not give any additional information. Legal authors suggest that all regulatory provisions in the financial sector should limit the home state regulation principle. This position was based on consideration of the E-Commerce Directive. The "country of origin" principle is not applicable to insurance business.

■ **Hungary.** Although the Directive had not been implemented, Act CVIII of 2001 on e-commerce is generally in compliance with Council Directive 2000/31/EC regarding certain legal questions of e-commerce, with certain exceptions. The 1996 Banking Act and the 2001 Capital Markets Act also contains provisions concerning e-commerce, but these are mainly in relation to consumer protection.

The 1996 Banking Act states that a financial institution must unambiguously and clearly inform customers on the conditions of the services provided. If services are also provided in an e-commerce form, the information shall continuously be available to customers electronically. The 2001 Capital Markets Act states that investment service providers and commodity brokers are required to post their Standard Service Agreement in an electronic format where the services are provided through electronic channels.

■ **Italy.** The Directive has not yet been implemented. Existing provisions on the marketing of investment services via the Internet represent a derogation to principles set out in the Directive. Consob Regulation 11522/1998 concerning investor protection has provisions considered as of public interest and therefore cannot be derogated from or superseded.

■ **Netherlands.** The Directive has not been implemented.

■ **Poland.** The Directive has not been implemented. Some steps were taken before Poland became a member of the EU to harmonize Polish legislation with EC law. These relate to the provisions of the Civil Code and the Act on Electronic Signature regarding forms of acts in law, electronic signatures, and entering into contracts.

■ **United Kingdom.** The directive was implemented on August 21, 2002 for financial services as the Electronic Commerce (EC Directive) Regulations 2003. Its provisions affect all service providers. They must make certain information available to all recipients of their services in a way that is "easily, directly and permanently accessible." These provisions include:

● Their name, geographic address and contact details (including an e-mail address).

● References to prices must be clear and unambiguous, and indicate whether they are inclusive of tax and delivery.

Other requirements include:
- Those subject to VAT must provide their VAT registration number.
- Additional information is required from those who are members of a trade association or similar register, those exercising a regulated profession such as accountants or lawyers, and those providing a service where the provision of the service is subject to an authorization scheme.

These requirements are in addition to any obligations contained in other legislation such as the Consumer Protection (Distance Selling) Regulations 2000. They affect every commercial website.

What is required of those who promote their goods and services by sending unsolicited e-mails? Communications designed to promote a business or other commercial activity are known as "commercial communications." Qualified organizations and those who promote such communications must ensure that they clearly identify:
- that a communication is a commercial communication
- the person on whose behalf it has been sent.

This ensures that anyone receiving unsolicited commercial communications must be able to identify them upon receipt. The UK Department of Trade and Industry (DTI) guidelines even suggest using the word "unsolicited" in the message title. Where a communication contains information about a promotional offer or game, terms and conditions must be obvious and easily accessible.

Every commercial website is affected, so this will have an impact on virtually every bank at retail level. It also increasingly affects wholesale banking, where corporate actions and trade information is supplied to investors via secure websites. While many of these "back office" sites do not charge directly, their provision is usually included "bundled" as part of a broader custody service. The regulations affect suppliers of an "information society service," which is defined as "any service normally provided for remuneration at a distance by means of electronic equipment for the processing (including digital compression) and storage of data at the individual request of the recipient of the service." The DTI claims this covers anyone offering online information or commercial communications (such as advertisements), or providing tools for searches, access, and retrieval of data.

There are five derogations relevant to financial services regulation in the United Kingdom:
- small e-money institutions
- insurance companies
- advertising by operators of UCITS
- the permissibility of unsolicited commercial communications sent by e-mail

● contractual obligations concerning consumer contracts.

Where the FSA has made use of these derogations, the rules can be found in the FSA Handbook under the E-Commerce Directive source-book (ECO). Derogation for insurance companies means that the existing regime for insurers has not changed, except for the minimum information and other requirements that apply where a service is provided by electronic means.

Practical tips for investors

Investors can research the adequacy of a company's compliance by simple inspection of its website. This may not seem to be a major issue initially, but it is an area of regulation that is likely to lead to considerable litigation in the near future. The omission of appropriate information has to be part of the company risk strategy.

Website inspection should indicate the degree of compliance pursued by the issuer. Best practice dictates full compliance. The investor has to take a view on the exposure of the company in this arena, since many companies will not have formally included these requirements in a risk analysis.

Practical tips for issuers and intermediaries

Broadly speaking, the regulations apply to all forms of commercial activity conducted online. It is probable that the regulations will apply to intermediaries, especially those with service portals, involved in:

■ advertising and selling goods or services online
■ the promotion of goods or services online
■ the transmission or storage of electronic communications
■ the provision of information society services—the means of access to a communications network.

Intermediaries must ensure the site contains appropriate text to cover the requirements.

Issuers have to conform to the regulations both as outlets for product goods, and as elements within a supply chain. They should:

■ check that other members of their supply chain are compliant
■ enforce requirements as internal policies
■ educate staff so that customers are informed of their rights to classes of information under the regulations.

From this same perspective, the UK implementation (under Regulation 4 of the Electronic Commerce Directive (Financial Services and Markets)

Regulations 2002—rules relating to a consumer contract requirement) means the FSA requires that certain information be provided about:

- rights of cancellation and withdrawal from a consumer contract; these must be published in sufficient detail
- features of the product or service; but with enough information not to be misleading
- compensation schemes; if any
- charges and fees, as clearly stated as possible.

The FSA has also made a "safe harbor" rule so that providers in other Member States may comply with the rules of their country of origin, where these rules correspond to the FSA requirements.

EU Framework Directive for Electronic Signatures (1999/93/EC)

What is it?
EU regulations that cover the supervision of certification service providers (CSPs), the issuers of certificates or related services for electronic signatures.
What does it do?
It implements measures towards a European framework for electronic commerce and assisting legal recognition within a technological context of electronically "signed" certificates.
Who does it affect?
All organizations controlling the issuance of electronic signatures in business.
Why does it exist?
It is part of the EU framework on controlling the use of electronic signatures.
Will it change?
As the use of electronic signatures become more widespread it is likely to be extended.
Who are the regulators?
National jurisdictions.

The provisions of this legislation cover the supervision of certification service providers (CSPs), who issue certificates or related services for electronic signatures, and address their liability and data protection regulations.

A central idea is the certificate, defined as electronic attestation linking data that verify a signature to an individual and confirm the identity of that person. Qualified certificates advertise themselves as such and identify the issuing CSP. The detail on the provisions is contained in the EU Framework Directive for Electronic Signatures. All organizations using electronic signatures in business are affected.

Implementation of these measures is covered in the United Kingdom by the Electronic Communications Act 2000.

Key elements of the legislation

These can be summarized as:

- **Legal recognition.** The Directive indicates that an electronic signature cannot be legally discriminated against because it is electronic, and that it is valid in legal proceedings.
- **Liability.** The Directive establishes minimum liability rules for the validators of certificates.
- **Technological context.** The Directive stipulates legal recognition whatever the technology used (such as cryptography of biometrics).
- **International dimension.** It allows for mutual recognition and co-operation over electronic commerce certification between third parties on a global basis.

The issue of electronic signatures is of major concern to both investors, as it raises privacy questions, and intermediaries, as it raises operational efficiency issues as well as privacy.

Many of the regulations covered in this book, and indeed many that have not yet been covered, include an element based on the identification of customers: in this context, investors. That identification element is underpinned in most regulation by the requirement to hold original documentation which demonstrates the validity of the identity. In many cases, such "attestations" or self-certifications require an original signature.

The difficulty arises from the nature of the financial services model, which often requires that such documentation is transmitted between the primary holder and some other intermediary, who must use it as the basis of another consequential action. In the tax process part of the back office, this is exemplified by the provision of W-8BEN or W-9 forms from non-US and US investors respectively, first to demonstrate their residency and status to a withholding agent, and second to claim the benefits of a beneficial tax rate under double tax regulations.

The use of electronic signatures has been very slow to take hold in financial services, mainly because of the wide variance in the level of technical sophistication of sending and receiving parties. There is no doubt that the conversion of a paper form into a data packet with an electronic signature would save millions of dollars a year for intermediaries. Unfortunately, even with these regulations, there is no ISO standard that has been implemented by intermediaries generally.

The most common misconception is that an electronic signature is actually a digital certificate. While these are proliferating, financial services has yet to adopt them for the technical reasons given. In 2001 a proposal was made to the US Internal Revenue Service to use a data packet combining the holder's tax and country identifiers with the investor's similar details into a "signature alternative." This simple mechanism meets the requirements of the legislation, would save significantly on costs, not least mail costs, and has even been included by SWIFT into message formats that are the equivalent of those forms W-8BEN. Presently, they remain on the shelf.

This, therefore, is one piece of critical regulation that would afford massive benefits, particularly given that the use by the intermediary industry of the secure SWIFT network eradicates privacy issues from a transmission perspective.

Practical tips for investors

At this stage investors have to recognize that the use of electronic signature is patchy. However, there is the Directive and its work in defining certificates, and the responsibilities of the CSP are aiding the cause of electronic trading at this level.

Practical tips for issuers and intermediaries

Those entities that wish to use signatures can do so within the framework of the Directive. Cross-border harmonization is not yet a reality. However, agreements do exist for the acceptance of certificates.

ASIA/PACIFIC

Financial Transactions Reports Act 1988 (Australia)

What is it?
Australian regulations dealing with money laundering.
What does it do?
Establishes reporting procedures for suspicious transactions, establishes a monitoring body, and defines penalties.
Who does it affect?
Australian firms dealing with financial transactions.
Why does it exist?

> To prevent money laundering.
> **Who are the regulators?**
> AUSTRAC—the Australian government.

This Act provides for the reporting of certain transactions and transfers, establishes an Australian Transaction Reports and Analysis Centre, and imposes obligations on "cash dealers" (what are elsewhere known as intermediaries) in relation to accounts. The FTR Act requires cash dealers to report:

- suspicious transactions
- cash transactions of A$10,000 or more or the foreign currency equivalent
- international funds transfer instructions.

The FTR Act requires cash dealers to verify the identity of persons who are signatories to accounts, and also prohibits accounts being opened or operated in a false name.

Cash dealers are defined in the FTR Act, and include:

- banks, building societies and credit unions referred to as "financial institutions"
- financial corporations
- insurance companies and insurance intermediaries
- securities dealers and futures brokers
- cash carriers
- managers and trustees of unit trusts
- firms that deal in travelers checks, money orders, and the like
- persons who collect, hold, exchange or remit currency on behalf of other persons
- currency and bullion dealers
- casinos and gambling houses
- the Totalizor.

There are also requirements for members of the public to report cash transfers into and out of Australia of A$10,000 or more, or the foreign currency equivalent.

The legislation provides penalties for anyone evading the reporting requirements, and also penalties in respect of false or incomplete information. It also has penalties for persons who facilitate or assist in those activities.

The reporting and identification requirements, backed by penalties for offences, are like other money laundering deterrent regimes in providing a strong deterrent to money launderers and facilitators of money laundering. These provisions effectively increase the level of risk associated with abuse of the Australian financial system by tax evaders and organized crime groups. It also adds to their costs of doing business, and in particular in laundering their illicit profits.

The legislation also sets a standard which must be met by the cash dealers. Failure to meet the standard places the cash dealer at risk of being used in the process of money laundering, and thus subject to consequential penalties when detected. Penalties include pecuniary penalties and imprisonment.

The legislation in this one Act, requiring both intermediary and public action, is the equivalent of that provided in the United Kingdom by the Money Laundering Act (dealing with intermediaries and others in "regulated" business) and the Proceeds of Crime Act 2002, which includes the imposition of responsibilities on members of the public.

India and data protection

Most of this book is concerned with regulations and the impact of how their structures overlap. However, there is an important aspect of the new global regulatory landscape that, if we were to follow this remit exclusively, would be missed. The issue is what to do when there are *no* regulatory structures covering certain markets, regulatory issues, or both.

The biggest issue for investors and intermediaries flows from the increasing use of outsourcing of back-office processes. It is in these processes that most cost lies for intermediaries, and also the most risk.

From 2003 India has been at the forefront of financial services outsourcing, and so it is important to mention this jurisdiction in connection with data protection, mainly because India has little or no data protection structure, and yet today personal data on EU as well as US and other investors is being sent to India as a matter of normal processing, together with their financial transaction history. Much of this is being done on the basis of flimsy legal terms in account set-up documentation which does not even meet EU suggested levels.

Even though the Indian government has a strategic objective to increase inbound outsourcing business from the United States and European Union, it has decided that enacting a comprehensive scheme of data protection may not—at least in the immediate future—be the best plan of action.

To understand the Indian perspective toward data protection, it is necessary first to appreciate the importance to India of outsourcing. Outsourcing is the act of transferring a function from one location or company to another. As the term has come to be used today, it applies to the transfer of jobs to other nations—usually to a nation where the salary structure is much lower. Inasmuch as the primary rationale for engaging in outsourcing is cost-saving, it is not surprising that most of it takes place to developing nations. China, for example, is a rapidly growing destination for outsourcing, but the number one outsourcing destination today is India. India has a unique combination of a relatively low salary structure and a multitude of highly trained individuals who are comfortable speaking English, which makes it especially attractive to many outsourcers.

As the level of outsourcing has increased, it has become a political, as well as an employment issue. The US states of Connecticut, Maryland, New Jersey, and Washington are considering legislation that would place restrictions on outsourcing, and India has indicated that it would bring any such statutes to the attention of the World Trade Organization. While the Indian outsourcing industry is attentive to attempts to legislate a reduction in outsourcing, some seem to believe, and take comfort in the view, that continued outsourcing from developed nations is economically inevitable. Thus, outsourcing today comprises a significant and rapidly growing segment of the Indian economy. And because of the importance of outsourcing to the Indian economy, concerns about maintaining and increasing the level of outsourcing are driving the development of Indian data protection law.

Much of the early outsourcing to India was from the United States, which has no comprehensive data protection laws. As a result, great quantities of personal data were, and continue to be, shipped from the United States without the complications that arise where cross-border transfer restrictions apply. However, an increasing amount of outsourcing now involves data that is subject to the laws of the Member States of the European Union. In its 1995 Data Protection Directive the European Union mandated that each of the Member States must have in place a strict national data protection law that, inter alia, precludes the transfer of personal data from within the European Union to a location outside the European Union, except where one of several specified restrictions is met.

From the perspective of the data exporter, the easiest of these restrictions to satisfy occurs where the laws of the transferee nation have been deemed "adequate" by the European Union. Once the European Union has designated a particular nation as having "adequate" data protection laws, data may be transferred to that nation without a violation of law. The European Union has been rather stingy in designating nations as "adequate," and thus far has designated only a few. Many in India believe that the amount of outsourcing work emanating from the European Union would grow dramatically if India made it onto that list, or otherwise conformed to the requirements for lawfully hosting data from the European Union. The pressure on India to adopt some form of a basis for lawful transfers from the European Union has been heightened in recent months by the fact that many US companies are now considering, as outsourcing alternatives to

India, Eastern European nations such as the Czech Republic, Russia, Romania, and Hungary (all of which have data protection laws in place and may offer even greater economies than does India).

Some firms have executed the standard contractual clauses approved by the European Union for cross-border data transfer, but the use of such clauses is problematical. For one thing, use of these clauses opens the data importer to suit in the European Union by any data subject who claims that his or her data protection rights have been violated. Such use also may subject the importer unnecessarily to the jurisdiction of an EU Member State data protection authority (DPA). And if the parties depart from the approved language in an attempt to eliminate these undesirable ramifications, they run a real risk that the resulting contract may not meet with the approval of the appropriate DPA.

There is little specific privacy law presently in India. The Indian Constitution makes no specific mention of privacy, but the nation's courts have found an implicit and vaguely defined, but nevertheless basic, right of privacy in the Constitution. The Indian Information Technology Act 2000, intended to cope generally with e-commerce, contains a brief mention of privacy-type issues, but has nothing specifically directed toward privacy. That act focuses instead on computer abuse and evidentiary matters related to proving computer-related cases. And, although the banking statutes have no explicit provision imposing a secrecy obligation, a bank's obligation to maintain confidences is recognized on a practical level. Thus it can fairly be said that at present there is no specific Indian data protection law that applies to commerce generally, whereas a comprehensive specific data protection law is exactly what is required for an adequacy finding by the European Union.

The initial intention of the Indian government, espoused at least as early as early 2003, was to enact a comprehensive data protection law, so as to permit the unimpeded flow of personal information from the European Union into India. Obtaining an adequacy determination from the European Union is not a rapid process. As noted above, thus far only four have been given, and several jurisdictions (Australia, Guernsey, the Isle of Man, Japan, New Zealand, South Korea) are presently "in line" seeking such determinations for their data protection laws. It is estimated that generally the process takes about one and a half years. In spring 2003, the Indian National Association of Software and Service Companies (Nasscom) and the Indian Ministry of Information Technology prepared a draft of such a statute, meant to eliminate the barriers preventing the free flow of personal data from the European Union to India. That draft, said to be patterned after the EU Directive, was either not released, or has been released on only a limited basis.

Nevertheless, in late 2003 discussions between the Indian government, industry associations, and legal experts resulted in a "go slow" approach.

Instead of proceeding directly to a new comprehensive EU-type statute, it was decided to institute an interim regime that would either consist of a revision of the Information Technology Act 2000, or would emulate the Safe Harbor Principles agreed between the European Union and the United States.

As a result of these discussions, the industry offered an "action plan" which would commence with Nasscom identifying Indian companies operating in the European Union, and consolidating the data protection provisions in their contracts for dissemination to the Indian outsourcing industry. A group of legal experts would review the present legal framework and suggest modifications. The government would analyze the Safe Harbor arrangement in place between the European Union and the United States, so as to understand its comprehensiveness and the steps necessary for a dialog with the European Union on execution of a similar agreement with India.

In the data protection area, the winds of change are blowing across India, and they are likely soon to alter the landscape. But the new shape of that landscape is not yet clear. The near future is likely to see major modifications to the Information Technology Act 2000 and/or a proposal to the EU for a Safe Harbor India regime. The long-term shape of Indian data protection law may depend on the success (or lack of it) that the short-term solution enjoys. But, one way or another, Indian data protection law is likely to change dramatically in the next few years.

GLOBAL

There are some regulatory structures that are truly global. Often these are not actually regulatory in the sense that they attempt to control or constrain the probity of any given party. They are more likely to define processes or intentions at inter-governmental level. Many of the regulatory structures will come into this definition as time progresses, and governments seek to harmonize regulation within and between trading blocks.

One of the most well known of these inter-governmental structures, and one which has a significant impact on institutional investors, is the concept of double taxation, and the agreements (DTAs) between governments that codify the taxation of cross-border investments.

Double tax agreements

What are they?
Treaties between countries usually following a standard form model.
What do they do?
They establish "treaty" rates of taxation for various kinds of cross-border income received by investors.
Who do they affect?

All financial institutions acting as withholding agents, all financial institutions receiving cross-border income directly or indirectly, on their own proprietary accounts or those of their clients, and all investors in receipt of cross-border investment income.

Why do they exist?
To mitigate the effects of local taxation regulations which would otherwise lead to double taxation of income.

Will they change?
Treaty text tends not to change. Rates change frequently. New treaties are being signed monthly.

Who are the regulators?
Tax authorities.

Many counties recognize that there is a significant degree of trading and investment between their residents and institutional investors. The domestic taxation regulations of most countries normally require that any investment income received by either domestic residents or so-called non-resident persons be taxed. Such tax is called "withholding tax," and the amount varies by country but is typically between 10 and 30 percent.

So if an institutional investor—for example an Irish-resident unit trust—invests in a portfolio of companies across the major markets, when each company declares a dividend, the investor will receive the gross dividend minus the withholding tax applied by each country. Within the country, the withholding tax is sent to the local tax authority by the custodian representing the issuing company. This takes no account of the fact that when the income is received into Ireland (in this example), it will be subject to taxation under Irish law. Hence there is a potential for double taxation.

For those markets whose financial services industry relies on inward investment, this is clearly a barrier to investment, as investor returns will be significantly damaged. Double tax agreements (DTAs) exist in the form of treaties between many countries to alleviate this problem. Most modern DTAs follow a standard form, and provide for the mitigation of the double taxation of a variety of cross-border income, including royalties dividends, bond interest, and so on.

This is achieved in one of two ways. First the market agrees to allow investors to claim treaty benefits in advance. In other words, as long as investors (or their intermediaries on their behalf) can provide proof of their residency and status, the issuer's custodian can be instructed to distribute dividend income either gross or at the treaty rate as applicable. This is called relief at source (RAS). There are three RAS models, simple, intermediate, and advanced. The section on pages 87 to 98 on the US 1441 NRA Regulations outlines an example of an advanced RAS regime. The regimes only differ substantively in the complexity of the documentation and information that needs to be provided and managed prior to a net distribution being made by an issuer.

The other type of process available to deal with treaties is remedial reclaim. In the financial industry it is often the case that relief at source is either unavailable (a given market chooses which type of process to adopt, and this can vary by market, income type, investor type, and several other factors), or is available, but the investor or intermediary failed to provide adequate documentation in a timely manner. In either case, the entitlement to a treaty rate of taxation still exists for a specified period (designated under a statute of limitations). To file a remedial reclaim still requires documentation, but also in this instance some evidence that the person claiming treaty benefits actually received income at the wrong rate: that is, there must be proof of entitlement to a reclaim.

From an investor's perspective, relief at source is clearly beneficial, as the maximum return on investment is obtained within the shortest time period. Remedial reclaims can take from weeks to years. For institutional investors the amounts concerned can be truly huge. In particular for hedge funds, the impact can be extremely large.

Figure 3.4 shows the typical interactions of those involved in processing a remedial reclaim. It is clear that the process is complex, error prone, and only partly automatable.

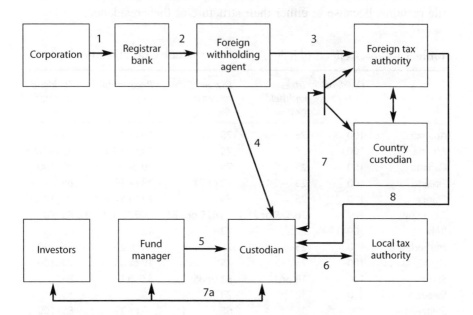

Figure 3.4 Process flow for a remedial tax reclaim
Source: the authors.

1   The issuer declares a dividend.
2   The relevant registrar notifies the issuer's bank (a withholding agent) to distribute funds.
3   The withholding agent bank sends withholding tax to the tax authority.
4   The withholding agent bank sends the net dividend to the investor's custodian bank.
5   The investor provides documentation to prove residency and status (this is usually done at account set-up).
6   The investor's custodian obtains a local tax authority certification of investor's residency.
7   The investor's custodian files a tax reclaim and advises the investor of the amount receivable.
8   The custodian receives tax reclaim funds and credits the investor's account.

Table 3.1 shows the effect that withholding tax can have in material terms across a basket of typical investment markets.

The situation can often be much more complicated, depending on the markets concerned and types of investor, and there are many instances of investors losing millions of dollars through failure to understand and deal with implications of these treaties. In the Irish unit trust example cited above, it is common for trustees of such funds and even their tax advisors to believe that Irish resident unit trusts are unable to benefit from RAS or file reclaims because of either their structure or their residence.

Table 3.1 Typical effects of failure to adhere to double tax agreements

Country	Dividend	Taxes withheld (%)	Dividend received %	Recoverable taxes (%)	Dividend received (%)
Australia	100	25	75	10 or 25	85–100
Austria	100	25	75	12.5 or 10	85 or 87.5
Canada	100	25	75	10 or 25	85–100
Finland	100	28 or 29	72 or 71	13 or 14	85
France	100	25	75	22 to 52.5	97–127.5
Germany	100	26.375 or 21.1	73.625 or 78.9	16.375 or 6.10	85–90
Italy	100	27	73	12	85
Netherlands	100	25	75	10 or 25	85–100
New Zealand	100	25	75	10 or 25	85–100
Spain	100	18 or 15	82 or 85	3.0 or 0	85
Sweden	100	30	70	15	85
Switzerland	100	35	65	20 or 35	85–100

Source: Globe Tax Services Inc.

Many institutional investors are also structured as "omnibus," or multiple in-depth sub-accounted structures. For example US hedge funds are typically partnerships. The structure of the custody service for these funds often means that they are over-taxed because those in place do not have access to the underlying partner or investor information to be able to file reclaims or RAS applications for them.

Double tax agreements have a very direct impact from the investor's perspective, in that failure to adhere to them or take them into account directly reduces investment income, sometimes by over 25 basis points. Conversely, institutional investors who ensure that this item is in the top five of their agenda items for safe custody will benefit from over 25 basis points of performance.

Practical tips for investors

- Make sure that withholding tax is explicitly defined and benchmarked in custody agreements.
- Where withholding tax services are not offered at a suitable standard or are not available, outsource the function directly to a specialist third party provider.
- If in any doubt, conduct a regulatory impact assessment with a specialist third party provider.

Practical tips for issuers and intermediaries

- Make investors aware of double tax agreements relating to their portfolio, and the impact of withholding tax, as well as the extent of intermediary services in this respect.

INTERNATIONAL FINANCIAL REPORTING STANDARDS (IFRS)

The IASC Foundation and IASB Framework

In March 2001, the International Accounting Standards Committee (IASC) Foundation was formed as a not-for-profit corporation in the State of Delaware, USA. The IASC Foundation is the parent entity of the International Accounting Standards Board (IASB), an independent accounting standard-setter based in London, UK. On April 1, 2001, the International Accounting Standards Board (IASB) assumed accounting standard-setting responsibilities.

General

The IASB members come from nine countries and have a variety of functional backgrounds. As its mission statement says:

The IASB is committed to developing, in the public interest, a single set of high quality, understandable and enforceable global accounting standards that require transparent and comparable information in general purpose financial statements.

As with most bodies with an international focus the IASB "cooperates with national accounting standard-setters to achieve convergence in accounting standards around the world."

Organization

The structure of the organization reflects its international basis, and establishes the lines of responsibility, the technical expertise of its members, its independence, and indicates how it represents the scope of its international community, balancing of the functions of the organization through their operational relationship. The oversight body (the Trustees of the IASC Foundation), the advisory body (the Standards Advisory Council), and the interpretative body (the International Financial Reporting Interpretations Committee) reflect the diversity of its geographical and professional scope. The standard-setting body (the IASB) reflects technical competence.

The IASC Foundation

The governance of the IASB and its related bodies is ultimately in the hands of the trustees of the IASC Foundation. There are 19 trustees who appoint the members of the IASB, the International Financial Reporting Interpretations Committee (IFRIC), and the Standards Advisory Council. Among other things, the IASC Foundation's Constitution provides (paragraph 6) that:

Each Trustee shall have an understanding of, and be sensitive to, international issues relevant to the success of an international organization responsible for the development of high quality global accounting for use in the worlds capital markets and by other users.

Note that the trustees are not responsible for setting International Financial Reporting Standards; this responsibility resides with the IASB.

The IASB

The IASB develops International Financial Reporting Standards (IFRS), and follows a rigorous open process. The IASB consists of 14 board members, each with one vote, appointed by the trustees. The IASC Foundation Constitution provides (paragraph 20) that the IASB shall:

comprise a group of people representing, within that group, the best available combination of technical skills and background experience of relevant international business and market conditions in order to contribute to the development of high quality, global accounting standards.

Standards Advisory Council (SAC)

Acting as a forum for organizations and individuals with an interest in international financial reporting, the SAC has about 50 members who contribute to standard-setting. Members have a variety of professional backgrounds and are drawn from many countries. Their appointment is renewable and for three years. The SAC meets the IASB at least three times a year in a public meeting. Both the IASB and the IASC consult with the SAC on matters relating to standards and constitutional changes. The main function of the SAC is to give advice on decisions and priorities in the IASB's work, and forward the views of relevant organizations and individuals involved in major standard-setting projects to the IASB.

International Financial Reporting Interpretations Committee (IFRIC)

The Standing Interpretations Committee (SIC), was reconstituted in December 2001 as IFRIC. IFRIC works closely with national bodies on accounting issues that need consensus and authoritative guidance. In developing interpretations, IFRIC works within the context of International Financial Reporting Standards (IFRSs) and the IASB Framework. IFRIC meets regularly, and technical decisions are taken at public sessions. The Committee addresses only issues of general importance, and the "interpretations" cover newly identified financial reporting issues not dealt with in IFRSs or issues where there may be confusion or lack of authoritative guidance.

International Financial Reporting Standards

Statements of International Accounting Standards issued by the Board of the International Accounting Standards Committee (IASC) between 1973 and 2001 are called "International Accounting Standards" (IAS). In April 2001, the IASB announced that its accounting standards would be called "International Financial Reporting Standards" (IFRS) and that it would adopt all of the International Accounting Standards issued by the IASC.

IFRS Summaries

The IFRS summaries cover IFRS, IAS, and Interpretations issued on or before March 31, 2004. IFRS are published by the IASB; these include the body of standards issued by IASC. The IASB also publishes a series of Interpretations of IAS developed by IFRIC and approved by IASB.

IASB Framework for the Preparation and Presentation of Financial Statements

IASB has a framework, the *Framework for the Preparation and Presentation of Financial Statements*, underlying its financial reporting standards and interpretations. The Framework defines the concepts guiding the preparation and presentation of financial statements for external users. It was approved in 1989 by IASB's predecessor, the board of IASC, and adopted by IASB in April 2001. The Framework involves:

■ the development and review of an IFRS
■ promoting the harmonization of regulations and financial reporting standards
■ assisting national standard-setting bodies in developing national standards
■ assisting those who prepare financial statements in applying IFRS.

The Framework itself is not an IFRS, nor does it define standards. Where there is a conflict between the Framework and an IFRS, the IFRS prevails.

Clearly these standards and the bodies that maintain them have crucial importance to investors, flowing as they do from the same concerns that led to the creation of corporate governance regulations. Large firms are already focusing on these standards, as they are directly affected. Yet even these large firms are having significant difficulty complying with them. Scope creep of these regulations to lower orders of firms is already under way, and its expected that the way will not be smooth for these firms.

The effect on investors and intermediaries is twofold, where typically these groups view it as a single issue. Investors are interested in issuers' compliance to the standards, because these are the companies in which they have invested. However, similarly although not quite as directly, the intermediaries between the investor and the issuer are also subject to the standards, and their probity in meeting these standards is related to their overall service provision—a provision that the investor pays for, usually in custody or broker fees. So while investors are correct to look closely at reporting standards compliance of their issuers, they are currently overlooking the same regime with the intermediaries to which they pay fees.

As for the intermediaries, they too are guilty of tunnel vision. Their focus in terms of financial reporting standards is usually vertical: that is, they are interested in their own financial performance (which cross-links of course to Sarbanes–Oxley issues). The reality is that the activities of the intermediary impact the issuer and the investor, as well as vice versa.

Part of the Global Regulatory Impact Assessment (GRIA) described in Chapter 4 highlights how these alternate views must be monitored in order to avoid a "black hole" quite capable of creating the next WorldCom.

Part III

Part III

CHAPTER 4

Regulatory Overlaps and their Impact

The previous chapters have now given the reader a basic understanding of a number of different regulatory frameworks that affect the global financial services community and global investors. With this basic framework in place, we can now spend some time reviewing how some of these regulatory frameworks impact each other. Typically these impacts include one of more of the following factors:

- Nominal impact—some cost savings for intermediaries from compliance to multiple regulations with single procedures.
- Significant impact—difficulties for investor/intermediary relationships, added cost, risk and liability for intermediaries, financial loss and/or loss of confidentiality in transactions for investors.
- Major impact—exiting business sector or geographical sector for intermediaries with consequent loss to reputation, fiscal growth, and increase in competitive threat; scandal at senior levels in investor community, loss of reputation, and ultimate failure of investors.

It is clear that the range of impact of multi-regulatory structures is great, and that at its ultimate extent, the combination of one or more regulatory structures and the failure to deal adequately with them can lead to the ultimate failure of both intermediary and investor.

Even in this book, we do not cover every piece of regulation that affects the financial services industry. However, even within the limited scope of the regulations we do discuss, there are significant areas of overlap. The various regulations act in a similar way to the way that two waves interact when they combine. The overlap can be constructive, null effect, or destructive. In a constructive overlap, each regulatory framework either deliberately (rare) or accidentally (common) strengthens the overall impact. These types of overlap are good inasmuch as their synergy often means that, for the financial services community and investors, costs of compliance can be minimized and the resultant impact is nominal.

Where the overlap is destructive, the structures and procedures of one framework do not match similar aspects of another. The result is increased expense of compliance for financial firms, since they have to ensure not just two separate systems of compliance, but also that any conflicts of overlap are resolved, which usually requires constant legal review.

Finally, in a null effect overlap, predictably, the nature of any differences that do exist is minimal or nil.

The difficulty with the concept of overlap is that it can occur at any one of several levels. The most complex of course is an overlap at a fundamental level, where the intent of the regulations may be the same, but the jurisdictional methodology is different. This is exemplified in the overlap between the United States and the European Union in respect of data privacy. At the other end of the spectrum the overlap may be simple. In such cases the overlap is not fundamental, but is more likely to be procedural. This is best exemplified by the double taxation agreements entered into by many countries for the avoidance of double taxation. Most new agreements and revised existing agreements now follow the OECD model, so at the fundamental level there is consistency of policy and intent. At the procedural level, however, tax authorities impose radically different methods to assure adherence to the treaties, ranging from relief at source to tax recovery of any income over-taxed, with many details of procedure causing enormous complexity, error, and labor for those involved in compliance and corporate actions processing in financial firms.

In our research for this book, we came across some significant overlap areas which many inside the financial services community are either unaware of, or have not addressed suitably from an investor perspective. Some of this is a result of a focus on the effects of regulation at the retail end of financial services, as opposed to the wholesale/custodial and investment management end. We have tried to illuminate these areas, and clarify for investor and financial firm alike what the key issues are, and what should be done to mitigate these problems of destructive regulatory overlap.

EU DATA PROTECTION DIRECTIVES AND US SAFE HARBOR ACT

The EU Directive on Data Protection of 1998 and the US Safe Harbor Act overlap not just in their methodology but also in their practical impact. Many European financial services firms have clients of varying residencies and statuses. In particular, the investment and custodial chain can be both long and complex, involving primary, secondary, and tertiary custodians, brokers, clearing utilities, as well as indirect recipients of data such as tax authorities.

For example, the US Section 1441 NRA regulations, otherwise known as the QI regulations, provide effectively for all non-US financial firms to be categorized as either qualified (QI) or non-qualified (NQI) intermediaries. This is because, simplistically, in return for being able to maintain the secrecy of their clients, QIs become unpaid tax collectors for the IRS. NQIs, which are either unable or unwilling to enter into a contractual arrangement with the IRS, must pass the personal details of all their clients once each year to a firm that is under IRS jurisdiction, usually a US withholding agent bank. Primarily this is so that, in the absence of a contract, the IRS can be assured that the US firm will verify that any US-sourced income sent to a foreign resident is properly taxed.

However, the implication of the regulation is that, in the case of EU citizens, it requires the transfer of personal data from an EU jurisdiction, to the United States. As we have seen, the US data protection regime does not meet EU standards, and such a transfer breaches the prohibition on such transfers under the Eighth Principle of the EU Directive. There are many such instances in banking and custodial procedure. This particular one by itself has been estimated to generate transfers of personal information for up to 900 million records per year, without taking account of duplications between different EU firms and the potential for differences between their data records.

Given that there are no US banks in the Safe Harbor list, we must return to the EU Directive to find any opportunity to be able to justify the transfer of client information from an NQI in Europe to a US withholding agent.

Figure 4.1 (overleaf) shows the decision tree that can be applied to decide whether a data transfer carries significant risk or is indeed prohibited. From a realistic viewpoint, the irony of the regulation in the European Union is that despite the detailed procedural aspects in which the Commissioner has given advice and guidance on how to comply, there is still, as a backstop, an ability for data processors—the people within firms designated to be responsible for compliance—to make their own subjective judgment on adequacy. If such judgments are likely to be good enough on a consistent basis, one would have to ask why the superior procedures exist at all.

So in the first instance, given that personal data processing is taking place, which in virtually all financial services firms it will, the first decision step is to decide whether any of the data is being transferred outside the European Union for any purpose. It is useful at this stage of risk assessment to establish the exact purpose, and to have to have any documentation, explicit or indirect, that the relevant clients have signed up to. The default decision, under best practice, if data is intended to be transferred outside the European Union, is that such a transfer is prohibited. Everything from this point on seeks to determine if there are any other factors that might mitigate this decision. This default methodology is "safe" under best practice because it ensures a net for the client's privacy which must be

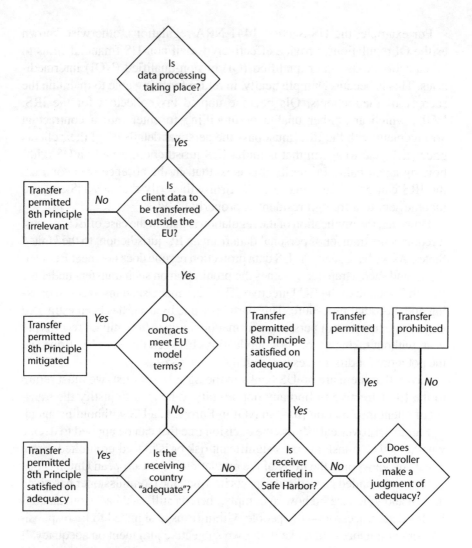

Figure 4.1 Risk mitigation in personal data transfer between the European Union and the United States
Source: the authors.

assertively removed: that is, a conscious and recordable decision must be taken to allow the personal data to be transferred.

The first level of possible mitigation falls from the EU Commissioner's advice that if there are suitable contract terms in place which clearly establish clients' knowledge that their personal data will be transferred outside the European Union, then the transfer can be permitted. However, this is a particularly sensitive area. Frequently financial services firms try to "cover" all situations with bland, generic statements, often on websites and in fine print. Such terms fall well short of the guideline contract terms published by the EU Commissioner. Financial services firms would do well to regularly review this regulatory overlap area to ensure that the their clients are aware what is happening to their personal data. Because the EU Commissioner has provided such detailed sample contract terms for this purpose, what looks like a subjective matter should in reality be very objective. It is not in the interests of financial services firms to take unnecessary risks by assuming or presuming that their own text is adequate to the task. If sufficiently explicit and suitable contract terms are not in place, again, the default position is that the transfer is prohibited.

The second level of mitigation comes from knowledge that the jurisdiction to which the data is to be transferred is "adequate" according to the EU Commissioner. In this instance, reviewing transfers to the United States, the default position is "no" as the US data protection regime is already deemed to be inadequate.

The third level of mitigation with respect to the United States comes from the existence of the Safe Harbor list, where the current list of certified Safe Harbor firms should be consulted. If the intended recipient is not certified in Safe Harbor, again, the default condition imposed is that in addition to the jurisdiction being inadequate in and of itself, the receiving firm does not have adequate protection for the personal data being transferred, and the transfer should be prohibited.

We come now to the fourth level of mitigation, and the first level at which the transferring firm should, under best practice, have any freedom. The fourth level allows the transferring firm's data processor to make a judgment of adequacy based on the knowledge that the data processor holds about the intended recipient. This level carries the highest risk. In essence, all other levels of control, even those recommended by the regulator, are being replaced by the internal judgment of the firm holding the data. There are clearly issues of concern relating to control and undue influence which could affect the quality of decision that any internal data processor may make. In addition to these issues, it would be necessary for data processors to have very well-documented evidence detailing the reasons not just that the internal processor made a judgment of adequacy, but also that these judgments may have been at variance to independent assessments. Data processors should take great care before adopting this fourth-level strategy since it is arguable that operational risk and thus liability for the firm increases.

MLR 2003 AND THE PRINCIPLE OF CLIENT CONFIDENTIALITY

In many areas of financial services there is a continuing tension between investors' natural wish to have their financial transactions kept confidential, and the regulatory requirement for such information to be available for the purpose of ensuring that no irregularities are present. In other words, the many are subject to sometimes conflicting disclosure requirements in order to identify the few who are allegedly abusing the system.

A typical example exists with accountants, auditors, solicitors (lawyers), and other financial intermediaries when it comes to MLR. MLR requires a person in a relevant business to report any suspicious transaction, whether financial or not, that might ultimately be related to money laundering. The ever more natural instinct of intermediaries is to protect their probity, sometimes to what a normal person would consider an illogical degree.

When MLR came into force in March 2004, the process of reporting had two facets of concern. The first was a requirement to report any suspicious activity to the National Criminal Intelligence Service (NCIS) using an appropriate form. The second, and more insidious, was that the report of such activity must not be revealed to the person or entity being reported.

In and of itself, this should not cause a problem as long as the judgment of suspicion is reasonable: that is, it is founded on concrete facts that would lead to a concern over money laundering. However, this did not take account of the natural conservatism that pervades the financial services community, nor of the almost paranoid concern over compliance that is increasingly part of any financial services transaction. The combination of these two effects means that, if any kind of discrepancy takes place that may ultimately affect accounting, there can be no guarantee in the mind of the MLR officer within the firm that the discrepancy is not part of some form of money laundering.

In March 2004 this was highlighted outside the financial services arena in the retail sector, when supermarkets came to do end-of-month stock takes. Since any discrepancy in the stock take could theoretically be caused by pilfering, which is consequently linked to black market sales and thence to money laundering, virtually every supermarket branch in the country filed a report to the NCIS. They did this not because they seriously considered that money laundering was occurring, but because the filing of a report absolved them of any liability in case any of the events actually was linked to money laundering. This ludicrous position has led since March 2004 to the NCIS being flooded with reports on a monthly basis.

Returning to the financial services sector, there are two areas where investors should be concerned. The first is an outgrowth of the paranoia demonstrated in the retail sector. Rather than face the risk of liability, many accountants, auditors, and other relevant businesses have sent a list of their entire client base to the NCIS and reported them all. In this way, they are absolved from liability by passing the buck to NCIS.

The second issue flows from the first. The investor or client will not have been told that a report has been filed. Many clients will, even now, have a report filed on them at the NCIS without their knowledge. With-holding of this information is not optional for the MLR officer concerned, it is mandatory: that is, they *must not* tell clients they have been reported.

Now most clients, investors, and so on are completely law-abiding. They are liable to find the thought that the aversion to liability of their interme-diary has led to their being reported to NCIS without their knowledge disturbing, to say the least.

The second and more interesting scenario relates to the oft-quoted "client confidentiality" principle. Most investors are firmly of the opinion that, as long as they are fully compliant with local law, they need have no fear that information provided to their agent intermediary will, without their knowledge or consent, be passed to a third party. Consider however the consequences of clients asking an intermediary directly whether a report has been filed on them with NCIS, perhaps to obtain assurance that they have not been included in a "blanket" filing. Irrespective of whether the intermediary has made such a report, he or she must perforce either lie to their client or evade the question. In either case, the net effect is a serious erosion of confidence from the investor community.

More recently, new agreements from accountants and intermediaries have included wording to make it clear that such disclosures will be made. A typical example is shown below:

In accordance with the Proceeds of Crime Act and Money Laundering Regulations 2003 you agree to waive your right to confidentiality to the extent of any report made, document provided, or information disclosed to the National Criminal Intelligence Service (NCIS).

You also acknowledge that we are required to report directly to NCIS without prior reference to you or your representatives if during the course of undertaking any assignment, the person undertaking the role of Money Laundering Reporting Officer becomes suspicious of money laundering

Source: Witney and Co.

SARBANES–OXLEY AND MLR 2003

In many cases, the intent of governments to internally control financial activ-ity meets with the market reality that financial activity is increasingly a glob-alized phenomenon. Thus many sets of regulation have implications beyond the borders within which their inventors have a remit and authority.

Sarbanes–Oxley is fundamentally about corporate governance and probity. Its remit is often thought to be the United States only; however its real effect is global. Firms outside the United States that trade their shares in the form of American depositary receipts (ADRs) are directly subject to it. Also directly subject are the auditors of such firms. Increasingly, because the issue is one of corporate information and probity, boards of directly affected firms outside the United States are requiring their suppliers to meet the requirements of Sarbanes–Oxley even though they are not directly subject to it.

MLR 2003, while a UK Act of Parliament, makes no direct statement that a financially suspect transaction must be of UK origin or have an UK end-point in order to be subject to the Act. The only criterion is that a relevant business becomes aware of, or suspects, such a transaction. The nature of the criminal investigation services is effectively global, and information sharing is a fundamental principle

Of course, by simple logic, a suspicious financial transaction under the terms of MLR 2003 is also a reportable issue under Sarbanes–Oxley.

FREEDOM OF INFORMATION, THE DATA PROTECTION ACT, AND MLR 2003

Under MLR we have seen that intermediaries (with the exception of legal advisers) have the regulatory requirement to report suspicious (or what they determine to be suspicious) transactions to the National Criminal Intelligence Service (NCIS). This is right and good as far as it goes. However, as has been mentioned, many firms to avoid contingent liability have a policy of reporting all their clients as a matter of course. Even without this policy, there is a high likelihood that many of the reported transactions will prove to be completely innocent. However, this raises a conflict. NCIS might now have one or more reports on an investor's activities, all completely innocent, of which the investor is unaware. The Data Protection Act gives data subjects the right to know what data is held about them within the computer systems of commercial firms. So the overlap, indeed conflict, exists inasmuch as an investor's intermediary may not disclose that a report has been submitted, but the data subject—the investor in this case—has a right to know that there is a report to be verified. If the investigation finds the data to be not linked to any suspicious activity, should there be a means by which the report is destroyed?

FREEDOM OF INFORMATION AND DATA PROTECTION

Section 40 of the UK Freedom of Information Act gives a blanket exemption if any request is made by applicants for information which relates to themselves. To this extent therefore, individuals cannot use the Freedom of Information Act to find out whether a public body has information about them. However, once made, such an application is deemed to be a public access request under the UK Data Protection Act. This will actually be transparent to an applicant, since the guidelines for freedom of information officers notify them that they should automatically treat the request as made under the Data Protection Act even if the Freedom of Information Act is cited as the basis for the request.

THE USA PATRIOT ACT, SECTION 1441 NRA REGULATIONS, AND MLR 2004

This overlap would, in other circumstances, be considered to be of purely US interest. However, the structure of these forms of regulation, and in particular the way in which their procedures are defined, creates a potential conflict which affects all non-US financial intermediaries directly, and US intermediaries and non-US investors indirectly.

The implementation of Section 1441 of the NRA regulations established the concepts of QIs and NQIs, and was designed originally, in addition to relief at source taxation procedures, to identify US investors investing in US companies via a non-US intermediary and thus gaining a more favorable "treaty" based tax rate on their investments—so-called "treaty shopping." In order to find this minority, the regulations as passed affected anyone deriving US-sourced income. The result was that the IRS would have been deluged with information.

The principle of the QI contains one key element—confidentiality. Investors deriving US-sourced income can keep their identity secret from the IRS by ensuring that the custodian of their assets and income is contracted with the IRS as a QI. A more exhaustive explanation of the regulations can be found in *International Withholding Tax: A practical guide to best practice and benchmarking* and *Relief at Source: An investor's guide to minimizing internationally withheld tax*, both by R McGill, published by Euromoney Books.

So while the Patriot Act as well as several other regulatory structures define the way in which information must be shared or disclosed, these regulations have at their heart the principle that a non-US recipient of US-sourced income can remain anonymous.

Intermediaries that are also QIs can aggregate the income and taxes payable by tax rate on behalf of all their beneficial owner investors so that the IRS gets income and tax information without knowing to whom it applies. NQIs must disclose such information to the IRS or to another QI. This confidentiality is based on the QIs' contractual agreement to document their investors to a satisfactory level.

The Patriot Act as well as Gramm–Leach–Bliley, Sarbanes–Oxley, and MLR 2004 all take the opposite tenet, of disclosure to be basic. For investors, this is very confusing. Many intermediaries have based their status as QIs on the principle that, commercially, it places them at an advantage since they are able to cite client confidentiality as a benefit for clients investing in the United States. However if transactions are made within certain limits, this confidentiality is at least suspect, and at most, clearly broken. A typical example would be an investment in the United States, in dollars, which represented more than €15,000 as a one-off transaction. This would be confidential as far as the intermediary's status as a QI with respect to the IRS was concerned, but might trigger a report to NCIS in the United Kingdom as a suspicious transaction.

Also, given that the Section 1441 NRA regulations permit a non-US person to maintain their beneficial ownership of US securities as confidential as a base presumption, the Patriot Act in Title III Subtitle A Section 3.11 has text, "Information relating to beneficial ownership," which allows the Secretary of State to require disclosure by a domestic financial institution. The way in which the markets work, using domestic correspondent, custodial, or withholding agent banks, makes this an over-arching disclosure requirement that places an immense responsibility on financial institutions to make judgments about the probity of every financial transaction that flows through their books, irrespective of the protections that seem to be offered under other domestic regulation.

The situation is further highlighted in section 3.25(3) relating to concentration accounts (often used by withholding agents on behalf of intermediaries as aggregation accounts where all the income relates to some operational parameter, such as the tax rate):

> The Secretary of State may prescribe regulations ... in order to ensure that such accounts are not used to prevent association of the identity of an individual customer with the movement of funds of which the customer is the direct or beneficial owner.

This rather conflicts with the principal operating mechanism of the intermediaries that are QIs under Section 1441 NRA, and that manage tax-rate-level concentration accounts at US withholding agent banks without information on the beneficial owners in their possession. While the information is technically within the government's access since QIs are liable to audit, such audits are contractually every three years, by which time any such funds movement will be old history. The potential impact on intermediaries is immense.

UCITS III AND US DOUBLE TAX AGREEMENTS

UCITS effectively sets up the framework for Europe-wide sales for open-ended unit trust types of investment. The objective is to remove competitive barriers and widen the concept of the European financial services market. As a result, it is entirely possible for a resident of one country to purchase units in a fund resident in a second country, as long as both are within the European Union. While this may be laudable, it can create difficulties in interpretation which ultimately affect investors. Two factors create the problem:

■ Most unit trust-type vehicles are treated by tax authorities as "opaque," that is, they have a separate existence for tax purposes, and the fund is taxed by a foreign tax authority on its income based on the fund's residency, amongst other factors, and not that of its underlying unit holders who are the owners of the trust. This is different for example from US hedge funds, which are typically structured as partnerships, and similar to pension funds, which are taxed at fund level.
■ Purchasing units in a unit trust is not the same as buying shares in the fund. Unit holders are not beneficiaries for tax purposes of the income from shares in which the fund invests (hence the reason they are considered opaque).

UCITS III does not create a problem at this stage within Europe. The effect however is that more and more European funds will have larger and larger proportions of unit purchasers from different (third party) countries within their investor base. Technically this means that, while its not the objective of UCITS III, an investor could theoretically pick and choose investment vehicles based on which country provides the lowest tax rate on investment income for its resident UCITS-type funds—a form of treaty shopping.

Unfortunately US double tax agreements include provision for special terms known as "limitation of benefits" or LOB clauses. These clauses are designed specifically to allow the IRS to deny lower levels of taxation (based on treaty rate entitlements) if the authority believes that the investor's primary objective is treaty shopping. These clauses are structured based on the proportion of the fund whose ownership is based on foreign investors—just like the UCITS III model.

So on one hand the IRS deems these funds to be opaque for tax purposes because the investors are not actually individually the beneficial owners of the income. On the other hand the same tax authority can deem the fund to be transparent for tax purposes in order to decide that the fund is not qualified to receive fund-level treaty rates, on the basis that the structure is designed to permit treaty shopping based on its ownership.

The resolution is often pragmatic, and linked to the degree of aggression the tax authorities have in the pursuit of treaty shopping as an abusive tax mechanism.

Ironically, because of generic ignorance, typically UCITS funds are in any event taxed at source based on the high domestic withholding rate, and not at any lower perceived treaty rate. The issue therefore is not the original taxation for the fund, but the availability of remedial tax reclaims. It is arguable that if the tax authority deems a UCITS III fund to be transparent, this decision will necessarily mean that the fund cannot recover any tax. It does however consequentially mean that the underlying investors can recover tax based on their individual residencies. While this sounds great, the difficulty is then of course that the unit holder has no direct relationship to the shares which generated the income on which the tax was levied, and without such a causal relationship the tax authority concerned would probably refuse to pay.

So while UCITS III may well open the doors to a more free intra-European market in financial services, for those funds that invest in companies outside the European Union there may significant tax disadvantages. The investor might be better off investing directly and being taxed at a lower level than investing via a unit trust vehicle. For institutional investors the amounts concerned can be very significant, over 25 basis points difference across a typical portfolio.

Intermediaries have no effective way to penetrate this conflict. While the answer is actually to ask the relevant tax authorities directly, so that a more definitive fund by fund determination can be made to the benefit of investors, many advisors do not do this, and trustees are woefully ignorant of such complexities. An example may help to explain:

1 An Irish-resident unit trust is set up as a UCITS fund. This fund invests heavily in US stocks. The fund has no US individuals as unit holders, but because it is a UCITS fund, it can have unit holders from anywhere in the European Union.
2 The US-Irish double tax treaty has a limitation of benefits clause to prevent funds obtaining treaty benefits based on their Irish residency (15 percent as opposed to 30 percent), and the exemptions provided in the clause may not apply.
3 Because the fund is UCITS it falls under the LOB clause, and so the fund is not qualified to reclaim 15 percent of the tax it has suffered in the United States.
4 While the unit holders do "own" the fund, they cannot file claims for over-withheld tax because they cannot demonstrate individual beneficial ownership of the shares that created the income.

In these circumstances, if the investors know that the majority of their investment will be in the United States, this UCITS structure will mean that their income from units will be lower than expected because neither they nor the fund are able to recover tax.

Since under no circumstances can the unit holder file a reclaim, because of the structure of the investment vehicle, the only potential way out is based on whether the tax authority makes a judgment that the LOB clause is active in a particular case. In other words, is the fund a qualifying person? The US model explicitly details the basis on which LOB clauses will have effect, although many misinterpret the definition of qualifying person.

In the case of an Irish resident unit trust, Article 23 (d) (i) states that a unit trust is qualified to receive treaty benefits where:

i)   the principal class of units in that person is listed on a recognized stock exchange located in either Contracting State and is substantially and regularly traded on one or more recognized stock exchanges, or

ii) the direct or indirect owners of at least 50 percent of the beneficial interests in that person are persons referred to in subparagraph d) i) or e) i); e) a company, if: i) the principal class of its shares is substantially and regularly traded on one or more recognized stock exchanges, or ii) at least 50 percent of the aggregate vote and value of its shares is owned directly or indirectly by companies described in subparagraph e) i), or by persons referred to in subparagraph b), or by companies more than 50 percent of the aggregate vote and value of which is owned by persons referred to in subparagraph b), or by any combination of the above; f) a person described in subparagraph c) of paragraph 1 of Article 4 (Residence), provided that more than half of the beneficiaries, members or participants, if any, in such organization are qualified persons.

So in the example cited, as long as the fund is listed on either the US or Irish stock exchanges and is substantially traded, it would qualify for treaty benefits. Unfortunately, this last criterion often causes the trip. Many funds are listed but not for trading purposes. The lack of trading removes their entitlement to treaty benefits.

SARBANES–OXLEY AND THE TURNBULL GUIDANCE

An instance of regulatory overlap that illustrates both similarities and differences between the United States and its European counterparts is the way the Sarbanes–Oxley Act is being approached. The SEC is well aware that a number of companies listed in the United States are non-US entities; this is especially pertinent, given the degree of external investment in the US economy. It has also been made aware that these foreign companies are already regulated under national or regional legislation and guidance, and that inevitably there is a degree of overlap with the SOX Act and what is already in place elsewhere. Indeed many foreign national regulators have looked closely at the Act as a potential model for shaping their own regulation. In the light of this the UK Turnbull Report, with specific regard to guidance on internal controls, has been identified as a relevant piece of regulatory information that qualifies for recognition.

As was noted in Chapter 3, the Combined Code on Corporate Governance, published in July 2003 by the Financial Reporting Council, (FRC) incorporates the guidance of the Turnbull Report, *Internal Control: Guidance for directors on the Combined Code*. Since its publication in 1999, the Sarbanes–Oxley (SOX) Act of 2002 has been enacted in the United States. The SEC has been monitoring compliance with Sections 302, 404(a), and 404(b) of the Act . In particular, Section 404(a) requires the management of a listed company to make judgments regarding the effectiveness of material controls over financial reporting. These reports and statements have to be made in the context of a suitable framework. In examining UK-based listed companies, the SEC has recognized that the Turnbull guidance is such a framework.

In December 2004 the FRC published a guide to help non-US companies that are SEC registered, what the FRC calls "SEC registrants," who have chosen to use the Turnbull guidance as a framework for Section 404(a). It outlines the relevance of the two pieces of guidance and legislation, and how best to get the most from working to compliance with both. Within our terminology we might see this overlap, at first sight, as a "constructive overlap" with a "nominal impact." However, in examining the practicalities of implementation we might arrive at a different picture.

At the outset the FRC warned that its guidance was to be taken carefully, and that organizations should spend time and effort studying the implications of the original SOX legislation. Immediately we are aware that the Turnbull guidance is a reference framework. In the United States the PCAOB recommended the COSO framework and its approach to managing internal controls as an effective reference for those seeking compliance with SOX. Certainly Turnbull and COSO have elements in common:

- They focus on internal controls within an organization.
- They capture best practice for managing these internal controls.
- They are comprehensive in addressing risk, information management, and the importance of monitoring processes.

But these common elements serve to stress that while Turnbull is a useful reference, it is not a substitute for a fuller compliance program. By satisfying Turnbull a company will not be satisfying its obligations under SOX. This is stressed throughout the FRC's guidance paper.

The Public Company Accounting Oversight Board (PCAOB) set up under the SOX Act issued an Auditing Standard no. 2 as a guide for auditors covered by Section 404(b) of the Act. The requirements of the Act under Section 404(a) were implemented by the SEC within Rule 33-8238, and it is this that governs the way non-US listed companies need to consider their responsibilities. Essentially, senior management, or "principal executive" and "principal financial officers," have to assess the effectiveness of the issuer's internal controls over financial reporting. The framework on which this assessment is based must be "a suitable, recognized control framework." Internal controls are defined as a process that is designed, with senior management oversight or input, to "provide reasonable assurance regarding the reliability of financial reporting." They must further record and maintain records about transactions that support the financial reports, and include information on events that materially affect the information in the financial statements.

In the bigger picture we see a relationship emerging that is characterized as in Table 4.1. Here we note that the Turnbull guidance is only a part of the picture, a contributor to Section 404(a) rather than a substitute for it. In terms of overlap and impact there are a number of points to observe:

- The requirements to comply with all the SEC rules stemming from the Act indicate that although the overlap here is constructive (that is, work and investment in making the company compliant with Turnbull can be reused for compliance with SOX), the impact is more than nominal. It is more of a "significant impact" than "nominal," in that there is added cost in the bigger process of compliance.
- The SOX emphasis on responsibility settling on the shoulders of "signing officers," and the SEC focus on "principals" such as the CEO and CFO, differ from the broader responsibility in the UK context and governance climate. The Turnbull guidance does place responsibility on the board of directors, but it also places it on management in general. This is a disparity in emphasis which has very significant punitive consequences. Some believe the focus of SOX and the potential for imprisonment is the driver for so much governance action in the United States. It remains to be seen if a non-US CEO could be prosecuted. There is a

Table 4.1 Sarbanes–Oxley requirements and Turnbull

SOX sections	Requirement	Reference	Applications
S404(a)	Management assessment	Evaluation framework	COSO Framework Turnbull guidance
S404(b)	Auditor's attestation	Authorised frameworks	PCAOB Auditing Standard no. 2

Source: the authors.

destructive impact here in the way incomplete compliance could create problems for the non-US company in a US context, and the need to put in place longer-term monitoring of US legislation and case history, as well as consultative auditing and legal fees.

■ The FRC notes that there is a big difference in the "spirit" approach between the United Kingdom and the United States. The Combined Code emphasizes a fairly benevolent approach, based on "comply or explain"—and explain in your own words. This is not something endorsed by the SEC.

■ Perhaps an overlooked impact, which is a hidden significant impact, is that compliance with Section 404(a) requires a great deal of thorough preparation. Turnbull places these activities in the context of risk. Risk is really what SOX is also about. The focus is on building in as much oversight and monitoring as possible to ensure good governance. In the United Kingdom, such governance is encouraged rather than punitively mandated. The SEC and SOX moves place importance on testing and documentation; Section 302 of the SOX Act saw a tremendous amount of activity on documenting processes to meet compliance. This overlap can be seen as constructive, depending on how far the UK company has gone with its compliance plans. It they conflict or miss the requirements of the SEC, there is a great deal of additional cost and budgeting to consider.

■ The SEC rules insist that any "material weaknesses" in internal controls should be included in the report. This alone has had an impact on the public perception of the company, including share value, and is something most companies will work hard to avoid. The US and UK views of material weakness vary in emphasis. This, along with the documented evidence of how management arrived at its assessment, provides a body of detail a company may not wish to share so publicly.

■ The SEC rules are specific about internal controls, which are defined and refined in its Rule 33-8238. A potentially destructive overlap exists in that the SEC internal controls are specific to financial reporting. In the United States, many consultancies have made much of this as an opportunity for a listed business to explore controls throughout the organization, and review how the company's governance works within its overall business model. This is quite a challenge for an international company with multiple subsidiaries. However, the focus is on these specific controls. In the United Kingdom, Turnbull talks of all controls, having a broader governance concern. The danger is that work on controls under Turnbull may be thinly spread, whether as a result of limited resources or as a result of a different analysis of what is needed to comply. This work would then need to be revisited in more depth to satisfy the SEC rules.

Nevertheless, the SEC has accepted the Turnbull guidance as a reference framework, satisfying its demand that such a framework include qualitative and quantitative criteria that can measure a company's system of internal control for financial reporting.

Turnbull has specific advantages which it brings to the overall process of compliance:

- It gives guidance on how to review effectiveness, and hence contributes to the management assessment.
- It establishes the importance of documentation to support the review.
- It broadens the picture by including an examination of the risks identified during the process of compliance. These act as inputs to a risk strategy to help fine-tune the company's "risk tolerance." Such risks also identify, usefully from the point of view of SEC compliance, material weaknesses and significant failings in the controls themselves. Using SEC definitions, the SEC rules only mandate the inclusion of material weaknesses in the financial report.
- It identifies remedial action needed to mend failing controls.

Many of these points have a constructive impact if the requirements are analyzed and planned for in advance. But, as we have indicated, they can result in a destructive impact if the compliance processes are not effectively coordinated.

Issues for institutional investors

Given the similarities and disparities between the regulatory approaches typified here, an investor needs to assess the way a company is approaching regulation. The principles of overlap and impact provide a mechanism for measuring the risk involved from this perspective. They are not scientific, but based on such evidence as is available, and they allow other material to support or be included in a judgment. However, all this has to be considered within context. For example, under SEC rules, the management assessment of a company cannot conclude that its internal controls over financial reporting are effective if they report a material weakness. This does not mean that the financial report is an inaccurate statement of the financial health of the company and not worthy of investment. Yet it is a serious status under the SEC rules, and remedial action is required. This does not mean it is a failing company. Equally, the SEC has not specified the exact detail it requires in the report in order to avoid giving a "fixed" feeling to company reports. This is closer to the spirit of the Combined Code "comply or explain" approach. Thus a company may report a sound and effective system of internal control for financial reporting, yet still have some systemic problems elsewhere in the organization. Under Turnbull, these other areas would be addressed.

As the FRC concludes in its paper, "The Turnbull guidance as an evaluation framework for the purposes of Section 404(a) of the Sarbanes-Oxley Act," published in December 2004:

> Whilst the Turnbull guidance is a suitable framework for the purposes of S404(a) of the Sarbanes–Oxley Act, nothing in the Turnbull guidance reduces SEC registrants's obligations to comply with US laws and regulation.

The Turnbull guidance does address the processes, procedures, and criteria that assist compliance with US legislation. Nevertheless, management still has to carefully consider what compliance really means under the SOX Act, and build in an ongoing monitoring process to maintain compliance over the longer term. And, we might add, with an eye on compliance to Section 409 in the near future.

CHAPTER 5

Compliance

A FRAMEWORK FOR COMPLIANCE

Central to any discussion of the regulation of financial services is the concept of "compliance." The *Concise Oxford Dictionary* lists compliance as "action in accordance with request, command, etc." So it has the force of something that leads somewhere, an active approach to a suggestion. The dictionary also adds a secondary definition, "(degree of) yielding under applied force." This is a more passive action, a sense of being cajoled into doing something. In reality, we can see both definitions at work in the relationship between regulator and financial institution. Some organizations work willingly to meet regulation; others more reluctantly, only doing the minimum to avoid punitive action. For those regulations not enforceable by law, a two-step process often is necessary:

- A case has to be made to ensure acceptance of the benefit of the investment in compliance.
- Compliance is scoped, planned for, and implemented.

Letter and spirit

Any discussion of compliance inevitably reflects on the way those subject to regulation approach the process of making themselves compliant. This frequently translates into a "letter and spirit" debate. The meaning of a piece of regulation or legislation can often be found in the context in which it originated. That is, the climate, or series of events evoked a response that resulted in the legislation. Its "meaning" in this sense can often be lost as the intention is translated in enforceable enactments that then have a life of their own. Generally there is an intent to not simply to force an issue and direct a company to fulfill certain requirements; it is often the intent to change behavior. This indication of "spirit" is often contained in the text of a regulation—it is the "effect" desired by a "cause and effect" chain of aspiration. The spirit is achieved through concrete, verifiable actions that can be made subject to enforcement, reward, and punishment. Simply reacting mechanically to legislation can be a short-sighted view of compliance. Nevertheless the approach adopted by many who support organizations entering the compliance trail is that of a "policy and procedure" fix as a mechanism to ensure "letter" compliance.

This is very much an approach rooted in creating, mending, streamlining, and generally improving operational activities:

- It takes a view that the compliance requirement can be satisfied by mechanical improvements to the system, using methodologies and tools either currently available in the organization or vendor market place, or in the process of being made available.
- Its ideal is the automation of processes and monitoring activities, preferably with minimal manual intervention.
- It is centered on the organization as a functional entity for doing business.

This is a very valid approach. It determines that by making the organization effective through its processes and controls, it satisfies compliance. How far does this deliver transparency and disclosure as envisioned by regulation?

In contrast to this is the approach that sees compliance as a web of "players" and their links, or relationships, as the threads that will bind the business community to a more transparent mode of disclosure and deliver good corporate behavior. Unlike the operational approach, this way includes key players such as investors in its scope:

- It implies that compliance is about something other than organizational effectiveness in delivering reports.
- It implies that the relationship between the players is subject to continual scrutiny and fits more properly into the realm of corporate governance, with its investment in transparency and outward information flows, to ensure investor credibility and effective data for decision making.

One might add that a third way of viewing compliance, perhaps a way that encompasses the operational and relationship views outlined above, is to see successful compliance as a result, or product, of a well-run organization or business, in much the same way as an effective quality system is at the heart of good business practice. This view also marries well with the intentions of regulation, as the means to achieve good corporate behavior.

Compliance and regulation

With what, then, does a company or an intermediary have to be compliant if it is to meet the requirements of regulation? What elements are driving the compliance debate? We believe there are two main factors:

- Size of company—the scale of response is a function of the complexity of the organization or its business processes.
- Information flow—the degree to which external information about a client organization is fed consistently from the intermediary into both the organization and the auditor, who will ultimately attest to its veracity and impact on the organization's numbers as a whole.

However, it must be remembered that information passing from an intermediary to an organization subject to regulation is a high-risk issue. It is high risk for both parties if the intermediary is not directly subject to regulation. This interface with external firms, especially financial services firms, presents a significant secondary risk.

Avoidance and evasion

As well as the distinction between "letter and spirit," the subtleties of "avoidance and evasion" also color the response to regulation. In fact, a considerable amount of effort is normally accorded to reducing the ambiguity of legislation. However, it is equally true that critical areas are left open to interpretation through vaguely worded expressions in the text of the statutes. These are then only clarified through case law, which is a little late for those organizations trying to measure up to the demands of compliance.

Few companies would claim they intend to "avoid" compliance, but most would put some effort into considering how they can reduce the compliance burden, if necessary through "evasion." Even with the tightest of controls and vigilant enforcement, deliberate malfeasance will occur. If someone wants to mislead, regulation will certainly be a deterrent but no more. After all, regulation is a response to events, and in that sense, a remedial tool; it is at its most effective in the context of applied good governance.

The regulators

Regulators have very specific roles when it comes to compliance. They are tasked with:

- identifying violations
- rooting them out
- punishing violators
- ensuring the offences are not repeated.

A major part of their effort is in the timely gathering of evidence once violations are identified. But how much is enough? The answer is, as much evidence as is relevant to ensure a conviction if need be, for long enough to cover the period of violation, and with as much untouched detail as possible. An organization in violation cannot hide or tamper with critical evidence in the event of a prosecution. In the face of penalties, fines, and share value loss, the organization will minimize its risk by implementing systems that ensure compliance and acquiesce in the storage of incriminating information. The assumptions underlying this move are focused on the interests of the regulator. This perspective is investigative and inquisitorial. It seeks to find out and question. It is the aggressive side of compliance.

The investor

Regulation, as a whole, is about maintaining investor confidence in the probity and good management of financial services. In this the perspective of the investor, private, public, or institutional, is paramount. The transparency of regulatory measures and the accountability of boards of directors are designed to ensure investors can see and be assured that their investment is being well managed and is not at risk from corporate misdemeanor.

Objectively, making a profit is the primary aim of investing; social responsibility is secondary. Investors entrust the delivery of that commodity to the companies in which they invest, and quite rightly, they have an expectation of high return and of high standards of behavior. The former is a natural trait, the latter is a more strategic acceptance of the fact that failure to have high standards of behavior will ultimately prove to be detrimental to the objective. In effect, the investor's perspective is close to that of regulation itself.

Reporting

Perhaps the most obvious aspect of regulation is the emphasis placed on reports. Indeed the processes that dominate the path to compliance through the management of internal controls are focused on generating a report, or rather, a periodic financial report. Reporting covers:

- financial statement reporting
- pro forma reporting
- performance management reporting
- forecasting and planning reporting.

Reports also include the advice and guidance the executive provides to the market, and its reports to external authorities.

The challenges of reporting relate to when reporting is due. There are two types:

- periodic reporting—such as monthly, quarterly, and yearly
- non-periodic reporting—ad hoc events, internal and external to the operation of the business.

Financial reporting

Periodic financial reports are generally governed by the formats commonly defined by national regulators. In the United States they are documents such as Forms 10-QSB/A, and are either a quarterly report under Section 13 or 15(d) of the Securities Exchange Act of 1934, or a transition report between specific dates, and filed accordingly. These reports follow a standard pattern since they attempt to present key information to investors and shareholders and the public as a whole. They contain financial Information and general company information such as:

- statements on the stock balance, for listed corporates
- a condensed consolidated balance sheet
- a condensed consolidated statement of operations
- a condensed consolidated statement of cash flows
- notes to condensed consolidated financial statements.

Such a report may include a "Management discussion and analysis of financial condition and results of operations," which gives a summary overview of the condition of the company, its strategy in the market, and a section on liquidity and capital resources. The US version has a section on "Quantitative and qualitative disclosures about market risk" and a section entitled "Other information," which covers legal proceedings, directors' dealings, and so on. All in all it provides a substantial snapshot of the state of the company, of value to shareholders, potential investors, and regulatory bodies. Reports tend to be at the very sharp end of the whole discussion. Key forms are Forms 10-Q and 8-K. They have a universal significance in that many international companies have a US base and are generally familiar with these reporting mechanisms.

Advantages for financial services companies

There are market advantages to the exposure of such important company information. It is very much a level playing field in that most companies have to divulge similar information. However, the quality of information is the focus of much regulatory inspection. The Sarbanes–Oxley Act in the United States, and other legislation in the United Kingdom and elsewhere, have focused on just that.

It can be useful for firms providing services to firms subject to regulation to be aware of their partner's circumstances. Opportunities for marketing advantages abound. For example, a company observing regulations is seen to be more transparent than one that is not. Suppliers to such companies will up their transparency to match, promoting their worthiness as partners and their commitment to observing similar standards of behavior.

For financial intermediaries, this creates new ways to leverage IT expenditure and compliance with standards such as SWIFT. Anything that helps keep existing clients and gain new ones is a bonus.

For their part, financial intermediaries, as supplier companies to regulation subjects, and perhaps even regulation subjects themselves, are already well aware of US reporting issues, and have already had to deal with the clone scenario of regulatory "creep." So financial intermediaries should be well positioned in meeting the corporate governance issues raised by regulation, and should find that their previous history of regulatory compliance stands them in good stead as good corporate governance partners. Issuers and investors would do well to question their intermediaries about their experience in this area. Such questioning provides valuable insights which may reduce or control costs, and should give the issuers and investors insight into the degree of probity that can be expected from any given institution.

Documentation and information

The past decades of legislation have underlined one fundamental reality of modern financial systems—that business is based on information, and the creation, maintenance, and control of this information is vital to the success of the business. This information comes in many forms. The data that underpins the business itself is the raw material (and often the product itself), expressed as information is in many media forms, hard and soft. This mass of material is presented to the world at large for consumption. Regulators, not unnaturally, are concerned with this. We have seen how the focus on company reports is really about the quality of the information released for investors. The value of this information lies in the extent to which it helps an investor make a decision.

In a sense all business information is about decision making. Quality and quantity coincide to assure the best decision is made. Of course, the decision is made in the human dimension, which has as much to do with psychology and temperament as with clear, well-presented information. Nevertheless, it is generally considered that transparency and quality information can help avoid more Enrons, and help shape a productive future for financial services. Documentation is the practical expression of this ideal, and a fundamental concept for regulation. Traditionally document management has been a kind of workflow across many areas of the business, and it is a well-understood discipline, witnessed in the widespread use of methodologies structured around business process management (BPM), enterprise resource planning (ERP), and other frameworks that insist on the importance of documenting their elements.

At a practical level a document is "proof" or "evidence" as a recording of ideas, facts, transactions, or images. From the point of view of regulators, this emphasis on evidence is the primary function, underlying the investigative nature of regulatory activity. Material becomes authoritative and reliable once officially recorded and passed into a records management system, and these documents carry their meaning as a summary of the context in which they were devised. Here, we see it as the product of a process of creating, distributing, and retaining management or business information.

Regulatory requirements for documentation

In the United States a number of regulations guide business control over documentation and information. The sections of the Securities Exchange Act of 1934 are Rules 17(a)-3 and 4, and NASD 3010 and 3110. These define the need for technical and procedural controls to ensure the:

- authenticity
- accuracy
- accessibility

of stored electronic records for review and audit.

In 1997, the 17a-4 rule was extended to allow broker-dealers to store records electronically, including electronic messaging.

Traders in securities, brokers and banks, securities firms and financial institutions trading in securities, have to observe the rules on:

- retention
- non-rewriteable storage
- ease of retrieval.

Among these rules are requirements to create policies and maintain management of customer records and transactions, with a strong regulatory focus on access.

The SEC has made clear that "records are the primary means of monitoring compliance," and recent cases involving the deletion of e-mails and other electronic records "have affirmed the need to have measures in place to protect record integrity." Major dealerships, brokers, and securities organizations have all fallen foul of inadequate e-mail retention procedures. To be compliant, organizations must have written and enforceable retention policies, the capability to store data on non-rewritable media, data formatted for retrieval with searchable indexes, and stored offsite. Organizations respond through a combined strategy of leveraging existing in-house IT systems and outsourcing certain IT functions. In some instances, for Sarbanes–Oxley for example, the requirement to use external agencies is mandatory. Arrangements with designated third parties (D3P) enable SEC regulators to arrange access to an organization's stored information. The objective is to ensure there is access to archives in the event of an uncooperative violator or a business that has folded.

Document retention

When it comes to keeping documents as evidence, there are considerable cost implications. Managing storage costs is a preoccupation of IT departments. In the United States alone, there are over a thousand retention requirements set out under federal laws, and many more under state laws. Internationally there are many more.

We can see three practical areas of activity in the retention of documentation:

■ the defining and documentation of business processes
■ the retention of the evidence and the need to archive effectively
■ the enforcement of retention policies.

These activities are in line with the emerging industry framework model that defines how the burden of managing company documentation is handled end-to-end: information lifecycle management (ILM). This model has been adopted and developed by a number of vendors, and recognizes the challenges of regulation by providing a framework that assumes a mix of core competencies from a range of vendors.

Financial services executives' responsibility for compliance/information

The management and protection of vital information assets is a growing responsibility for executives. Safeguarding vital data is more than just a moral and business responsibility. Many regulations, some directed particularly at financial services, require this. Business and regulatory demands for data protection are linked. Governmental agencies create and enforce regulations that dictate the orderly, fair, and transparent operations of financial services firms. Regulation that benefits the public, government, and the firm requires that data and information are accurate, complete, and safe. Regulation especially requires that it is available. The fiduciary responsibility is to ensure the safekeeping of that information.

All institutions have information assets that hold considerable value:

■ customer records

- sales transactions
- product information
- marketing research data.

Information availability

For executives, the process of ensuring compliance with this body of regulation is often seen as a matter of simply making information available. This is often tied to a business continuity strategy. It also offers straightforward guidance on how to develop an effective information availability strategy.

Accurate, timely and complete business information is the foundation of compliance with each recent regulation. Information availability in this context is based on two requirements:

- effective IT systems—covering the functionality required to implement and maintain a compliant organization and protecting data from destruction
- available IT systems—ensuring the business operation is working.

The degree of protection and availability necessary often varies according to application. Some systems require constant availability, while others can be offline for hours without significantly impacting the business function or the capacity to comply with regulations.

If lost data is critical and wide-ranging, it can be destructive to the firm, its business, its customers, and its shareholders. Temporary loss of access to data may not be as severe as permanent loss; however, in real-time, "just-in-time," and short-term batch processing environments the downtime of systems can be very damaging. Such events may have limited effects at the time, but when reported as ad hoc events that affect business, or are identified as the result of failures in the system, such reports can affect confidence and ultimately share value. These temporary losses can happen for a variety of reasons:

- An internal hardware failure might force a business critical application offline.
- Operator error may accidentally close a system.
- An external power failure may close trading systems.
- External links in a supply or value chain may fail.

Temporary failures are often harder to guard against than permanent ones. Generally, disaster recovery planning is better prepared for a full fail-over response.

Executive responsibility

The importance to senior executives of effective controls is emphasized. For the purposes of compliance, the signing officers should:

- establish that the internal processes are measured by internal controls
- personally avow to these processes and controls
- ensure effective communications between the responsible managers and operations staff, and with subsidiaries.

From the investor's perspective and that of "public interest," anything that affects the business should be declared. There are assumptions that the kind of events that should be reported are "material changes," or events that change the financial condition of the company in some way. These events are identified under the frameworks that cover internal controls, which figure so prominently in much of the current regulation. For senior executives this is no longer an option—it is a mandated imperative.

Information value and loss

Lose information assets, or lose access to them, and you lose their inherent value and your business capital. If anything, in the financial services sector, information assets tend to have even greater value than in other sectors. When dealing in currency, securities, or insurance, a firm is in reality working with information. Customers' assets are held electronically; they are stored (using ILM) and managed. Regulations stipulate what should be held, the accessibility, and for how long. Loss of these assets undermines the confidence all regulation is trying to build.

BENCHMARKING AND ASSESSMENT METHODOLOGIES

In such a complex area with so many regulations to consider, extensively identifying practical issues of compliance by each regulatory framework is clearly extremely difficult. There are however some general issues that flow.

The two types of issue that flow are, first, those whose source is the fundamental regulatory structures themselves, and second, those whose source is one of the three types of overlap (constructive, destructive, and null effect).

The Global Regulatory Impact Assessment (GRIA) methodology is a proprietary analytical method of the authors, described generally here for the first time, and designed to enable investors and their intermediaries to assess and mitigate regulatory impacts.

Global Regulatory Impact Assessment (GRIA)

These types of methodology will become fundamental to most intermediaries in the next five years. The term is self-explanatory, but usually represents a compliance function activity rather than an operational one. Even so, most compliance functions are still focused only on regulatory impact assessment (RIA). These are two-dimensional RIAs, assessing the impact of one set of regulations against a specific set of investor portfolios. As this book sets out, it should be immediately clear that there are a very large number of permutations in data and activity in which an intermediary is engaged on behalf of a client, where multiple regulations may have a constructional or destructional effect. Some of these will affect investors directly. Others may also have severe affects on regulatory compliance for the intermediary.

GRIAs are a practical extension of RIA concepts which deal with these permutations with a combination of mapping and analytical tools. A GRIA has two basic threads which are analyzed separately and then combined—the intermediary thread and the investor thread.

Figure 5.1 shows an overview of the analytical process map using the intermediary thread. The investor thread is similar.

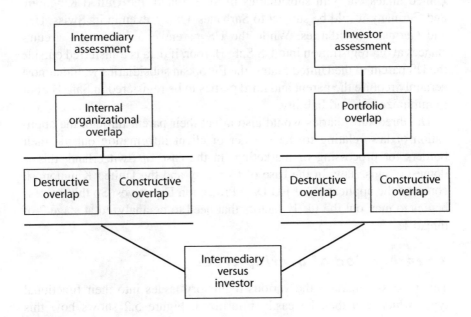

Figure 5.1 An overview of the GRIA analytical process map using the intermediary thread
Source: the authors.

1 Intermediary assessment

This establishes the scope of intermediary activities in terms of the firm's activities, and the jurisdictions it may be subject to. In particular, the map must be made of the position the intermediary takes contractually with its counterparties. In many financial services activities, the global financial model is very complex. Intermediaries can interact in several ways. As we saw earlier with respect to tax operations, a custodian bank can be a "withholding agent," a "qualified intermediary," a "non-qualified intermediary," and an "in-country agent bank" all at the same time. At this stage of the analysis, the investor is irrelevant. The issue is to identify the potential regulatory issues flowing only from the nature of the intermediary, and how it has set up its operations and links with other entities. This provides a map of direct and indirect risks: direct from regulations applying directly to the parent or subsidiary, and indirect from regulations that apply to other intermediaries and flow through to the intermediary.

2 Internal organizational overlap

This is the second phase of GRIA. However complex the external relationships may be, there also exist internal relationships which have a capacity for risk. So for example a listed global custodian headquartered in the United States but with subsidiaries in Switzerland, the United Kingdom, and Germany would be subject to Sarbanes–Oxley, even in its Swiss, UK, and German subsidiaries. While the US parent could in some circumstances avoid registration into US Safe Harbor, if data is transferred outside the US parent in the United States, the European subsidiaries would almost certainly require the parent and third parties to be registered in Safe Harbor to minimize risk and liability.

The three subsidiaries would also affect their parent through the application of law relating to the transfer of client information outside their borders for processing or marketing. In the case of Switzerland, this is domestic Swiss law. In the case of Germany and the United Kingdom, it concerns the application of EU Data Protection Directives. So this process begins to map out the likely factors that need to be analyzed at stage 2 of thread 1.

3 Segregation of overlap types

This process separates the various regulatory issues into their functional types which can then be easily prioritized. Figure 5.2 shows how this process of segregation overlap begins.

The analysis must first establish a range of applying factors, in this case jurisdictions. These are jurisdictions which have regulatory structures that

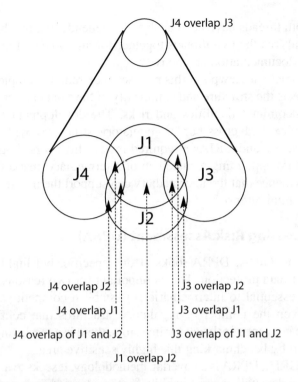

J4 overlap J3

J1

J4   J3

J2

J4 overlap J2   J3 overlap J2
J4 overlap J1   J3 overlap J1
J4 overlap of J1 and J2   J3 overlap of J1 and J2

J1 overlap J2

Figure 5.2 Segregation of overlap types

may have some effect on either the intermediary's operations and compliance, or that of its investors. In the example, just three jurisdictions to consider create several potential overlaps in addition to domestic compliance. For each "drop down" in the diagram, a map must be constructed for relevant intermediary operations: for example trade, safekeeping, tax operations, and treasury. Two lists need to be applied to each: documentation and activity, which specify what documents are held, and what activity is performed relating to them.

Care must be taken at this stage to be inclusive rather than exclusive, to avoid liability. For example, those subject to Sarbanes–Oxley, even indirectly, must include e-mail transmissions and receipts in their map, and "activity" must include a relationship to the CEO and accounting policies, as both of these are fundamental to Sarbanes–Oxley.

Note the complexity and permutations of this three-element model. Most intermediaries have relationships in at least the main 12 global markets, and the largest may have over 100 different relationships.

The investor thread must be analyzed similarly. Typical investment portfolios are often in the 9 to 20 range, and so this analysis is often less complex than the intermediary thread.

Once both threads have been analyzed independently, the third and final process analyzes the two threads together for any potential overlap issues relating to documentation and activity.

From a practical viewpoint this may seem extremely complex. However it only reflects the structure and complexity of the financial services model, and its concomitant liabilities and risks. The development of more and more complex and cross-border regulatory structures will make RIAs quickly obsolete and GRIAs a required model. Investors should therefore ensure, before appointing a custodian or intermediary, that a GRIA report provides evidence that the intermediary can support the investor's intended program at minimum risk.

Data Processing Risk Assessment (DPRA)

In contrast to GRIA, DPRA looks at one specific, but highly important area, that of data protection. This is important for two reasons. First, good practice is essential to intermediaries to establish competitive advantage. Second, given the number of regulatory structures that conflict with or damage the concept of privacy for investors, there is a marketing advantage to be gained by benchmarking this highly sensitive area.

As with GRIA, DPRA is an overlap methodology. It seeks to assess the risk that personal data will create a liability for the intermediary as a result of:

- the fact of its possession
- the nature of its storage
- its accuracy
- its transmission to third parties.

This effectively assesses a numerical risk associated with each of the Principles of the EU Directives, or other regulation that applies, such as the US Safe Harbor Act.

AUDIT

One of the natural developments of governments' increasing wish to know more about their own, and everybody else's, citizens has clearly been the increase in regulations whose effect crosses national borders. This creates a problem of information gathering and management for those governments that do not have the resources to support such activities. Typically, in the financial model, intermediaries are used to fulfill this purpose, since their commercial existence depends on their ability to support a global economy. This model is also useful because governments do not have resources to check the probity of every financial transaction. The net effect of these forces is that most cross-border regulatory structures now place a responsibility on intermediaries to collect and manage information, not for the benefit of their clients, but for the protection of various governments. This clearly gives the intermediaries a conflict of interest with those who pay their bills, the investors.

In the absence of resources at government level, intermediaries are most commonly required to check the probity of their activities, as we have seen, across multiple permutations of regulatory overlap. The way in which governments verify these activities is through audit, with sanctions coming close behind, ranging from fines through pecuniary damages to delicensing or contract cancellation (often amounting to the same thing).

Two examples of this occur in tax compliance within intermediaries relating to cross-border investments of their clients. For selected securities and in selected countries, US investors can obtain so-called relief at source from high taxation via the Depository Trust's Elective Dividend Service (EDS). DTC, a US utility, has negotiated arrangements on behalf of its intermediary members (participants) with several government authorities to allow this relief to be granted even though the government concerned has no documentary evidence to support lower taxation. Acting on behalf of its participants, DTC ensures that intermediaries contractually agree to collect and store such documents under pressure of audit by a foreign government. If they fail the audit, they can be, and have been, ejected from use of the utility generally, and fines may also be imposed by foreign tax authorities.

In the second example, in a similar move the US Internal Revenue Service (IRS) established a complex three-phase audit process over at least 2000 non-US financial intermediaries to ensure correct reporting and collection of taxes on US-sourced income (under Section 1441 NRA: see Chapter 3). It is worthwhile for intermediaries and investors to understand the audit process model for these regulations, because it has an impact on them, and it is a model that is likely to be more widely used in future.

In the 1441 NRA model, two layers create the audit framework, which minimizes cost for everyone concerned and assures deterrence. The first layer defines who is authorized to perform audits. In the instance under analysis, this can be any one of three types of body. The first is an independent internal auditor, the second is an independent external auditor, and the third is the IRS itself. From a cost perspective, the first option is clearly the most effective from the intermediaries' and the investors' viewpoint, as long as there is already such a function in place, so the additional work involved has effectively no incremental cost. External auditors are expensive, the more so because these types of regulation require not just expertise but continuous research into changing rules and interpretations.

This model is likely to be replicated on a global scale. In and of itself it can create an entirely new layer of costly compliance and risk management. Intermediaries now must not only assess the operational impact of failure to comply with regulatory overlap, they must also assess the operational impact and liabilities of putting in place an expensive audit compliance system. It is estimated that one of the top four accounting practices made over $30 million in just six months from such audit compliance work on qualified intermediary regulations for just one jurisdiction.

The second layer deals with the way in which the audit is performed. For the 1441 NRA regulations, the IRS requires a three-phase audit process. The first is a "spot check," where a statistical sample is taken to assess compliance on a range of issues. Notably this includes compliance not just to the letter of the contracts but also to the spirit. So in this case, spot checks will include checks on data veracity, and also on the training given to support ongoing compliance within the firm. The degree of liability at Phase I is limited to correction of any problems found within the statistical sample, although attention will be given to making sure that the principle of any issues is resolved on an ongoing basis.

Figure 5.3 outlines the extraterritorial audit process.

Each of the phases in this audit model are dependent on the failure of compliance at the previous level. So if the Phase I audit is passed, no

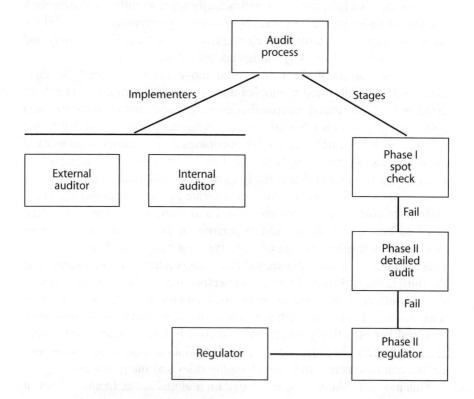

Figure 5.3 Extraterritorial audit process
Source: the authors.

further audit activity is required. If it fails or there are serious problems, a Phase II audit is required. In this phase the intermediary must do more work. The general scale and scope of compliance is analyzed in more detail, and the issues that failed in Phase I are addressed specifically. In other words, this is a more detailed audit. If the auditor is still not satisfied either that the issues are being or will be addressed, or feels that the intermediary is incapable of becoming or remaining compliant, then a Phase III audit is required. This is euphemistically termed "a discussion directly with the IRS," and would seem to be self-explanatory. The regulator will engage directly with the regulated company on the basis of the two audit phases that have been failed.

In a third example, we look at the destructive overlap caused by the differences between the European Data Protection Directives and the US Safe Harbor Act, and the practical impact of the audit compliance requirement of Sarbanes–Oxley and its developing European equivalents.

Audit is often, unfortunately, the first time that an intermediary (or an investor) ever finds out there is something wrong with its assessments. In researching this book with both the regulators and the financial services community we came across a frightening range of presumption, and what can only be described as "advanced ostrich mimicry." We received responses including the following, all from major custodian banks in the United States and in Europe, self-admittedly transferring client personal data from the European Union to the United States, and thus subject to both Safe Harbor and Data Protection Directive regulation:

What is Safe Harbor? Never heard of it.

We don't have to be in Safe Harbor because we are regulated by the Financial Services Authority (FSA).

We've no idea what this is all about. When you find out can you tell us?

We have general disclaimers that mean we're allowed to transfer personal data anywhere when we need to.

Our contracts with clients all have a clause to allow us to transfer data.

The impact of Sarbanes–Oxley solutions for corporate enterprise has meant an increasing focus on auditing not only the fact but also the content of information passing across, into, and out of an enterprise. Financial services firms face an enormous task because they are in themselves corporate enterprises with financial results that will, under the US and developing European regulations, require transparency and disclosure. They (the financial services firms) are also part of the enterprise web formed of their clients' businesses, so that client information, as opposed to internal bank information, must be tracked in order that the financial firm can ensure that it is a compliant part of its client's enterprise externally, as well as its own internally.

If we recognize for the moment the broader aspects of this audit requirement, we can overlay this onto the data protection issue. The data protection issue is generally at the client level at present, albeit many firms are treating it at enterprise level. In the latter, financial firms mistakenly presume they can be compliant if they use general, small disclaimers about data transfers. In the former, more robust model, information about data protection is dealt with at the client level through specific, well constructed, regulatorily compliant clauses in contacts and service level agreements. However, the principles of Sarbanes–Oxley act at transactional level, and so it is predictable that eventually, data protection will need to be tracked and audited at transactional level also.

In this most robust model, data protection will still be established at client level with properly compliant contractual clauses. However, audit of compliance will be performed at the transactional level, so that systems will identify both home and destination jurisdiction of data, and assess the relevant regulatory impact of the two jurisdictions. The system will also identify at what point the compliance was established, whether by inference of systemic procedure (for example the recipient is in Safe Harbor, therefore transfer is permitted) or by subjective judgment (the judgment of the data processor in the absence of compliance to any other decision element, which is most risky).

Systems will also track each and every data transfer, identifying what was transferred and its purpose. By this means, the data transferred can be both qualitatively and quantitatively audited for compliance to the principles espoused in the regulations. We expect these changes to take place over a period of three to four years, given clear air in which to migrate and develop suitable systems on a voluntary basis by the industry. That time frame may be shortened if there is a significant legal "issue" raised by sufficient clients in something similar to a class action suit taken against a major custodian or investment manager, by say a hedge fund or similar fiscally transparent vehicle, where large numbers of sensitive citizens have their personal investment data transferred to an inadequate jurisdiction.

Audit control in these circumstances will become increasingly burdensome, and we would remind readers here that this is just an example of one area of regulatory overlap. There seems to be no easily identifiable end point to the increasing complexity and cost that this will involve for custodians. Effectively, everything that anyone does within any financial services enterprise must be automated, recorded, and held intelligently against decision or rule-based systems, simply in order to protect against future unlimited liabilities such as we have already seen from Enron and Parmalat.

Given the importance of process, internal controls and their verification, and the primacy of audited company reports, it is no surprise to discover that the role of the auditor is a preoccupation of regulation. The audit process is a key area of scrutiny, and the opinion of the auditor is now being used as a monitor of the means of establishing true transparency of operation; almost an adjunct of the regulatory arm. For some regulation, the focus on internal controls and testing for effectiveness by auditors is the main practical dimension.

Many financial services companies rely on their internal auditors to document and test their controls. There are a number of points to note as newer legislation takes hold:

- When internal auditors function as a part of the company's internal control system, the independent auditor will not be able to place as much reliance on their work.
- Independent auditors will have to test the work of internal auditors in each area they wish to examine.
- Independent auditors will need to make independent tests of the controls.
- Confidence in the effectiveness of systems will derive from the external auditor's own procedures, and not those of internal auditors.

The consequences of a failure to adequately document or test internal controls may result in the report of "weaknesses," which can have a severely detrimental affect on the value of the company.

Although auditors have always documented controls as part of their activities, increasingly the level of documentation is wider in scope. In keeping with the severity of penalties for some legislation, the audit tends to be more thorough, covering a broader spectrum than was generally the case for financial reporting. The corporation under audit must inevitably budget for more time and resource; past experience is not an entirely reliable guide.

Internal auditing

As a matter of course, most financial institutions rely heavily on internal auditing resources. The work of these internal auditors, their documenting and testing, forms the basis for the assurance that management seek when they make their assertions on the nature of their internal controls and prepare their company reports. There is a trend in current regulation to separate the work of internal and external auditors to ensure a truly objective perspective on the work done. When an external auditor comes to perform the audit, practice is shifting to their often repeating the work that has been carried out internally. US legislation, such as Sarbanes–Oxley, is clear that the external auditor's "attestation" of the supplementary "assessment" made by a company board about the effectiveness of its internal controls must be objective and independently arrived at.

External auditors cannot simply use existing auditing evidence as the basis for their report. They may, however, use this input, which can then be verified. It is also common practice for auditors to introduce their own tools and testing methodologies, and internal auditing results are subject to these.

For the internal auditor, the pressure to get it right first time has increased. The risks of failure to present an accurate and fair picture of the operation of the company have escalated; the only reliable source of information for the final report is the audited information. The role of auditing has expanded, and there is now more emphasis on a thorough assessment and testing of internal IT processes to ensure compliance with company policies.

External auditors

In the United States, SEC independence rules do not allow external auditors to perform tasks for clients that result in their functioning in any way as management, or any activity that might cause them to be perceived to be auditing their own work. These rules were reinforced in December 2004 when the PCAOB (set up under the Sarbanes–Oxley Act as its oversight board) proposed ethics and independence rules concerning independence, tax services, and contingent fees "to promote the ethics and independence of registered public accounting firms that audit and review financial statements of US public companies." These proposed rules treat a registered public accounting firm as not independent of an audit client if the firm, or an affiliate of the firm, provided a range of services for a contingent fee or a commission, or "received from an audit client, directly or indirectly, a contingent fee or commission." The proposed rules detailed further instances covering "planning, certain tax advice or services." The PCAOB also proposed a general rule: "requiring registered public accounting firms to be independent of their audit clients throughout the audit and professional engagement period."

The clear message from this and other legislation is that external auditors are not permitted to document and test controls for management if they are engaged in auditing activities. The emphasis is placed on internal resources, and any shortfall has to be made up by buying in expertise.

However, if they are carefully positioned within such guidelines, external auditors can offer a significant and cost-effective advantage:

- They can provide up-to-date information on the mass of requirements in the current regulatory system.
- They are specialists in best practice, and can indicate effective ways of addressing compliance.
- They have considerable domain knowledge specific to financial services that enables them to understand the business as well as the regulatory context.
- They contribute to advisory groups or closely monitor legislative developments.
- They can work as part of the documentation effort.
- They understand testing, and have a range of effective tools based on their experience, best practice, and domain knowledge.

As auditors work within the framework of current legislation and observe its strictures on their behavior, many sources have commented on an apparent growing estrangement between them and their clients. This relationship has changed. Auditors have become more "conservative" in their dealings with customers. The use of external agencies, generally auditors or auditing arms of larger agencies, has undergone considerable change, and observations center on a shift in the relationship:

- Where an auditor has operated as a business partner and stressed this aspect of the relationship, regulation has worked to reduce this.
- While there is an overall increase in the number of conversations between client and auditor, the content of the conversation is more limited.
- Dialog which was once open is now limited to the specifics of the auditing process.
- The advice on best practice and implementation that was once part of the value-add of the relationship from auditor to client has been curtailed.
- Auditors are more inclined to give up long-standing clients if they are perceived to be a "risk" to their own activities.
- Clients are more inclined to give up long-standing relationships with auditors if the latter are seen to be focusing on increased fees with reduced value-add.

The major auditing companies have responded to legislation by restructuring to allow separation of function. As some of these are large consultancies with multiple arms of expertise, such an activity has even meant spinning off entities to ensure independence and avail themselves of the market opportunities associated with incorporation and listing. This poses a dilemma for them in determining how far they have to go to ensure these identities are separated. Legislation also lays responsibilities on the financial institution to ensure it observes this separation in employing agencies, and manages any conflict of interest. For the financial institution there are some mixed consequences:

- The separation of functions between firms is another operational cost, since the corporation no longer benefits from economies of scale in employing a single supplier to cover a range of allied tasks.
- However, the severance of traditional ties and control by a single agency of an account means that the financial institution can benefit from a competitive tendering process.
- In turn, this is mitigated by the available skills shared among a limited number of suitably equipped agencies.

As yet the true advantages and disadvantages of this situation are not clear. However this develops, over time this could have a significant impact on compliance projects.

GOVERNANCE

The need to monitor and control the behavior of organizations became the central concern of regulatory initiatives over the last decades of the 20th century. As corporate entities, financial services firms are subject to these concerns, and, if anything, such legislation as that generated to control corporate misdemeanor is directed at the world of finance. As a heavily regulated sector, the finance sector is very aware of the implications of governance. It handles not just the interests of its shareholders, but the very substance of a nation's wealth tied up in savings and investments.

Institutional and corporate scandals

The shock waves of the Enron scandal in the United States are only now beginning to subside, but the effects have a legacy written into the statute books. However, regulation is not new. In the United States, the SEC laws of 1934 onwards have their origins in the Crash of 1929 and the need to protect the investing public. In the United Kingdom, throughout the 1970s, 1980s, and 1990s there were numerous scandals, debacles, and not so public financial disasters. These have all generated reactive legislation that has sought to mend, fix, and bolster the finance sector. The moves have vacillated according to culture and political will between self-regulation and persuasion, and legislation and punishment.

The collapse of Enron, a US major energy trader, took down a partner, Andersen, the high-profile US accounting and auditing firm. The experience has been shocking, especially for the United States. Many consumers had invested in Enron and its like, and relied on Andersen to introduce a degree of trust in corporate management. As Andersen imploded, the shock wave ran through Wall Street and across the rest of corporate America, and the damage to the reputation of the world of accounting stretches far beyond the beleaguered auditing firm. As well as the sudden collapse of a huge and seemingly profitable company, there was the realization that US accounting standards—the Generally Accepted Accounting Principles (GAAP)—were no insurance against malpractice, and certainly no longer better than those of other countries.

The time had come, said Harvey Pitt, chairman of the SEC, to rethink the US system of financial disclosure. The US President announced a review of corporate disclosure requirements, and the Financial Accounting Standards Board moved to speed up work on issues raised by the Enron case. Moves had already been taken to reform US financial reporting, and top of the list of issues to deal with were the "quantity, complexity, and lack of easy retrievability" of accounting regulations.

US financial reporting, unlike that of European and other countries, is based on the supremacy of rules rather than principles. At face value this would seem to make the US regime much tighter than any other, but the focus on detail enabled financial departments to massage the figures to fit.

Governance is as much about relationships as spreadsheets, and financial reports contribute primarily to investor perception. If they serve as the basis for assessing both good governance and investor confidence, they alone are not enough. The challenge was, and is, to establish financial reports that make another Enron impossible.

Auditors focus on what they need to address. They establish a figure, a set of percentages, and the work is done, using techniques such as benchmarking as a familiar way to measure performance. But it is the grey areas in between that really give pause for thought on what regulation is really about.

The United States: FASB

In the United States, the FASB has been the recognized private sector organization defining financial accounting and reporting standards since 1973. Its mission statement summarizes its role:

> The mission of the Financial Accounting Standards Board is to establish and improve standards of financial accounting and reporting for the guidance and education of the public, including issuers, auditors, and users of financial information.

The relationship with the SEC is governed by the status of the SEC, which has statutory authority to establish financial accounting and reporting standards for publicly held companies. In practice, the SEC has relied on the private sector to define the standards in the public interest. The standards set by the FASB are officially recognized as authoritative by the SEC. They are also recognized by the American Institute of Certified Public Accountants (AICPA).

Over the years the trend on developing standards has been largely reactive. They tend to be drawn up in haste in response to sudden issues and weaknesses in the system, and being legislative by inclination, the SEC tends to seek rule-based solutions which simplify decision making for investigation and enforcement. However, such simplicity is not necessarily effective. Legislation in the United States tends to be knee-jerk, and pushed through Congress under public and political pressure.

A background consideration is that the legal culture in the United States is notoriously litigious. This generally shapes legislation to be specific and narrow in focus, to reduce ambiguities and assist in shortening time in court. Another background consideration is the public perception of the auditing profession being seen to fail in its duty of maintaining independence and monitoring financial correctness. The Enron case highlighted all these issues and gave them a very public airing. The Sarbanes–Oxley Act is a reaction to this, and an example of the way standards have evolved in the United States—as another check to a process largely left to its own devices.

Corporate governance

In a sense, all regulation has, as its ultimate aspiration, an improved behavior. This is manifest as good governance. For financial service companies this is represented by corporate governance. The International Chamber of Commerce defines corporate governance as:

> the relationship between corporate managers, directors and the providers of equity, people and institutions who save and invest their capital to earn a return.

The "corporate" nature of the definition focuses on the organizational responsibilities of boards of directors to ensure that "the corporation itself conforms to the law and regulations."

This corporate perspective defines governance as the relationship that links those who invest and those who generate a return on the investment. This relationship succeeds or fails on the notion of trust. "Trust" is something that can not be legislated for, only encouraged. Regulation ensures that corporate enterprises manage and return that trust. Technology has introduced new areas of business activity and broadened the scope for governance. The spread of e-commerce has meant that transactions occur simultaneously, and create challenges in a time frame that is very difficult to "govern." This shift in emphasis signals the advent of corporate governance over systems that operate without human intervention and at speeds controlled by technology.

The concept of governance as a matrix of relationships operating in the interest of investment and return is a very human one. It is close to the insights associated with psychology rather than business and finance. Nevertheless, these relationships are held together by trust, and it is clear that the primary aim of regulation as a whole is to engender and nurture trust: in the firm, in its executives, in its products, and most importantly, the system it operates within. The process of disclosure is a gesture to encourage trust. Transparency of information reinforces this gesture, making possible the exchange or transaction that is the purpose of the financial exercise. Through business activity, self-interest is translated, at an organizational level, into this matrix of dependent relationships: organizations and agencies acting on behalf of either themselves or others in pursuit of the financial interests of all. Regulation focuses on this, and its many manifestations serve one side or the other in this exchange, with a stated belief that this should work to mutual benefit.

Governance assumes accountability for the setting of organizational objectives and their realization. It also examines the objectives as well the way they are set, and ensures that relationships operate in a way that conforms to expected behavior. It does not define what this behavior is exactly, but seeks to ensure that it does not put at risk the greater good. The statutory instruments and directives that define regulation set up agencies to monitor and administer this framework for behavior. They responsibilities of those linked in this way, for example the accountants and auditors, become part of this picture. The investor is positioned as an end point in this sequence. From this position the links should be "transparent," that is, nothing should be hidden. A prime objective of corporate governance is to ensure that all the relationships are characterized by such transparency. The investor who is making an investing decision needs this. Deprived of critical knowledge or fed with inaccurate or false knowledge, the investor is at risk. Thus one critical aspect of corporate governance is that it seeks to minimize the risk of relationships with corporate entities.

Part IV

Part IV

CHAPTER 6

Other Operational Issues

OPERATIONAL COMPLIANCE

The biggest difficulty faced by both investors and their intermediaries is not cost. If the relative returns of investing in a particular market or markets are high enough, money will never be a problem. The problem is the on-the-ground operational day-to-day business of remaining compliant with multiple, overlapping regulatory requirements. Realizing the nature of the problem is followed closely by appropriate and ongoing training and retention of key strategic expertise. Most of the regulatory structures currently in existence, as well as most of those known to be in development, have one common thread—information. The requirement is its:

- collection
- accuracy
- storage
- protection
- transfer limitations
- use.

These lie at the heart of virtually every regulatory system.

Regulators in many jurisdictions have over the last few years been increasingly willing to impose severe penalties on firms, often for failure to keep or maintain accurate client records. Where this has not been the case, it is usual that such failure has been a significant indirect factor. This would seem strange at first glance, since compliance to multiple structures can be most easily and cost-effectively maintained by getting it right from the start: in other words, in the account-opening process. Several regulations cover this aspect as part of their control requirements.

There are of course two conflicting pressures in this process. Investors on the one hand are renowned for being slow to respond to requests for information, and intermediaries are often frustrated by this tendency. Investors in the past have had a natural aversion to providing too much information, because the intermediary is often an easier route for a regulator, or more often the tax authorities, to use in order to get investor-level information.

Intermediaries on the other hand are less than open about the reasons for the collection of such information, being far more likely to cite "regulatory requirement" than "client benefit." Yet intermediaries do have two roles to play with the information they receive: compliance to regulations and also maximizing investor returns. The first creates the aversion, but the second is often invisible to the investor, being packaged as part of a custody or investment management process.

One of the key aspects of such information gathering is documentation during account opening, and subsequent maintenance of such documentation. For domestic investors (those investing only in their country of residence), providing documentation is relatively easy and familiar: for example a passport for individuals, or formation documentation for corporates and funds. However, the vast majority of institutional investors are portfolio-based, often investing in between 9 and 15 countries. Some of these other countries are prepared to accept the "home" jurisdiction's account-opening process, others are not and require specific documentation. The United States for example, in its cross-border taxation regulations, "approves" account-opening processes on a jurisdiction by jurisdiction basis. Even so, the United States has its own specific documentary requirements which overlap this approval. So while an intermediary may open an investor account under its own regulatory process and documentation, the investor, once known to be receiving US-sourced income, will be required to complete separate documentation (such as Form W-8BEN) to self-certify its status and residency, in addition to the documentation already supplied.

Once spread over the portfolio of countries, this can make the account-opening process extremely onerous for both intermediary and investor. However, there are significant advantages to be gained from investors taking a positive approach to such matters. Apart from making the intermediary's compliance easier, there can be financial advantages to the investor. In the example cited, if the investor does not provide adequate documentation or work closely with the intermediary to maintain the currency of such documentation, the investor's US-sourced income is likely to be over-taxed by as much as 15 percent.

Unfortunately many intermediaries, in order to make the account-opening process as simple and speedy as possible, reduce the documentation at this stage to a minimum. While this has some marketing and competitive benefits, there are far greater benefits to be gained in both marketing and compliance terms from a more rigorous analysis of regulatory overlap and documentation requirements at this stage, as it applies to the specific portfolio of the new client.

Account opening is also a time of maximum risk for regulatory overlap in data transmission. Typically, where investments are expected in multiple markets, supporting documentation is obtained to satisfy the needs of each market's regulatory authority. However, the structure of the financial services industry often requires the transmission of this information not just to regulatory authorities, but also to other intermediaries in the investment chain that perform related "local" support custody services. Thus the operational compliance problem involves not just obtaining the documentation, but also controlling the flow of information resulting from the account opening. The problem is complex. Some countries (such as Switzerland and Germany) prohibit the transfer of information by law. In other cases there is regional over-arching regulation such as the EU Data Protection Directive, which constrains how and to whom such information may be divulged, even though the resultant failure to divulge can damage the investor's portfolio performance.

The policy to be adopted with respect to operational compliance is one of risk management, careful planning, and minimization of replication. If account-opening documentation has several options, some of which are time-sensitive and some of which can be used to support several jurisdictional needs, it clearly makes sense to perform a portfolio compliance overlap analysis (PCOA). Unlike the more traditional gap analysis, PCOA identifies the required documentation and its attributes for any given portfolio, so that the most effective use of resources can be deployed to open the account, and minimum stress placed on the investor in the process.

Figure 6.1 (overleaf) shows the key elements of a typical PCOA analysis. The process establishes the documentary requirements for the investor's portfolio at local, regional, and portfolio levels. At each level, operational needs include the requirement to ensure there is an internal process to make sure time-based documentation is tracked for renewal, and that storage and retrieval systems are capable. This much is basic, and most intermediaries already have such processes in place. Three important areas often overlooked are:

- mapping of local, regional, and portfolio regulations that will apply to this investor and which may cause either destructive or constructive risk
- a data transfer risk map to identify any part of the portfolio where a data transfer is required, which might create a conflict with home or other market regulations with regard to data privacy
- a documentation overlap map to indicate where documentation can be minimized across multiple markets, thus reducing costs, risk and effort.

INFORMATION TECHNOLOGY

There is no doubt that, for intermediaries, IT is seen as the only way in which multiple regulatory structures and liabilities can be managed

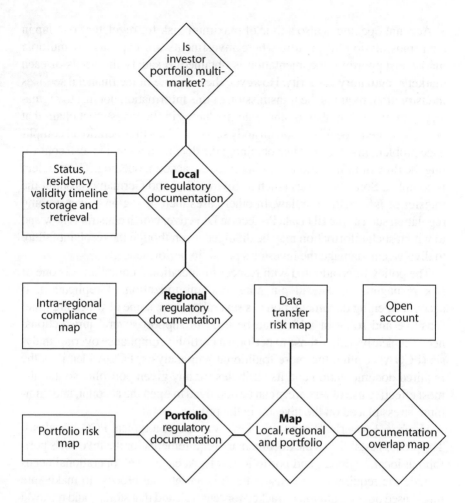

Figure 6.1 Key elements of a typical PCOA analysis

effectively. Most banks and brokers have had strategies in place for some years to dematerialize their paper-based systems, retaining them only as books of record and disaster recovery backup processes. Institutional shareholders are somewhat further behind in this process, and consequently they will need to expend more in the next few years to reach a point where they can gain the advantages of systemic IT—that state of IT at which the business could not run effectively for more than 24 hours without it.

Most "professional" intermediaries have already invested in imaging systems to collect and retain documentation, as well as the data contained on such documentation. However, one of the largest hurdles to complete dematerialization remains the requirement by most regulators to have documentation signed by an officer of the company, or by the investor personally. This applies as widely as the Sarbanes–Oxley regulations and its European clones, through US tax regulations, to the UK's MLR regulations. Intermediaries may collect, store, and directly act upon data provided by investors, but when it comes to regulatory overlap, in most cases original documentation is required primarily to satisfy the regulator that the original investor, resident in another country, has some link to the data and its veracity.

A notable exception is the United States, which has some limited acceptance of the need for electronic "signatures." However, while this is laudable, the way in which the relevant regulations are written restricts the transfer of an electronic signature between two parties rather than allowing such transfer up or across a chain of investment. The latter is actually the way in which the market is structured, and so such moves, while good as a starting point, need to be extended. This may seem a small thing, but in actual fact it is the single largest impediment to efficient processing that still exists in today's investment market.

Most regulatory systems require a statement of residency and status from account openers, supported by evidence to prove that they are who they say they are. Consequentially the greatest area of overlap is in the way such statements are made acceptable in different markets, and how these statements are transferred between intermediaries in such markets in order to enable investment to take place legally.

There does exist an international proposal for a signature alternative (SA) in many markets, although to date it has not been officially adopted. The principle of the signature alternative is based on two issues. First, the level of technology used for transmission must be based on the lowest common technology denominator. Second, a regulatory authority needs to be able to trace either the person certifying a particular form, or the intermediary that holds the original documentary evidence. The format of the SA is shown in Table 6.1.

In most jurisdictions the identifier will be the tax identification code of the entity concerned. However, there are some jurisdictions where there are legal restrictions on the age at which an investor may legally hold shares. Therefore it may be that in some jurisdictions, the account holder does not yet have a tax identification code, so that some substitute must be made, such as a social security number.

Table 6.1 The signature alternative

Country code	Type of identifier	Identifier	Country code	Type of identifier	Identifier
GB	TID	YY 00 00 0X	GB	TID	YY 11 11 1A

In the example in Table 6.1, the first half of the SA comprises the details of the country of residence and unique identifier for the account holder. The second half represents the same data for the institution that holds the original of the form on which the SA is used. So if a receiving regulatory body or intermediary were to receive a data packet representing a form, this SA would allow the intermediary or regulator to either identify the account holder directly via his or her tax authority, or contact the institution holding the original of the form (signed by the account holder).

As documentation is a fundamental principle of virtually every regulation system affecting financial services today, developing a globally acceptable smart signature system is critical to reducing costs for intermediaries through enabling more efficient straight-through processing (STP). It will also remove the onerous task placed on investors to have signatures on multiple documents repeated over time. This will be replaced by a single power of attorney enabling the intermediary to append the signature alternative to subsequent evidentiary documents.

The use of such technology will be critical to the development of sound platforms of cross-border investment. The partial development of STP has already revolutionized the investment and custody community in terms of trade efficiency. The final link to make STP a reality will include signature alternatives as a natural step to increasing the automation of back-office processes, which are inextricably linked with compliance across the global regulatory framework. The degree to which regulatory authorities establish and adopt such standards, and the degree to which the investment community uses them, will define the degree to which cross-regulatory compliance can be made effective in the next decade.

INTER-DEPARTMENTAL LIAISON

It has been anecdotal for some time in the investment management, and particularly the custodial, community that the control of business at an operational, and to some extent at strategic, level has been resident in the IT department. Having gained the majority of the operating budget some years ago, IT departments have, through the project management and queuing of key projects, successfully controlled what was done and when. In future, however, that political control of the business will move (and to a large extent already has moved) to the risk and compliance function. A good test for CEOs and chairmen of where the real decision making lies in their businesses is to take a hypothetical project which has real commercial value to the firm, which leverages opportunities from regulatory developments (perhaps jurisdictional anomalies), and which needs IT resource to implement. The result, almost across the board, will be three competing internal political pressures:

■ Commercial: the CEO and sales team want it now to exclude competitive threat, maximize brand image and increase the top line.

■ IT: want to add the project to the back end of the existing project queue to increase the reliance of the business on their expertise, to avoid the additional work of reorganizing other projects already in hand, and to increase job stability in their department long term.

■ Compliance: want to make sure that nothing happens without their approval, to mitigate or minimize the firm's potential liabilities.

These three motives are clearly conflicting, and internal politics can easily result in the CEO not being in real charge of the business as a result of "corporate inter-departmental inertia." The relative power of the three factions in the commercial mix is constantly moving, but there is no doubt that at present and for the foreseeable future, IT and commercial are in consolidation, and compliance is in the ascendant.

Most of these factors arise because of the sheer size of corporate businesses in the financial services sector, and smaller firms tend to display these effects to a smaller degree. However, as the major IT infrastructure developments are now in place, the pressure is on the commercial and compliance functions to find a way to work together to meet business objectives rather than place impediments in the way of the process.

The wave of new regulatory structures discussed in this book can thus be viewed either as an opportunity or as a threat. In the same way that the objective of this book is to discuss and encourage planning of regulatory compliance at a global level, intermediaries need to recognize the importance of inter-departmental liaison, with the constructive objective of keeping the business moving forward commercially while remaining compliant. Part of the problem is the departmentalized structure of most intermediaries, which at worst precludes, and at best inhibits, cross-disciplinary thinking. Yet it is only by getting different departments to think about their own function as it relates to others that there is the hope of catching some of the more dangerous conflicts between regulations.

The most common sharing of information typically includes no more that two departments out of a mix of five—sales, operations, compliance, IT, and legal. It is vital that all departments are represented in regular meetings to discuss projects as well as agenda items specific to each function. Unfortunately this all too often occurs at too high a management level to be really effective as an operational strategy. At operational level, legal functions need to make others aware of impending legal issues that might affect projects or processes. Similarly compliance needs to update the others so that manual and IT-driven projects can take account of this changing area. While many may infer that this is obvious and must happen, it simply does not, and most costs of compliance with regulatory structures are the result of "after the fact" information, rather than any form of pre-planning or good internal departmental liaison.

From an investor perspective, such inter-departmental liaisons can make account set-up and management much simpler and less onerous, and therefore client documentation may be easier to acquire in a timely manner.

RISK PROFILING VERSUS LIABILITY

Risk profiling is now a mature operational tool for most intermediaries, and many investors are aware of the process. However historically it has been used in rather a narrow way, mainly to determine the attitude to risk of an investor with regard to a given set of portfolio return objectives. Risk profiling in the context of this book is more extensive, and applies not just to the overall business model, but also to the degree to which regulatory issues have been assessed appropriately, alone and in concert.

We have already seen that most investors and intermediaries tend to think of risk on a market-by-market basis. That, after all, is the way in which the portfolio is managed for the most part. Balancing risk by restructuring the portfolio minimizes risk from loss of investment income, but this is still a rough use of the tool.

Risk profiling for regulatory compliance has much greater potential impact. This process looks at each permutation of market in which an investor is involved, and assesses the degree of overlap, the degree to which the primary and secondary aims of the regulatory structure interact, and finally the degree to which internal intermediary systems are structured to meet those issues. The equation that describes this profiling is not simple nor is it mathematically exhaustive, having within it the requirement for judgments of processes. However, it can act as a good tool to make assessments of liability that may flow from a high index. Some of these overlaps can lead directly to financial losses at investment level, such as over-taxation of income because of inaccurate or inadequate documentation. At worst they can lead to exclusion from a market or markets, or even business failure if, for instance, the overlap and liability relates to Sarbanes–Oxley compliance.

$$\textbf{Global regulatory risk (GRR)} = \textbf{pn}^n \int_1^q f(m)$$

where

n   is the number of markets in a portfolio

$f(m)$ is the degree of compliance to regulatory objectives 1 to q

p   is the degree to which the intermediary has adequate systems to meet the requirement.

OPERATIONAL RISK MANAGEMENT

Operational risk is of especial relevance to banks and financial institutions. It is centered on the notion that processes and people are error-prone, resulting in unplanned and unwanted impacts on the business such as system failures, transaction mistakes, and miscalculation in payments. Some mistakes are small and easily rectified, others are systemic and require great expense to fix, while yet others can be disastrous and life-threatening for the business.

Defining, identifying, planning for, and dealing with risk is a major business discipline in its own right. We looked at risk and risk profiling earlier. Risk is now a subtext for most regulation:

■ It informs every requirement for information. Accuracy of information reduces the risk of disadvantageous decisions being made.
■ It shapes the response of companies to regulation based on their risk tolerance, or how they balance the overhead of compliance with the imperatives of the business.

The Basel Accord defines operational risk as "the risk of loss resulting from inadequate or failed internal processes, people and systems or from external events."

Within financial services, operational risk is recognized as being distinct from market risk and trade risk. Its focus is on the risk carried by the failure of internal operational processes. These are wide-ranging and include:

■ the functional processes that dominate business
■ the staff and the skills that make up the intellectual energy of the business
■ the security of systems and information.

Internal controls and operational risk

To a large extent the focus on internal controls in US and EU legislation places operational risk at the forefront of boardroom concern. For intermediaries, these internal controls and operational processes drive the business. Their intermediary nature requires effective and efficient systems for taking and delivering; their transactional business base is dependent on the operation of these processes, predominantly electronic and reliant on a secure communications system. Internal controls are not only vital for formal reporting, but underpin a level of confidence in these systems themselves.

The US regulations centered on the Sarbanes–Oxley Act greatly emphasized the importance of effective internal controls. In the United Kingdom, failures in the 1980s of regulatory regimes to control pension scandals such as that of Robert Maxwell have forced UK regulators to lay a similar emphasis on the production of financial reports.

The Cadbury Code emerged in 1992, and was eventually superseded by the Combined Code. We have seen how these sets of recommendations have tied together common elements of regulation. In particular, the Combined Code helped clarify the recommendations on internal controls issued by the Cadbury Report. The Code insists that the board "should maintain a sound system of internal control," and the directors should review its effectiveness annually, reporting on this to shareholders, including all controls as they exist for the financial, operational, and compliance control and risk management functions. In 1999, the Turnbull Report added to this explicitly in its title: *Internal Control: Guidance for directors on the Combined Code.* Turnbull brought a focus on risk, and risk assessment as a manifestation of the practical meaning of a system of internal controls. This reinforces the view that compliance, for financial services firms, should be considered as the overall business risk strategy and factored in accordingly. By considering that operational risk is as important as other forms of risk, the firm recognizes the significance of electronic commerce as its business, its reliance on intellectual capital, and its dependence on the electronic markets to which it contributes.

The exposure to operational risk is variable and wide-ranging once it is fully acknowledged:

- A changing financial environment introduces not just market risks but operational risks in the new processes needed to meet the new opportunities.
- As customers and investors assume such risk management is in place, downtime becomes even more unacceptable as the expectation is to trade and benefit in real-time

This approach allows all risks across the business to be identified and managed in a controlled way.

Two further concepts are important for the discussion of operational risk: "loss" and "probability." Both of these have a significance for regulation. If we see loss as something that affects the business materially, then we are close to the regulatory concern of deficiencies and material weaknesses. These are then refined by the idea of their likelihood, or probability of happening, a key factor in risk assessment. Managing these concepts within a risk framework allows a firm to marry the priorities of compliance and the business, positioning them in a context that makes sense internally and clarifies their determination to be effective externally to regulators and most importantly, investors.

Governance and standards

In the United Kingdom, from the Cadbury Report to the Turnbull Report there has evolved a view of governance dominated by risk. The Turnbull Report guidance specifically states that:

- Risk management is the collective responsibility of the whole board.
- The company should have a sound system of internal control to safe-guard shareholders' investment and company assets.
- Management needs to review these controls at least once a year.
- Risks should be assessed regularly, and the assessment should include risk management, operation, and compliance, as well as financial controls.

In 2002 the FSA issued a consultation paper dealing with the management of operational risk (CP142: *Operational Risk Systems and Controls*). This paper draws on the Basel Committee's suggestions, and includes a discussion on business continuity management and operational risk in general.

Uncovering damaging risk is vital. Risk can have a significant or major impact, according to our terminology. Remediation is a valuable process, and another central aspect of regulatory initiatives. Risk reduction inevitably becomes a central concern throughout the organization, addressed through three approaches:

- Prevention: proactively enforce risk-based policies.
- Containment: limit the effect to departments, firewall and separate through information boundaries.
- Mitigation and remediation are understood steps in the compliance process and the ongoing commitment to maintaining compliance.

Nearly all regulation makes some reference to this, and some place a great deal of emphasis on a company getting back into shape. For some regulatory measures this is the purpose in the first place.

CHAPTER 7

Investor Issues

Investors continue to seek maximum returns on investment. However they are faced by increasing regulatory controls on their activities, and lay a significant proportion of this responsibility off onto their intermediaries. This chapter looks at several key issues from the investor perspective, and gives practical advice about how to ensure that the intermediaries concerned have the right tools in place to minimize risk to the investor.

TYPES OF CONSUMER

Understanding what influences consumer behavior is important. Types of consumer are also significant, as are the skills required to make investments. Investors are not as easy to categorize as they once were. They do not necessarily fall neatly into wholesale and retail investors. For example, there are many investors who—for reasons of size or expertise, which may vary from product to product—are wholesale for some purposes and retail for others. Others may be big institutions, such as fund managers, but in practice they place the funds of myriad small investors.

The smaller investor

The thrust of many new products on the market has been to push the responsibility for making intelligent assessments onto ordinary consumers, who are generally far from being expert on financial institutions and markets. For this type of investor it is critical that appropriate education is made available.

The stated objectives of most financial regulation are to protect the investing public from fraud, exploitation, and mis-selling. Behind this is an assumption that these investors or consumers cannot protect themselves from bad judgment. This is reasonable given the degree of bad judgment displayed by institutional fund managers. However, there is a responsibility on the consumer to make an informed choice. "Caveat emptor" applies in the financial services sector as in any other retail environment. The emphasis on proper and accurate disclosure that runs as a common thread through financial regulation implies that properly disclosed information is suited to the intended audience. In a sense the regulatory effort is bent on protecting the smaller investor from him or herself.

The European Commission has worked on a Communication which clarifies the definition of investors of this type. But as the financial services market mutates, the situation becomes ever more complex, with investor types splintering as some investors become marginally more expert and a new generation enters the market, and the types of investor lobby for a greater range of information and more regulation.

Institutional investors

The reality is that the greater bulk of investments on the internal stock and securities exchanges are made by bodies such as institutional investors, which employ sophisticated expertise to scrutinize issuer disclosures, and make informed choices based on extensive market knowledge. It is this investor that dominates the discussions surrounding regulation and consumer protection. To a large extent it is the macro elements in the system that define how the system works, or should work.

Changing investors

But at root, all investment comes from the small investor. It is individual savings and investments, drip fed into the many products, packages, and accounts (and taxes), that are the basis for all financial activity. Aggregated further on in the process, they form the funds that the institutions use to power economies. This layer of investor had relatively few investment options in the past. Now they have many, and often of a degree of sophistication once only available to institutions. It is not clear how far regulatory regimes, either national or transnational, have addressed this reality. More than ever, individual citizens are being asked to look after their own finances—select insurance schemes, determine best banking practice for themselves, and judge the future options of competing pension schemes. For the small investor, information is important, but education is critical. For large investors information, not education, is critical. It is clear that by far the greatest emphasis in recent regulatory measures is on information.

REDRESS

For financial markets, national or regional, to develop competitively on an international scale, they must provide all these services for their consumers. The looming pensions crisis in the United Kingdom is a case in point. There has to be a population of consumers confident in their options, and confident that, if they invest across borders, protection against malpractice will be strong and they can gain effective redress. This is something that currently has to be pursued through courts, and often in local national courts; this has a huge overhead in costs, time, intractable language, and custom complications. This makes such investment something of gamble beyond the initial gamble of investing itself.

Routing complaints through native national institutions may or may not bring effective redress at present. Efforts have been made to make accessible these routes of redress through ombudsmen, but much progress needs to be made to make such a smooth passage a reality.

For institutional investors the picture is different. Individually substantial, these are often wooed by issuers and markets. Grouped, they form strong pressure groups that can bring a great deal of clout to any regulator. But as companies operating in a regulated market they are not unaffected by consumer activism, and the risks are escalating for them.

CONFIDENTIALITY

If investment is simple and single jurisdiction, it may be possible to establish practically the degree to which confidentiality can be kept. However, most investors have a portfolio of investments across several countries. In such circumstances, even provided an intermediary has opened the investor's account in accordance with local "know your customer" rules, it is by no means certain that investors can rely on their information or activity remaining confidential. There are two issues: the operational location of back-office processing, and intermediary status.

Many of the largest intermediaries are global in reach. As a result they often process transactions outside the jurisdiction in which the account was opened, usually for reasons of cost abatement. This leads to potential risks from inter-regulatory reporting. For example, if a transaction is suspect, there are at least two and sometimes more places that this suspicion may become evident—primarily in the country where the account was opened. Second, however, there is a risk that such a transaction may be identified in the country where the data is processed, caught perhaps by an IT system performing sanity or consistency checks for other purposes. In addition, what constitutes a suspect transaction in one country may not trip the same rule in another.

Under such circumstances, the confidentiality of data and activity cannot be guaranteed. Typically if investors are not aware of the regulatory structure of the markets in which they invest, they must ensure that their intermediary does understand the structure. Investors must also take extreme caution when entering contracts with intermediaries regarding the powers they cede to intermediaries for transmission of information outside their direct control to third parties, especially when the third parties are outside the account-opening jurisdiction.

Many intermediaries use contracts with very generic text, giving them powers to do pretty much what they like, with little or no attention given to the controls that should be in place. Even when the party to whom such information is transmitted is within the vertical structure of the intermediary (for example, the US branch of a UK institution), investors must remember that information about their activity is now ruled by a different jurisdiction.

With many intermediaries using either the United States or India as processing centers, this is an important issue.

DOCUMENTATION

Documentation continues to be the bane of both intermediary and investor, and neither seems to have grasped the fundamental issue causing the problem. Investors are renowned for being tardy with the return of documentation even when it is time-sensitive. This is, in great part, the result of a failure of communication between intermediary and investor at relationship management level.

When requests for documentation arrive with the investor, they are perceived to be an administrative function (which they are), but there is frequently insufficient emphasis or explanation given at the time of their delivery on the reason for the documentation, time deadlines associated with it (if any), and the consequences of failure to deal with it in a timely manner. All this falls to the intermediary's relationship manager. Compliance typically has some hand in this process, but most often the only action taken is to prepare some generic, short text, included in a covering letter, noting that a failure to return documents may have "consequences" for which the intermediary will not be responsible. From the investor's perspective, for many years this has been accepted and just as promptly ignored, based on the principle that no one ever explained or linked any loss or risk directly to the investor's failure to deliver documentation.

In today's financial climate, investors no longer have this luxury, particularly at the institutional level, where reporting depth is increasing and the opportunity to hide behind the "I didn't know" or "I didn't realize" excuses no longer exist for either investor or intermediary. Intermediaries in the face of growing investor knowledge can also no longer hide behind a bland generic disavowment of responsibility. Many of the regulations described in this book either explicitly or implicitly increase the responsibility of intermediaries to meet "deemed fiduciary duty" in a much more comprehensive way than heretofore. Investors in the United Kingdom are for instance subject to the potential reporting of their normal activities to the National Criminal Intelligence Service without their knowledge, while at the same time their personal data and financial transactions may be being transferred to "inadequate" jurisdictions in the course of an intermediary's business. If the financial information is of sufficient import it may also be reported by the intermediary under Sarbanes–Oxley. In view of what the intermediary may do with investors' data and documentation, often without their knowledge, let alone explicit consent, it is imperative that investors ensure that, where possible, their interests are protected through effective policies and procedures with their intermediaries, that ensure they the best possible degree of knowledge about the uses and risk involved with documentation. This is a typical example:

> *Policy 1: When requesting documentation in relation to my account(s), you must explicitly, and in direct proportion to the potential risk or loss involved, inform me of the reason for the provision of documentation and the consequences of any delay in its return.*

EDUCATION

As we have seen, the degree of liaison between relationship management and investor can be critical. Many intermediaries now provide "education" to their investors in a variety of forms, including newsletters and regular updates. While this is laudable, the information provided often falls short of giving the client enough information on which to base typical investment decisions. At the heart of this is the custodian's role to act on the instructions of clients but not to offer "advice," on the basis of the potential liability this would incur for the intermediary.

Unfortunately, there is a large amount of information that either falls into a gray area, or that would not form the basis of investment advice. All of this is lost to the investor because of the aversion of the intermediary to giving advice. The answer lies in investor policies which recognize the degree of aversion intermediaries have to giving advice and risk, while placing on the intermediary a direct responsibility to compile and disclose information which may be relevant to the investor's decisions.

Some typical policies for investor education are:

- *Intermediaries must understand the types of regulatory information that will be relevant to investors.*
- *Intermediaries must provide that information in as complete a form as possible, recognizing that complete information may not be available at any given time.*
- *Intermediaries must provide the information in a form which readily supports the investor's decision-making process without being seen as advice.*

It is quite clear that intermediaries face a huge and complex task, with very strong forces pulling them in opposite directions. The net result is that their activities, and thus their products and services are more and more constrained. Replacing the risk of "advice" with a much stronger policy of education will continue to protect intermediaries to the extent that they wish to be protected in the market, while giving investors a much better base of information on which to make decisions.

This must not of course be abused. Deluging an investor with information does not help the investor. Irrelevant information will not give the impression that the intermediary has a close interest in the investor, and a lack of follow-up will make the information useless.

Education is of course only a first step. There are three steps in the process to ensure that investors get the best possible service from their intermediaries:

■ Education: inform investors of issues.
■ Facilitation: help investors understand regulatory conflicts.
■ Access: solutions, internal or external, to maximize returns.

Increasingly intermediaries are aware of regulatory issues, and where these constitute too much operational risk for their own infrastructure, they are partnering with third parties who have sufficient experience to mitigate the risk—a form of outsourcing. This is a global policy that investors may wish to require of their intermediaries:

Intermediaries should:

■ *know about the effect of regulations as they pertain to their investors*
■ *facilitate the education of their investor clients about the material effects of their decisions*
■ *provide access to solutions which can mitigate any loss in return on investment that would otherwise occur.*

FINANCIAL LITERACY

The importance of education as an enabling concept for the well-being of investment and the eventual success of financial service regulation is now well documented. International bodies, national bodies, regulators, and consumer interest groups have all repeatedly stressed the importance of having educated and informed investors, with expertise pooled in competent and transparent institutional investors. What does this mean in practice for the way regulation now works?

Two of the statutory objectives in the UK Financial Services and Markets Act are consumer focused. These are promoting public understanding of the financial system, and securing the appropriate degree of protection for consumers. In the United Kingdom the Financial Services Consumer Panel is an interest group that was established to advise the FSA on the interests and concerns of consumers. Being independent of the FSA it can raise concerns directly with the regulator, research issues of public importance, and publish reports.

Given the connection between education and investor protection, education has a number of benefits:

■ It helps investors make informed choices.
■ It enables them to manage their planning more efficiently.
■ More generally, it should lead to an increase in investor pressure.

Investor activism is a product of an increased awareness of investors in the way the markets operate, and a grasp of how well their particular investment is doing. This pressure should be a stimulus to more competition.

To achieve this increased level of investor awareness there are several processes at work. One is education that makes the investor more critical, that is, able to question and analyze based on a sufficient knowledge of how the investment chain works. A second is education as information and advice, where investors are provided with quality information for planning investments and building the knowledge base for critical choices.

In its comments on education, the FSA notes that "over the longer term, we are working to ensure ... financial literacy" (FSA website). On what area or areas are the interests of this educational processes to fall? The FSA talks of its emphasis on markets for financial products such as:

■ banking services
■ insurance services
■ pension schemes and investments.

It emphasizes its focus on the requirement to address the needs of those inexperienced with financial services and vulnerable to mis-selling. This clearly does not include established players such as institutional investors, who actually dominate the market and represent the bulk of investment decisions, even though they are using the accumulated funds of small investors. The key concept is the investment decision. And this takes us straight back to regulation, and the importance attached to the information flowing from issuers and financial institutions in the form of company reports and product brochures. Making sense of these is a primary concern of consumer education. This is one area where the impact of regulation is felt.

CHAPTER 8

The Future

DRIVERS FOR CHANGE

We began this book by commenting that most regulatory change at present is the result of concerns about:

- corporate governance
- money laundering
- international terrorism
- investor activism.

INFORMATION AND IDENTITY

From a regulatory standpoint, the two largest areas that underpin all regulations flowing from the set of issues are information and identity. It is in these two areas that most change will take place the next ten years.

Information

Of these two, information is a "glissile" subject: that is, the information, what it is and who has it, changes according to the particular regulatory and/or jurisdictional issues concerned, even with the financial services model. Corporate governance information is concerned with who knew what when, and what was done with that information: most importantly, whether it impacted on share price and return on investment. Money laundering information is concerned with what information exists and whether it represents a transaction that is illicit. Impacts on share price are irrelevant, it is the tracing of the movement of funds that lies at the core.

There is already an ISO standard for information transfer run by the interbank network SWIFT, which will probably form the basis of the global regulatory highway for financial services. Already SWIFT has recognized that while its members, banks and funds, are adopting SWIFT technology for intra-firm information management, there are many bodies that interact with such firms and are unable to access or leverage the security and validation that the SWIFT network offers. Its likely that in the next few years SWIFT's network will be globalized, both in terms of extensions to its existing ISO 15022 messaging into corporate actions processing, and also into different communities, notably including tax authorities and corporates.

The global regulatory highway

Everyone is familiar with the global information superhighway and its insecure "tarmac," the Internet and World Wide Web. The need to develop harmonized structures for regulation, based on the consistency of information and identity policy, defines what we like to call the regulatory highway.

The information highway concerns itself with information as its primary building block. This is why security was and continues to be the information highway's greatest threat and greatest challenge.

The regulatory highway will be a development of decades, and is best described as a convergence of information management systems and identity management systems, overlaid with regulatory compliance rules. We are already seeing the beginning of this trend in Sarbanes–Oxley compliance, where technological "solutions" in a very fragmented way seek to define information and identity in a way that "enables" or "warrants" regulatory compliance.

Regulatory convergence on the regulatory highway will ultimately mean a single basic framework for the identification of information, and a similar framework for the structuring of information and its transmission. While each jurisdiction may have local specializations based on its history or particular social peculiarities, the greater the use of the base model, the lower the cost of implementation for intermediaries, the easier the documentary load for investors, and importantly, the lower the number of variables to be considered when making changes to meet new perceived threats.

This means an ISO standard for structuring financial information, and validation rules to define what is "suspicious" at a technological level and also by jurisdiction. The infrastructure already exists. Some steps have already been taken on the buy-side of financial services, but this needs to be built upon.

Typically, if SWIFT is used as a the template, financial instructions and information would flow over a secure network with enhanced validation rules that would establish where the information had come from, where it was going to, and apply not just financial validation to the contents of the messages but also regulatory validation. For example, if a single transfer of over a certain sum in one jurisdiction is defined as suspicious, the system should be able to hold a regulatory "memory" of the transaction history of the investor as well as the regulatory requirements of the destination (or sending) jurisdiction. This would require a level of integration between regulators, intermediaries, and investors that does not currently exist. However, like identity cards and biometrics, the technology is there, only the political will is so far dormant.

Identity

Identity is a static or "sessile" issue. Regulators, in order to assess information, need some bedrock against which to measure glissile issues. The bedrock is identity. Who are the people who are moving information that impacts the governance issue? Who are the people who are moving money?

Even in 2005, we see the United Kingdom moving inexorably towards a single form of identity card at the very same time that identity theft is becoming the single largest crime growth area. The United States has already moved to a biometrics-based form of identification at consumer level. Most of the regulations discussed in this book have information and identity at their core. It is notable that in 2005, these regulatory issues are so far away from harmonization that overlaps can exist to the degree presented.

No one doubts the need for regulatory controls. Such domestic regulation has been with us almost as a basic tenet of civilization. Until recently, even cross-border regulation was clearly needed, but just as clearly, its simplicity was understandable and its translation into operating practice relatively easy and not costly.

The last ten years has seen an explosion not just in crime but in types of crime and scales of crime. The problem is now not just one of scale, but one of kind. The development of modern civilization has at its heart the transfer of information, but we no longer use quill pens and written ledgers. The speed with which a crime can be committed and the ways in which it can be covered up are fast exceeding the regulatory authorities' capabilities to detect and deter. It is a truism that what science can invent, science can circumvent. And so regulatory structures, like law enforcement, are continually trying to catch up with the ways in which a small minority seeks to subvert our global financial systems.

Yet the problem remains for financial services and investors alike. The relative number of potentially criminal acts in the financial services industry is small in comparison with the total number of transactions. There is an argument that this is partially because of the sophistication of regulation itself, but it is also just as true that in a market led economy, it is not good business to do things badly.

The challenge for regulators is to make "smart" regulations that leverage information technology to minimize costs for investors and intermediaries, protect the privacy of investors, and yet primarily deter, and secondarily detect, the misuse of financial services. This is a tall order, and one that is not in the nature of today's regulatory systems as they are "siloed" by jurisdiction.

It is natural then that as regulators speed up their attempts to control what is almost uncontrollable, regulations will become more complex, more difficult to interpret, more broadly interpreted by regulators, fundamentally more likely to contain internal and external inconsistencies, and therefore more costly for intermediaries and investors.

Two issues lie at the heart of managing information and identity as a methodology to deter and punish criminal activities: harmonization and information-sharing technologies.

In the United Kingdom, it has historically been a base tenet that information held by one agency of government cannot be accessed by another, and this is replicated around the world. Today, most regulatory structures are beginning to permit intra-departmental data sharing and comparison. On a cross-border basis, agencies themselves need to work more closely together before the data flow can be used effectively. Most investors are of course completely honest, as are most financial transactions. It is a reality however that it can take a much smaller event today to create a much bigger disaster. As the financial markets grow and use technology more invasively, their reliance on it and its inherent weaknesses mean that intermediaries must spend and spend and spend in order to keep up with regulation, which in turn is changing and changing in its efforts to keep up with the minority of transactions that underpin criminality.

In 2001 the International Monetary Fund (IMF) estimated that money laundering constituted 2 to 5 percent of global GDP, amounting to US\$600 billion a year. The value of assets under custody by the top 46 global custodians in 2004 was close to US\$60 trillion (source: www.globalcustody.net). If we presume money laundering to be a subset of "global corporate governance" inasmuch as the former fits into the probity requirements of the latter, it is clear that while the amounts at risk are significant in themselves, in comparison to the overall values of the market, the regulatory complexities being evolved could be described as a sledgehammer to crack a nut.

This is mainly because none of the various jurisdictions work together to create a single harmonic regulatory structure. In the last ten years we have seen only one example of harmony: double tax agreements, where most governments have now adopted the OECD model agreement. When it comes to data protection and corporate governance, there are no such models. This creates the complex regulatory overlaps that flow from different jurisdictional objectives, cultures, and methodologies.

- The cost of doing business will rise in all markets
- Profit margins for intermediaries will decrease, or prices to investors will increase, or both.
- Investors should assume that their financial data and activity will be shared on an international basis using rules.

GRIA

Regulatory impact assessment tools will need to develop significantly to take into account greater complexity within regulations, methods to assess risk, and critical operations points within regulations, as well as the overlap between different permutations of regulations. IT spend in this area will increase significantly in the next five years. Investors will become (as they are already) much more informed and educated about the activities of their intermediaries (which is one effect of regulatory reporting requirements).

ELECTRONIC SIGNATURES

Electronic signatures are already becoming a fact of life, albeit even these are treated in different ways in different jurisdictions. The difficulty for investors and intermediaries, even within the supposedly sophisticated environment of financial services, is that the degree of technology available is not consistent across the globe. One of the top three custodian banks in the world still receives over 40 percent of its instructions from clients on thermal fax paper!

In conclusion, there is an increasing need for jurisdictions to work together to create a harmonization of identity policy and information sharing. Such a utopia for the regulators has significant enemies amongst the civil libertarians. However, the argument for reductions in civil liberties to afford greater protection from the threats that use financial services as their conduit is likely to hold sway.

The single appendage to our financial services model that is ubiquitous across the world, and therefore is able to present itself as the platform for information and identity, is tax. The one fundamental and unavoidable principle of all financial activity is tax. Even those who are exempt must prove their identity to claim exemption. So it is likely that harmonization of the efforts in information and identity, while they may not be promulgated by tax authorities, will undoubtedly be used as the primary conduit to achieve compliance. Tax authorities have extensive domestic systems to track and trace their citizens' income, with equally ubiquitous identity management systems.

We believe that while investor activism and deterrence of terrorism may be the aims, the most effective tool to deploy is an extension and harmonization of tax structures. That is not to say that taxation itself must be harmonized. Tax can still be treated differently in different jurisdictions, as it has been for centuries. However, as the United Kingdom has seen in recent years, as long as there are effective rules for management of information, its centralization can only serve to enhance the regulator's ability to combine information to deter and capture criminals.

In summary:

- Regulatory compliance will continue to become more complex in order to respond to ever more circuitous strategies adopted by the minority.
- The global regulatory principles that provide deterrence and detection will converge using information and identity as the foundations of the regulatory highway.
- Until convergence is substantially achieved, global regulatory frameworks will continue to overlap, predominantly destructively.
- Occam's razor would hold that investors will, irrespective of yield, continue to see rising costs of doing business in global markets, fed by increasing costs of compliance.
- Intermediaries will continue to respond to regulatory change in a fragmented way, leveraging small elements of straight-through processing in a tactical rather than strategic way, until a unifying utility creates the playing field where regulatory convergence can occur without the effects of a commercial market.
- While the threads of compliance are so loosely structured, regulations so haphazardly connected, and the technological dots not joined up, global scandals will continue to occur, despite the regulators' ever more complex frameworks. The question is not whether, but when.

APPENDIX

The Regulators

UK

Financial Services Authority (FSA)

The FSA, created by the FISMA Act in 2000, regulates investment firms, credit institutions, collective investment schemes (UCITS), insurance companies, insurance intermediaries (handling long-term/life products), and fund managers. The Office of Fair Trading (OFT) deals with the issue of consumer credit licences.

Financial Reporting Council (FRC)

The FRC and its subsidiary bodies have responsibility for promoting high standards of corporate governance in the UK finance industry, "To foster in the public interest high quality financial and governance stewardship of listed and other entities and so support investor, market and public confidence."
It is to achieve this through "promoting transparent and full reporting of relevant and reliable financial, governance and other information and effective and independent audit."

It is also to act as the independent regulator of the accountancy profession, ensuring effective disciplinary systems are in place, overseeing the accountancy profession's regulatory functions, and overseeing the monitoring and enforcement regimes of the accountancy and audit profession. It works in partnership with the UK government in securing and implementing an effective statutory framework.

The FRC and regulation

- The FRC published the Combined Code on Corporate Governance in July 2003. It published at the same time its Regulatory Impact Assessment of the revised Code, and in June 2004 announced that it would be carrying out a regular review of the Combined Code.
- In the same year (2004) the FRC set up a new committee to lead its work on corporate governance, and to monitor the operation of the

Combined Code on Corporate Governance and its implementation by listed companies and by shareholders.
- In July 2004 the FRC announced that it would be reviewing the Turnbull guidance on internal control.
- The FRC intends to publish a guide for UK and Irish companies registered with the US Securities and Exchange Commission (SEC) on the use of the Turnbull Report to comply with SEC requirements to report on internal controls over financial reporting.

EUROPEAN REGULATORS

Committee of European Securities Regulators (CESR)

The CESR is an independent committee of European securities regulators, with one member from each EU Member State. Its role is to improve coordination amongst securities regulators, act as an advisory group to the European Commission, and to ensure more consistent and timely day-to-day implementation of community legislation in the Member States.

Austria

Finanzmarktaufsichtsbehörde (FMA) (Financial Market Authority): regulates banks, insurance companies, pension funds, securities, and exchange supervision.

Belgium

Commission Bancaire et Financière (CBF) (Banking and Finance Commission): regulates investment firms, credit institutions, and UCITS (but not the insurance sector).
Office de Contrôle des Assurances (OCA): regulates insurance companies.

Czech Republic

Czech National Bank: deals with bank supervision and control.
Ministry of Finance: regulates insurance institutions and investment funds.
Czech Securities Commission: handles securities/capital market supervision.

Denmark

Finanstilsynet (Danish Financial Supervisory Authority): regulates financial undertakings and securities.

Finland

Rahoitustarkastus (Financial Supervision Authority): regulates banks, brokerage firms, stock and derivatives exchanges, and management companies for mutual funds.

France

The main regulatory bodies are the:

- Banque de France.
- Comité des Etablissements de Crédit et des Entreprises d'Investissement (ECEI).
- Comité de la Réglementation Bancaire et Financière (CRBF).
  Commission Bancaire (CB): regulates credit institutions and investment banks.
- Commission des Opérations de Bourse (COB): regulates markets dealing in financial instruments, and asset management for third parties; the regulatory authority for financial markets.
- Conseil des Marchés Financiers (CMF): regulation and supervision of financial activities, with the exception of asset management; the French supervisory authority for financial activities.
- Commission de Contrôle des Assurances (Insurance Supervisory Commission): regulates insurance and reinsurance companies.

Germany

Bundesanstalt für Finanzdienstleistungsaufsicht (Bafin) (Federal Financial Supervisory Authority): regulates banks, insurance companies, securities and exchange supervision, and asset management.
Deutsche Bundesbank: regulates banks.

Greece

Bank of Greece: regulates credit institutions and financial institutions.
Hellenic Capital Market Commission: oversees operation of the capital market.

Hungary

Pénzügyi Szervezetek Állami Felügyelete (PSZÁF) (Hungarian Financial Supervisory Authority): regulates banks, specialized financial institutions, specialized credit institutions, cooperative credit institutions, financial enterprises, investment firms, investment fund managers, public warehouses, members of the Hungarian Commodities Exchange, the Budapest Commodities Exchange, Budapest Stock Exchange, Central Clearing

House and Depository Ltd, private pension funds, voluntary pension funds, voluntary mutual insurance funds, insurance companies, insurance brokerage companies, insurance cooperatives, insurance associations, venture capital enterprises, and venture capital funds.

Ireland

Central Bank of Ireland: regulates credit institutions, investment services, Stock Exchange member firms, and collective investment schemes.
The Department of Trade, Enterprise and Employment also has a regulatory role.

Italy

The main regulatory bodies are:

- Banca d'Italia: regulates banks, and financial intermediaries with a turnover of over €10 million registered with the "Special List" held by Banca d'Italia and fund management companies.
- Ufficio Italiano Cambi: regulates financial intermediaries with a turnover of less than €10 million registered with the "General List" it holds.
- Commissione Nazionale per le Società e la Borsa (CONSOB): regulates Investment companies and collective investment schemes (UCITS).
- Istituto per la vigilanza sulle assicurazioni private e di interesse collettivo (ISVAP): regulates insurance companies and insurance intermediaries.

Luxembourg

Commission de Surveillance du Secteur Financier (CSSF): regulates banks, undertakings for collective investment (UCITS), and professionals in the financial sector.

Netherlands

The main bodies are:

- De Nederlandsche Bank (DNB): regulates banks, investment institutions, and foreign exchange offices.
- Autoriteit Financiële Markten (AFM): regulates securities trading.
- Pensioen-en Verzekeringskamer: regulates insurance companies and pension funds.
- Sociaal Economische Raad: regulates insurance intermediaries.

Norway

Kredittilsynet (Banking, Insurance and Securities Commission of Norway): regulates banks, savings banks, insurance companies, finance companies, mortgage companies, investment firms, and pension funds.

Poland

The main bodies are:

- Komisja Nadzoru Bankowego (Commission for Banking Supervision): regulates banks.
- Komisja Nadzoru Ubezpieczeñ I Funduszy Emerytalnych (Insurance and Pension Funds Supervisory Commission): regulates insurance and pension funds.
- Komisja Papierów Wartoœciowych i Giełd (Securities and Exchange Commission): regulates public trading in securities, securities markets, and brokerage activities.
- Ochrony Konkurencji i Konsumentów (Anti-Monopoly Office): regulates competition and consumer protection.

Portugal

The main bodies are:

- Banco de Portugal: regulates credit institutions and financial companies.
- Comissão do Mercado de Valores Mobiliário (CMVM): regulates the securities markets (securities issuers, financial intermediaries, settlement systems, sinking funds, risk rating companies, and institutional investors).
- Instituto de Seguros de Portugal.

Spain

Banco de España: regulates credit institutions and the interbank, foreign exchange, and book-entry public debt markets.
Comisión Nacional del Mercado de Valores (CNMV): regulates stock markets and the activities of all the participants in those markets.

Sweden

Finansinspektionen (Swedish Financial Supervisory Authority): regulates banks, securities companies and fund management companies, stock exchanges, authorized market places and clearing houses, insurance companies, insurance brokers, and friendly societies.

Switzerland

The main bodies are:

- Eidgenössische Bankenkommission (Swiss Federal Banking Commission): regulates banks, investment funds, mortgage bond business, stock exchanges and securities dealers, disclosure of share holdings, and public takeover bids.
- Kontrollstelle für die Bekämpfung der Geldwäscherei (Money Laundering Control Authority): regulates self-regulating bodies and directly subordinated financial intermediaries.
- Bundesamt für Privatversicherungen (Federal Office of Private Insurance): regulates private insurance companies: life insurance, accident insurance, insurance against damage, and reinsurance.

UNITED STATES

The main bodies are:

- Securities Exchange Commission (SEC): set up by the Securities Exchange Act of 1934.
- Commodity Future Trading Commission.
- National Association of Securities Dealers Regulation (NASD).
- Internal Revenue Service.
- US Department of Treasury.

ASIA–PACIFIC

China

China Securities Regulatory Commission.

Hong Kong

The main bodies are:

- Securities and Futures Commission.
- Hong Kong Monetary Authority.
- Office of the Commissioner of Insurance.

India

Securities and Exchange Board of India (Sebi).

Japan

Financial Services Agency.
Ministry of Finance.

Korea

Financial Supervisory Service.

Malaysia

The main bodies are:

- Securities Commission.
- Central Bank of Malaysia.
- Labuan Offshore Financial Services Authority.

Singapore

Monetary Authority of Singapore.

Australia

Australian Securities and Investments Commission.
Australian Prudential Regulation Authority.

REST OF THE WORLD

Nigeria

Securities and Exchange Commission.

South Africa

Financial Services Board.
South African Reserve Bank.

Russia

Federal Commission for the Securities Market.
Central Bank of the Russian Federation.

Bibliography

Board, J., Sutcliffe, C., and Wells, S. (2002) *Transparency and Fragmentation: Financial market regulation in a dynamic environment*, Basingstoke: Palgrave Macmillan.

Buckle, M. and Thompson, J. (2004) *The UK Financial System*, Manchester: Manchester University Press.

Davies, H. (2003) 'Managing financial crises,' in P. Booth and D. Currie (eds), *The Regulation of Financial Markets*, London: Institute of Economic Affairs.

Goodhart, C., Hartmann, P., Llewellyn, D., Rojas-Suarez, L., and Weisbrod, S. (2001) *Financial Regulation: Why, how and where now?* London: Routledge.

Goodman, S. F. (1996) *The European Union*, Basingstoke: Macmillan.

Gorrod, M. (2004) *Risk Management Systems: Process, technology and trends*, Basingstoke: Palgrave Macmillan.

Herring, R. J. and Litan, R. E. (1995) *Financial Regulation in the Global Economy*, Washington, DC: Brookings Institution.

Howells, P. and Bain, K. (2004) *Financial Markets and Institutions*, London: FT Prentice Hall/Pearson Education.

Lamfalussy, A. 'Creating an integrated European Market for financial services,' in P. Booth and D. Currie (eds), *The Regulation of Financial Markets*, London: Institute of Economic Affairs.

Lander, G. P. (2004) *What is Sarbanes-Oxley?* New York: McGraw-Hill.

Liebenberg, L. (2002) *The Electronic Financial Markets of the Future*, Basingstoke: Palgrave Macmillan.

McGill, R. K. (2003) *International Withholding Tax: A practical guide to best practice and benchmarking*, London: Euromoney Books.

McGill, R. K. (2004) *Relief at Source: An investor's guide to minimising internationally withheld tax*, London: Euromoney Books.

Sampson, A. (2004) *Who Runs This Place? The anatomy of Britain in the 21st century,* London: John Murray.

Sparrow, M. K. (2000) *The Regulatory Craft: Controlling risks, solving problems, and managing compliance,* Washington, DC: Brookings Institution.

Zakri, I. M., Tay Pek San, and Chew Li Hua (2004) *Introduction to Cyberlaw of Malaysia,* Kuala Lumpur: Advanced Professional Courses.

Index